WHAT YOUR DREAMS CAN TE... ... ...

"At last, the definitive work on the scientific art of dream interpretation!

"Brilliant Alex Lukeman has written in a unique and original style that keeps the reader having fun while learning to be the detective in analyzing the message in one's dreams that will lead to success and bear fruit in your waking life.

"You will want to keep this manual on your night table for the ability to discover and understand the fascinating secrets your dreams can bring to you.

"This book is a powerful tool in understanding one's self — a way of connecting with all wisdom and knowledge.

"Every night can become an adventure; every night you can find a treasure trove. This book is the key to open the door to your personal Temple of Dreams."

— Jeraldine Saunders
Signs of Love

"One of Lukeman's major theses is that in each of us there is a factor that tries to communicate with the conscious portion of the self concerning the underlying patterns and needs of the self. One form in which this comunication occurs is dreaming. So, one important source of knowledge — even wisdom — for us is out dreams. As we follow Lukeman's clear guidance, we learn to access that deep source of our dreams — he calls it 'The Dreamer Within' to receive the messages presented in the dream imagery and patterns.

"Lukeman's use of 'key points' to emphasize important concepts, principles and techniques, plus his easy, almost conversational style make this book highly readable and rapidly rewarding. I cannot commend it too highly! I plan to use it in my teaching at the earliest opportunity."

— Kenneth P. Freeman, M.A.
Assistant Professor, Department of Philosophy
Colorado State University

About the Author

Alex Lukeman has been conducting workshops, retreats and classes focused on personal exploration since 1979. He attended Dartmouth College and Boston University. He brings to his work a broad background in psychology, mythology, history and the practice of alternative healing approaches. He is the creator of the audio cassette *Dream Mysteries*, a powerful tool for working with dreams, and of the audio cassette *Dissolve Into Love*, scheduled for release in 1991. He lives in Northern Colorado.

To Write to the Author

We cannot guarantee that every letter written to the author can be answered, but all will be forwarded. Both the author and the publisher appreciate hearing from readers, learning of your enjoyment and benefit from this book. Llewellyn also publishes a bi–monthly news magazine with news and reviews of practical esoteric studies and articles helpful to the student, and some readers' questions and comments to the author may be answered through this magazine's columns if permission to do so is included in the original letter. The author sometimes participates in seminars and workshops, and dates and places are announced in *The Llewellyn New Times*. To write to the author, or to ask a question, write to:

Alex Lukeman
c/o THE LLEWELLYN NEW TIMES
P.O. Box 64383–475, St. Paul, MN 55164–0383, U.S.A.
Please enclose a self–addressed, stamped envelope for reply, or $1.00 to cover costs.

What Your Dreams Can Teach You

Alex Lukeman

1990
Llewellyn Publications
St. Paul, Minnesota 55164–0383, U.S.A.

FIRST EDITION

Interior illustrations by Lynn Schrage
Cover design by Christopher Wells

Library of Congress Cataloging-in-Publication Data
Lukeman, Alex, 1941–
    What your dreams can teach you / by Alex Lukeman.
      p. cm.
    ISBN 0–87542–475–9
    1. Dreams. 2. Self–actualization (Psychology). I. Title
    BF1091.L83 1990
    154.6'3—dc20   90-45793
                                                         CIP

90 91 92 93   10 9 8 7 6 5 4 3 2 1

Llewellyn Publications
A Division of Llewellyn Worldwide, Ltd.
P.O. Box 64383, St. Paul, MN 55164–0383

ACKNOWLEDGEMENTS

All of the dreams presented in this book are real dreams told to me by real people. As you will see, when someone tells a dream they make themselves extremely vulnerable. Dreams reveal our most intimate selves. To protect their privacy, all of the names of the dreamers have been changed. I want to gratefully acknowledge their trust and help, without which this book would have been impossible to write.

I am especially grateful to two people in particular; Brugh Joy and my wife, Gayle. Brugh, because it was he who first introduced me to the deeper levels of dreams and inducted me into the experience of energies which hastened my understanding; Gayle, because she has unfailingly supported me when I needed it in this as in so many other things.

TABLE OF CONTENTS

FOREWORD

W. BRUGH JOY, M.D.

Anyone who has gained an insight into the meaning of dreams enters a small grouping of human beings who encounter a vaster stage in this most awesome mystery of being consciously aware.

It seems almost humorous when I hear people say they don't understand their dreams, implying that they do understand their outer sense of existence, not realizing that consciousness itself is a profundity beyond the explanatory capacity of contemporary science! As one journeys deeper into the psyche — the ocean which contains the underpinnings of reality — one is struck by the possibility that there is more to awareness than what is experienced at the conscious level. One discovers that consciousness is multi-layered and multi-dimensional. Multi-layered in that there are superficial ranges of intellectual cognition and much deeper and broader levels of intuitive understanding. Multi-dimensional aspects of consciousness appear to be independent of time and space, being both personal and collective in nature.

To be appreciated is that dreams and the sense of day-to-day reality are both derivatives of a deeper, totally unconscious field of influence and experience which the outer mind neither suspects nor has the resources to directly reveal. As both the sense of outer reality and the sense of dream reality originate from the same source they are fundamentally the same and are intrinsically related to the phenomenon of matter itself. This field of influence operating in time as the outer awareness and both in and out of time in our dream awareness, is the generator of what each of us calls our life experiences. To gain a larger perspective of what it means to BE, the dream level must be recognized and integrated, yielding a greater sense of self than one can have from only the perceptions of the awake awareness.

Alex Lukeman, in this lucid presentation of an approach to what one can learn from dreams, draws from his rich interpretive dream experiences to lead the reader in a clear, step-by-step manner into the dynamics of dreams — the dance of patterns in symbol form. Far from just a cookbook approach though, he guides the reader into the intuitive realm of dream interpretation — a superior level of dream analysis. The Dream Interpreter (as I term it) or Lukeman's The Dreamer Within is a leap in the art of dream divination as it requires the analyst to leave his or her own ordinary awareness and access a dimension of awareness not usually made conscious. This different aspect of a vaster self can easily understand symbol and pattern in any level or dimension, including those making up dreams and those making up the sphere of outer reality.

Lukeman's unique contributions to dream analysis include a guided imagery cassette tape which helps the reader to both remember and to call upon the Dreamer Within for interpretations of dreams, and a series of questions which directs the reader into stages of dream analysis.

The book itself is very informative, extremely interesting and well written with a good spectrum of the types of dreams and the layers of interpretation which each dream reflects.

As the material Alex Lukeman presents is worked with, the reader may suddenly see a pattern or an interpretive level not seen by the author. It is impossible to exhaust the interpretive potential of any dream or event (as lawyers well know). The perspective from which the dream analyst first views the dream determines the aspect revealed by the dream. Change positions in consciousness and the dream will reveal another hidden meaning.

Warning! Dream interpretation is addicting and extremely dangerous to the ordinary sense of self. Jump in! The water's great.

W. Brugh Joy, M.D.
Moonfire Lodge
Paulden, AZ 86334
©1990

INTRODUCTION

The world of dreams has fascinated me since I was a small child. I have always had vivid and complex dreams, and eventually I began to look for information which would help me understand them. Like most of us, I really didn't know what my dreams meant or what they were trying to show me. I found that the few books which were about dreams were not very helpful. They were either biased towards metaphysical belief systems which were intriguing but unprovable, or consisted of predefined interpretations of symbols and events which seemed leaden and lifeless to me. I was not at that time familiar with the works of Carl Jung and other seminal thinkers who had begun to explore the deep mysteries of the human psyche, and who had seen that dreams were a key to understanding.

The book you hold in your hand is the expression of many years of work in many different areas, directly related to the exploration of consciousness and self understanding. Not all of that work has been focused on dreams, but it is all relevant to the understanding of dreams. *What Your Dreams Can Teach You* reflects all of the influences, experiences, teachings, reading and exposure to different viewpoints and cultures which has been my life experience.

For years I had kept a dream journal and found that I was remembering as many as six or seven complex dreams almost every night. Some things became apparent over time. I saw that certain themes seemed to be repeated and that similarities existed between symbolic characters who appeared in my dreams. Sometimes I would wake with an electric sense of certainty and understanding about the message of the dream, which seemed to be born out when the message was applied to my waking life. I learned that there were sometimes emphatic variations in the dreams which emphasized the importance of the material. More often than not, however, I had no real understanding of what the dreams were about.

In 1979 I was handed a book which invoked the thrill of recognition which comes when one discovers a resonance of feeling and ideas and a confirmation of one's own experience. The book was *Joy's Way*, by W. Brugh Joy, M.D. The book is not principally about dreams but does contain a section about dreams which I felt was correct in its presentation.

I knew instantly that I wanted to explore further the stimulating material which was presented in this book. I began with a two week residential retreat in the high desert of California. It was an event which profoundly altered my experience of life and opened doors to understanding which have never been closed since that time. One of the areas which was worked with in that initial conference was dreams. It was at this conference that the deeper possibilities of dreams which I had always felt were present began to open themselves to me.

My work with dreams and the understanding of self has been deeply influenced by Dr. Joy. Some of his original approaches and ideas underly my own contribution to working with dreams. There are several fundamentally important ways of looking at dreams presented in this book which are either his or were first brought to my attention through his teaching. I want to take the time to point these out and acknowledge them.

Throughout this book you will find references to an inner energy of understanding which I call the "Dreamer Within." This aspect of our consciousness, once we learn how to access it, will lead us to an accurate and correct understanding of the material of our dreams and assist us with the dreams of others.

The fundamental principle which must be evoked for connecting to this aspect is a conscious "shift" of awareness. We can learn to move from our usual modes of perception to something which is felt within us in a much different way. It was from Dr. Joy that I learned how to do this. It applies the principle of self activated and expanded consciousness and the perspectives which it can bring to the interpretation of dreams.

Joy calls this aspect which understands dreams the "Dream Interpreter." Whatever one calls it, it is an aspect which truly does know how to interpret dreams. It requires practice to tap into this source within us, a willingness to explore and a developing sense of self trust and self love. It requires an honest and open receptivity to what dreams reveal when they are seen from the perspective of this inner aspect.

A controversial idea, not usually accepted in the conventional psychoanalytical sense, is the idea that dreams are "honest." I was skeptical of this approach. I had not yet done enough of the inner work which allows one to accept self on the difficult levels which can be seen through dreams. As my exploration and understanding of the psyche grew, it became clear to me that the idea was correct; dreams are honest and do not lie to us, because they are not coming to us from the areas of our psyche which are concerned about falsifying ourselves in order to obtain some advantage.

It is crucial to the understanding of dreams to take this on as an assumption, although it can not be proven in the scientific sense. If we begin to work consistently with dreams, we may discover the truth of this approach. This has been my experience. If it is true that dreams are truthful, then it becomes even more necessary to understand them if we are really interested in self discovery and inner growth. It also follows that any confusion about the message of a dream is based in the interpretive levels which are brought to bear by the conscious mind. This is important to remember when doing dream work.

Chapter 14 deals with the idea that life may be seen as a dream and that the information one gets from doing this is valuable for self understanding. It is not a new idea to consider that life might be a dream. For example, in the Hindu tradition the universe, life and all creation is seen as a dream of Vishnu. From there it is not a difficult leap to consider that one's individual life may also be seen as a dream. What is a unique approach is the idea that we may interpret real life events as a dream and use this as a way to understand dreams more deeply, as well as perhaps discovering something about our lives and how we live them. I was first exposed to this very effective tool of self discovery during that initial conference with Dr. Joy in 1979. Since then I have always found this to be a revealing way in which to look at reality.

An idea which is fundamental to working with dreams and using them as a focus of self growth and discovery is the concept of patterns within the unconscious. These patterns affect us in terms of our perception of life and our way of relating to life. Patterns of the unconscious are shown through dreams, if we know how to look. The idea of unconscious patterns within is basic to psychoanalytic approaches and may be seen in the pioneering works of Freud, Jung and many others who have sought understanding of the mystery of human behavior and consciousness. Dreams are a way for us to recognize and work with these patterns. I feel that Dr. Joy is an effective, original and powerful teacher in this area.

One of the most interesting and fruitful approaches we can bring to the interpretation of dreams is the concept of self as a multiple being. Joy is a contemporary pioneer in this work, presenting it in a way which allows anyone with firm intention to discover the reality of the idea.

I had often worked with the idea of inner dialog between different "voices" within myself which held differing agendas and perspectives. For example, I would act out younger "pieces" of myself in Gestalt work, ask them what they wanted, use them to dialog with my inner images of my parents and so on. Nonetheless, I always saw this as a sort of inner game for getting information and working with my feelings about the areas of my life and relationships which were unsatisfactory to me. I did not really feel the individual pieces as distinct aspects within.

When I finally broke through into the feeling levels of this radical concept of multiplicity, I was astounded at the recognition of truly different portions of myself within. I had always associated true multiplicity with a pathological state; the classic multiple personality disorder, once referred to as schizophrenia. If you are familiar with the movie *Sybil* you will have an accurate idea of my perception. It was exciting to discover whole new dimensions of self which were not merely products of an intellectual exercise in therapeutic approaches. I could see that this was a resource for empowerment and discovery which could never be exhausted. The multiple aspects of self may be seen clearly in dreams and bringing this perspective to dream interpretation opens a whole new range of possibilities.

One of the most powerful potentials that dreams hold for us is the possible discovery and resolution of the patterns we carry which lead to victimization, addiction and disease. It can be difficult to recognize that situations and problems which we find unpleasant or destructive in life can serve us in some definite way. As one integrates and expands upon this idea one crosses the border from the conventional and safer areas of psychology and science and enters a twilight zone loaded with booby traps for the unwary. The idea once grasped is interesting enough; the implications are staggering. Ultimately we are faced with the reality of our personal responsibility within any given situation.

In pop psychology and in much of the metaphysical literature which is available, variants of this idea about responsibility for our lives are frequently presented; but in a practical sense there is little we usually learn from these approaches in terms of real life. Sometimes powerful behavioral changes may be adopted, but it is difficult to change our perception of our responsibility in the world and our relationship to it and then implement practical results based on that new perception. This is particularly true when we are feeling victimized by life.

It takes only an unpleasant and uncontrollable event to shatter our fragile conceptions of responsibility and throw us into the role of victim. Often this conception of self as victim has been with us since our earliest memories, and we can always find confirmation externally for our perception of self in this way. Is there anyone who has not at some time felt victimized by circumstance and fate?

I spent years exploring various approaches which dealt with the issue of victimization and doing something about the feelings which go with it. By this you might deduce that I often thought of myself as a victim of different forces in my life, and you would be right!

It is not a trivial thing to feel deeply victimized. Whatever the reason for the feelings, it is a deep wounding of the soul, a scarring upon the psyche which must be healed in some way if a sense of the joy and spirit of life is to be restored or even perceived. Dreams are one of the most potent sources available to us for discovering the underlying patterns which lead to victimization and the fear and anger which go with it. We can learn to shift perception so that the secrets of the unconscious patternings that lead to victimization and their possible resolution may be revealed. This can lead to the healing. This work in fundamental in my approach to dreams, and it was Dr. Joy who showed me the way. For this especially, I am deeply grateful.

My challenge in this book was to in some way present my experience of the power of dreams as a tool for self discovery and change. More importantly, I wanted to present something which could be used and assimilated systematically, information which would have practical benefits and applications. Most of us do not have the benefit of extensive education or background in the fields of psychology or dream research. We are not familiar with the traditions of dreaming and the lessons they teach as seen in mythology or in primitive societies where even today dreams are still seen as important. That information is available to anyone who is really interested in those areas. What most of us do have is years of experience of dreaming, but without understanding. I have tried to bridge this gap between experience and understanding, and to present a practical manual for dreamers, a workbook which can be referred to and utilized as needed, a course in self discovery through the exploration of our inner selves as seen in dreams.

This book contains a systematic and proven approach to the understanding of dreams. It does not contain lists of symbols or interpretations for the dream images which may appear. Only you can discover what, exactly, the images in your dreams mean for you. The book does contain step by step information which can lead you to success with your dreams, success which will then bear fruit in your waking, outer life in the real world.

What Your Dreams Can Teach You is divided into two sections. Section One covers all the fundamentals you need to know to begin interpreting dreams. With the information contained in this section you will be able to immediately begin getting useful information from your dreaming consciousness. Section Two develops these fundamentals and brings in some additional ideas and tools for interpretation. Many examples of dreams are given which show how it is done through step by step analysis.

Throughout the book you will find sections or ideas which are emphasized by the phrase **"KEY POINT."** These important areas will be set aside from the main text and highlighted. If you pay attention to these key ideas you will quickly master the tools you need to interpret your dreams with increasing accuracy and understanding.

All of the information in this book comes from many years of practice and experience. Again and again, I have seen people who used this approach break into deep and excited understanding as the meaning of their dreams became clear to them. In turn, they took this new understanding and used the information they had discovered to affect their daily lives for the better.

This book contains a great deal of information about dreams. It is compact and specific. Expect to read it again and again, as you would any resource manual.

In this modern world, information is power. Your dreams offer you the power of understanding self, and through self understanding an avenue to the understanding of others. Dreams contain practical information for you and about you. As your knowledge grows your ability to move your life in the direction you choose increases, and you begin to take steps which can break down barriers to success and health, love and relationship.

You are about to embark on a journey into the rich and mysterious world of dreams. It is my hope that this book will assist you in understanding and discovering the fascinating secrets which your dreams can bring to you.

I wish you good fortune on your journey.

Alex Lukeman
Fort Collins, Colorado
Spring, 1990

Section One

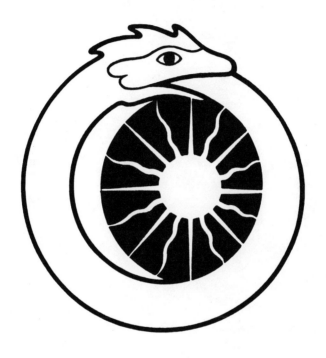

1
WHAT DREAMS ARE

Dreams have been with us since the dawn of human experience. The earliest myths and stories from every culture tell of dreams and their power to bring the dreamer information. In those tribal societies which survive today dreams are still seen as awesome and powerful messages from the gods or from supernatural realms. They are either sought for guidance or feared, according to the culture of the tribe.

Historically dreams have been emphasized at certain crucial moments. A famous example concerns the emperor Constantine. On the eve of the battle for Byzantium he is said to have had a dream of a fiery cross in the sky. He was told "In this sign shall you conquer." As a result of the dream he pledged that with victory on the coming day he would establish Christianity as the official religion of the Roman Empire. Constantine did conquer, and as a result Christianity was given powerful protection and support under his rule and the rule of succeeding emperors. Because of a dream the course of Christianity's evolution as a world religion was set firm and steadied.

In ancient Greece many came to the Oracle at Delphi. Kings and senators, merchants and soldiers petitioned the Oracle to have their dreams interpreted and thus to have the "messages of the Gods" made clear to them. In the Temple at Delphi, special rooms and benches were set aside where the supplicant would lie down to sleep and dream. The next day the Oracle would, with suitable ritual and offerings, interpret the dream for the dreamer. The Oracle was trained from an early age for the role she played. She knew something which we can re-discover;

KEY POINT

Dreams are an interface with a source of wisdom and knowledge not usually available to us in our waking consciousness.

Dreams are crucial for our everyday health and well-being. Studies by researchers in sleep and dreaming have shown that very bizarre things start to happen when people are prevented from dreaming. Exhaustion, confusion, hallucinations, irritability and physical illness begin to manifest. It is not just interrupted sleep which leads to these unpleasant results. People who sleep for very brief periods of time who do not have their dreams interrupted may be tired but they do not display the other symptoms of distress in the psyche. This seems to indicate that dreams provide an essential and fundamental balancing force within our consciousness which is independent of the body's need for sleep.

A deeper understanding of this balancing force within can lead us to a more balanced life and deeper understanding of ourselves.

The Language of Dreams

The language of dreams is symbolic. A symbol, by definition, is something which represents something else. It is not merely a substitution for something else. To be a symbol, the image or representation must contain many shadings and nuances of depth. A symbol contains meaning which goes far beyond the outer appearance. We have all heard the phrase that "a picture is worth a thousand words." We recognize that a picture conveys more information to us than even the best description. The same principle applies to dream images.

As with any unknown language, we must take the time to study and reflect if we wish to make sense of the communication. Would you expect to pick up a book written in an unfamiliar language and immediately begin to understand what it had to say? You would not know if you held a novel, a text book, a poem or a grocery list! You might recognize a word here and there which seemed familiar. You might then think you knew what you were reading. After learning the language you might discover that you were completely mistaken. So it is with dreams. The images presented to us in the dream may seem familiar, but we often make the mistake of thinking that the appearance of the dream image is literal in its meaning. This is a fundamental error in most cases.

KEY POINT

The images of our dreams always contain deeper levels of meaning which may have little to do with the outer appearance of the symbol.

This can be very confusing! For example, if your mother appears in a dream, you might have a tendency to think that the dream is about your real, physical mother. But if you pause for only a moment and begin to think of all the things mother means to you, good, bad and indifferent, you quickly realize that the image of "Mother" is far more than a simple picture of a person; it is a powerful and immensely complex range of possibility of meaning; it is a symbol.

KEY POINT

The symbols which appear as dream images to you are almost always personal in nature; therefore only you can ultimately interpret the correct meaning each image holds for you.

To successfully interpret a dream we need to discover the feeling and meaning which each dream image/symbol holds for us.

Later we will explore ways by which we can begin to understand our personal dream language.

The Conscious and Unconscious Mind

For the purpose of learning about dreams we can simplify psychology and divide the mind, or awareness, into two personal areas. We will call these the CONSCIOUS and the UNCONSCIOUS mind. For our purpose, the conscious mind is that part of our awareness which is functioning when we are awake and going about our lives. It is an observable and observing part of us and contains our outer personality levels, our outer ego structure or "I." It is the part which acts out the end results of all our decision making process. It is our perceptual interface with life and the world.

The unconscious mind is not so easily defined. In essence, it may only be defined in contrast to the conscious. In other words, what is not conscious is unconscious. By definition, if something is unconscious we are not conscious of it and therefore do not even know it exists! Right away we begin to see some of the difficulty when we try to get a handle on the unconscious. Since dreams arise from unconscious areas within us, they are a principle way to discover just what is going on inside on an unconscious level. The unconscious mind is usually not available to us without special training which allows it to be seen by the conscious part. Since the unconscious is just as much a part of us as the conscious, and since dreams show us something about the unconscious, dreams become a way for us to discover more of ourselves and more of who we are.

It is not a new idea to suggest or say that the unconscious part of our mind is by far the greater part. Nor is it a new idea to say that the unconscious never forgets anything that we have ever experienced in our lives. All the information of our lives is stored in the unconscious. It is probably just as well that most of it seems unavailable, or we might be overwhelmed by the amount of our experience.

KEY POINT

Dreams are a way for the Unconscious mind to bring information to us as needed. From the wealth of infor-

mation in our lives which has been stored and never forgotten, dreams access our own personal library of wisdom and present that wisdom symbolically to our Conscious awareness.

Dreams which are remembered are available to our conscious mind, and if we can understand the messages they contain we have bridged a gap between conscious and unconscious. Dreams are the easiest and fastest way to access the unconscious wisdom we all possess.

Later in the book we will look more deeply at the unconscious and see if we can understand why it presents material to us in dreams. Also we will try to understand why some of the dream material can be unsettling or frightening to us. The unconscious is a mystery which we can explore with some success, as long as we do not make the mistake of placing our conscious judgments and belief structures upon it.

Expanded Awareness and Wisdom

So far in our brief discussion we have been looking at the idea of the conscious and unconscious mind as a personal expression of who we are. This is sufficient for a good understanding of dreams, because we can see how there is plenty of material for our minds to work with. This is based simply on our life experiences. We contain a huge personal reference library of everything that has ever been presented to our awareness, every book, every film, every sight and sound, every feeling and sensed perception. All of this life material can be used by the unconscious to create scenarios which present information to us in our dreams. This would be more than enough for a rich dreaming experience.

What if there is another and impersonal dimension to be added? For example, there are many recorded instances of prophetic dreams foreshadowing events in the world which had not yet happened. Dreams have been reported which showed events occurring at a place far distant from the dreamer. These were dreams which could not have been based on the dreamer's personal experience. From the viewpoint of hard science, these kinds of phenomena are seen as "anecdotal." This means that they cannot be proven to have happened, since the report is based on a personal event and cannot be duplicated by scientific experiment. Each of us must make our own choice as to whether we feel this kind of dream has validity or not. It is easier for us to accept this if we have had a personal experience of prophetic or clairvoyant dreams.

There are also dreams which bring forth new discoveries and ideas. The discovery of Benzene is a well known example. The structure of this then unknown substance was presented in a dream. The formula for insulin was written down in the middle of the night after waking from a dream.

KEY POINT

Dreams may be a way by which we can connect to a greater awareness. This awareness is not based on or dependent upon our personal experience. This awareness may contain all wisdom and knowledge.

If this is true, then our unconscious mind is a powerful transceiver, capable of linking with a greater awareness and exchanging information with that awareness. In turn the information received may be communicated to us through the process of dreaming. Dreams bring the information one step further to our waking and conscious mind.

KEY POINT

Our unconscious mind is connected to powerful intuitive/ wisdom areas which exist independently of our "normal" awareness and experience. Dreams are a way for this larger area of awareness and information to make itself known to us.

2
HOW TO BEGIN WORK
WITH YOUR DREAMS

Step One:
Recording Your Dreams

Before you can do anything with your dreams you must first become skilled at recording and remembering them. Most of us remember occasional fragments of our dreams or even longer stretches or scenes. Often the dreams we remember best are those which shock or horrify us — the "nightmare." Nightmares are certainly a way of getting our attention, because the terrifying material imprints itself on our waking mind, even though we may not understand what it means or simply shrug it off as a "bad dream."

There is no such thing as a "bad dream." All dreams are useful to us. When we have a particularly shocking dream it usually means that the material is important for us to understand. It is the unconscious mind's way of trying to get through. It is possible to understand the message of a nightmare. Once the message is understood the feeling of horror transforms.

Fortunately for our comfort and rest, most dreams will not be like this. As we begin to consciously make the effort to remember our dreams a rich and intriguing world begins to open to us. Every night can turn into an adventure, better than going to the movies and cheaper, too!

9

Sometimes people believe that they never dream, or if they know they have dreams, they never remember them. If you are one of these people, be assured that you do dream and that you can learn to remember. As soon as your unconscious gets the message that you are really interested in what it has to say, you will be surprised at the number and depth of the dreams you begin to remember.

The first thing you must do is prepare yourself to record your dreams in some manner. There are three basic approaches to this.

1. Place a pad, paper, pen and small light by your bed when you prepare for sleep. A small flashlight works very well. With this technique you will teach yourself to wake up when you have a dream. You write down on the pad everything you can remember of the dream, or at least key events and scenes from the dream. The light is a good idea, as any of you who have tried to write in the dark and read your writing in the morning know! In the morning you rewrite the dream legibly with any extra details or events which you may not have put down during the night.

2. Get a small tape recorder which plays and records, such as a Sony Walkman or similar small machine. A voice activated recorder may be a good choice for you. You turn on the power at night and make sure there is a blank tape or space on the tape for the dream. When you have a dream and wake up, you simply turn on the recorder and speak the dream as you remember it into the built in microphone. This technique has the advantage of not needing a light or having to wake up enough to write something down. In the morning or at your convenience, you listen to the dream you have recorded and write it down if you wish.

3. When you wake in the morning you write down any dreams or fragments of dreams which you may have had during the night. Although this may seem the easiest method, it has the disadvantage of losing whole sections of the dreams which may vanish with waking consciousness. Particularly if you wake with an alarm, you may find that the dreams are driven right out of your waking mind, and they will be lost to you.

I have used all three of these methods and they all work. The tape recorder provides the most complete detail for me, although writing the dream down during the night can also be very complete.

KEY POINT

The first step to working with dreams is recording everything you can remember, no matter how fragmentary or unimportant the dream may seem to you at the time. Without recording the dream, memory rapidly fades and the information in that particular dream is lost to you.

Step Two: Remembering Your Dreams

Of course, recording dreams isn't much use if you don't remember what you dreamed. Then you would have nothing to record! Preparing to record the dreams is the first step because this alone may stimulate the memory. You must be ready to record any dream which you might have. Usually we need to do something to stimulate our ability to remember. Further along in the book is a meditation you may use to help you remember. Also you will find information about an audio cassette tape called "Dream Mysteries" which can assist you with this. It is not necessary to have the tape to be very successful at remembering. The important thing is to prepare the mind for the memory of dreams.

The most powerful time for us to consciously touch the bridge between conscious and unconscious mind is in the "twilight zone" between sleep and wakefulness. During this temporary period many of the filters which our outer mind imposes have been removed. The lines of communication are more open. Material can flow more freely between conscious and unconscious. This is a good time to tell yourself that you want to remember your dreams. Try this simple technique.

1. Lie comfortably on your back as you quietly prepare for sleep.

2. Be sure that you will not be interrupted or disturbed — not a bad idea for simply going to sleep!

3. Place your hand over the center of your chest, resting lightly and comfortably. Feel the warmth of your hand and your chest.

4. Say to yourself, "Tonight I am going to remember my dreams. Tonight I will remember my dreams. I want to remember my dreams."

5. Continue to repeat this to yourself for a few minutes. You may or may not say this out loud. Be aware of your hand resting lightly on your chest. The hand signals you that you are ready to remember your dreams.

You may vary the wording or phrase which you choose to repeat to yourself. For example, you might add your name to the phrase, telling yourself that you will remember your dreams. After you have done this for a few minutes, simply relax and drift off to sleep. Make sure that you have first prepared to record your dreams and that you are aware of this.

This simple approach is very effective for stimulating memory. I have had people who did this report to me that they began dreaming again after many months or years with no memory of dreams. They were excited by the detail and richness of what they were remembering. You can do it also.

Remembering and recording your dreams will become easier with practice. Don't be discouraged if at first not much seems to happen. Stick with it and the results will come. Don't be a taskmaster to yourself about remembering and recording. Set up a feeling for yourself of discovery and co-operation with something within you which dreams. You will be pleased when the results do come.

KEY POINT

The state of consciousness between wakefulness and sleep is a powerful time for helping you remember your dreams. By telling yourself that you wish to remember your dreams while you are drifting off to sleep, you will begin to let the unconscious know that you are serious about listening to the messages of your dreams.

Step Three: Keeping a Dream Journal

A dream journal is one of the best ways to work with your dreams. When you write down the final copy of the dream keep it in a special book for just that purpose. Blank books in various sizes and nicely bound can be purchased at any good bookstore.

The advantages to keeping a journal are several. It gives you a convenient place to keep a record of all your dreams. When you record the dream, leave a blank page beside it. Later you may have new thoughts and ideas about the dream which you may wish to write down. Often over a period of time a series of dreams will present a pattern of events and images. In the pattern of the separate dreams and their similarities will be contained a message for you which you need to know about. This may not be immediately apparent. The dreams could extend over months or even years, and you will probably have forgotten them. When you go back through your dream journal something may leap out at you as you find any similarities between the dreams. If you can learn to see the pattern of any sequence of dreams which relate to the same issue, you may be able to resolve that issue.

A pattern is always predictable in its result. When a shirtmaker uses a pattern to manufacture a shirt, the result is always a shirt. One never gets a pair of pants from a shirt pattern! If you can see a pattern, you can then predict the result. If you don't like the result, you can change the pattern. The pattern will reveal to you how you relate to whatever the subject is. This gives you the information you need to make any necessary changes.

KEY POINT

A series of dreams over time may present you with different but similar pieces of information about the same issue within your psyche. If you can see the pattern of the dreams and how they relate to one another, you may then be able to resolve the issue by taking action based on the advice which you have been given.

It is much easier to read all your dreams in one place than to shuffle through various sheets of paper and little notes to yourself. Take my word for it, a dream journal is one of your best tools for understanding.

Psyche

The word "psyche" needs to be defined. The traditional, Webster's dictionary definition describes psyche as "soul, spirit, mind; the principle of mental and emotional life." The word is Greek in origin and from this root come related words like psychology, psychiatry, etc. I think of the word psyche as our personal totality of mind, body and spirit — the whole ball of wax.

I am interested in discovering more of who I am in my totality. It seems to me that the more I understand about myself, the more options will be available to me in my life and the more I will be able to enrich my experience of life. Dreams are the most immediate and obvious tool for this inner exploration.

3
HOW TO BEGIN INTERPRETING DREAMS

Step Four: The First Interpretation

Now that you have remembered and recorded your dream, it's time to see if you can understand it. It's important that you tell yourself that you can do it! The part of our minds which is sure we can't do something is never able to accomplish the task at hand. You do have within you a part which knows very well how to interpret dreams. After all, you had the dream, didn't you? That dream came from somewhere in your unconscious. Something in your unconscious decided that the images of the dream had clear meaning and importance for you. It created images to communicate with you. It knows the meaning of the images, even if your conscious mind is not at all sure what those images mean. So something within you knows the meaning of the dream. Something within you knows how to get the meanings of the images clear to your conscious mind.

KEY POINT

Something within you brought you the dream. Something within you knows the meaning of the images of the dream. Something within you knows how to interpret the dream to your conscious mind.

15

I call this piece which knows how to interpret the dream "The Dreamer Within." We might think of this as an aspect of ourselves which is willing to help us understand the meaning of our dreams. The first thing I do when I want to interpret a dream is ASK for this part of me to come forward and help. Sound silly? Remember that we are dealing here with areas of our consciousness which are not clearly understood. I find that it is a great help to take the time to consciously ask for assistance from my own unconscious! In this way we set up a feeling of co-operation within, rather than a struggle to try and figure something out with a part of our mind which has no real ability for the task of dream interpretation. This is one of the reasons people have so much trouble understanding dreams. It is as if we were trying to mow the lawn with a snow shovel, or find our apartment in the wrong building. It won't work.

KEY POINT

ASK your unconscious to help you understand the dream. The "Dreamer Within" knows how to interpret the dream and will help you if you learn to work with it.

Developing a sense of the "Dreamer Within" is essential for understanding the deepest levels of a dream. To get to this piece within you it is necessary to shift from your ordinary state of consciousness to another level. In the chapter called "TOOL BOX" you will find information about the audio cassette *Dream Mysteries*. You can use this tape to help you shift levels of awareness and access the "Dreamer Within."

The first interpretation is usually not very accurate, but it will sometimes provide you with good information nonetheless. There are really three levels to be looked at in interpretation. This idea will be developed as we move further into the book. For now, think of the first interpretation as being on the "first level." On this level the images of the dream are interpreted by association with what is already familiar to you in your conscious mind. For example, a friend you know in real life appears in the dream. On the first level, you think the dream has something to do with this real person. This will be true but not in the way you think!

When you begin to work with dreams, it is very helpful to write down your first impression of what the dream might mean, especially your feeling about it. You may have a sense that the dream is more or less important, that the you feel happy, sad, thoughtful, angry, frightened, aroused, confused, or something else. Note this down.

Note also how you felt in the dream. As you know, when you are dreaming it seems just as real to you as your waking life. You have feelings during the dream just as you do in waking life. How you feel about something in the dream and how you feel in waking life may be significantly different. That is important information. Make a note of everything you can remember about the dream. You may have forgotten something when you first wrote down the dream. If so, write it down when you return to begin the interpretation. No detail of the dream is unimportant.

KEY POINT

All the images and details of a dream are important, no matter how insignificant they may seem at first.

Let's review what we have talked about so far in regard to beginning the interpretation.

1. ASK for help from your unconscious in interpreting the dream.
2. Remember that something in you knows how to interpret dreams.
3. Write down your first impression of what the dream means.
4. Write down how you felt during the dream.
5. Write down how you feel about the dream now.
6. Write down any further details which you may remember.
7. Write down what you think the dream is about.

It is important to remember that your dreaming consciousness is not the same as your waking consciousness. You in the dream does not necessarily know more than You awake. You in the dream may feel differently about something than you do when you are awake. How you feel in the dream is valuable information. How you feel about the same thing when you are awake can also give you excellent information. As you begin to interpret dreams this will become clearer to you.

KEY POINT

The differences and similarities between how you feel in the dreaming awareness and how you feel in your waking awareness provide you with valuable clues and information about the real content of the dream. This becomes clearer with practice and observation.

Step Five: The Deeper Interpretation

In some ways interpreting a dream is like reviewing a movie. When you watch a movie, you are presented with an array of images which establish setting, mood and feeling tones. There are characters in the movie, and you feel about them in certain ways. Each character has a role to play to fill out the story line. The actions of the characters combined with the setting and the story line establish the theme of the movie. The story line then develops to elaborate on the theme and create a whole which is the film.

An idea which I learned from Brugh Joy has proven very helpful to me in interpreting dreams. Simply put, the idea is that each dream will begin with a section which establishes the theme. This is just like the overture to a symphony or the opening sequence of a movie. It will contain the key elements of the entire composition. Sometimes you will sense that there has been something forgotten in the dream before the section which you remember. Generally the first part which you do remember will state the theme or central message of the dream. The rest of the dream will develop this theme and give you more information about the subject.

KEY POINT

The first part of a dream establishes the theme and symbolic "message" of the entire dream. If you can understand this initial presentation, you can understand the rest of the dream more easily. The remainder of the dream will generally develop the theme stated in the opening sequence.

How do we begin our approach to a deeper understanding of the dream? You have already made a "first impression" interpretation, looking at how you felt during the dream, what it first may mean to you and writing down whatever comes to mind about the dream. For the moment, set this first interpretation aside. It is important to let go of what you think the dream may mean at this point. Even if your first interpretation turns out to be correct, it is necessary to set this aside and take a fresh approach.

KEY POINT

Even if your first interpretation of the dream turns out to be accurate, you must seek a fresh perspective which views the dream anew. This can provide the insight and intuitive understanding which is necessary for successful interpretation.

Now we have to go to the "second level" of interpretation. The second level begins to make logical associations and deductions about the symbolic images and events within the dream which go beyond the surface meaning of the images. It is detective work, and can be a lot of fun. Let's begin by looking at examples of actual dreams to illustrate the points I will be making. There are always distinct sections in a dream. Each section will contain new elements which can be identified and worked with. At this stage in our journey I will give actual dream examples along with detailed interpretations. This is to give you a feel for how it's done. Later on you will use the worksheets presented in this book to make your own interpretations of dreams you may have.

Example Number One: Carl's Dream.

Something is missing or incomplete. I am in a large church, very dim, looking for something. I can't find it. As I turn to go out, I realize that what I have been looking for is a paper hidden behind the altar. I have been "listening" to find it and realize there was a flaw in what I heard, an extraneous noise. Now that I know this, I can find the paper. I am saying, almost shouting, "I can use it! I know what to do! I won't abuse it!" I go back in and am even willing to interrupt the service to get to the paper, but David stops me.

Later, I am relating this dream to John, who appears interested. I tell John that all my dreams lately deal with something missing or incomplete. True — he agrees.

You do not need to know anything about the dreamer in order to understand the dream fairly well, but any extra information is helpful. If you have a dream, the information is available. If someone you know has a dream, you can ask questions to help find out what certain people or images may mean for them. I will give you some background about Carl which will help with the dream.

Carl is a man who has spent many years on what might be termed a "spiritual quest." He has taken on the role of teacher for others who also are searching for deeper meaning and understanding in their lives. When he related this dream, he was noticeably uncomfortable with the material. He sensed that this dream might indicate some fundamental flaw in his work and perception. This was born out by interpretation.

KEY POINT

The interpretations which follow throughout the rest of this book are brought forward by the "Dreamer Within." This aspect speaks with certainty about the meaning of the symbols in any given dream. This does not mean that these symbols always represent the same thing. A symbol which appears in one dream may mean something entirely different in another dream. Since each dream is unique, and since each of us has a personal symbolic language, it is

a mistake to assume that a symbolic dream image always stands for the same meaning.

You can begin now to practice shifting levels of awareness and getting in touch with the "Dreamer Within." Close your eyes, and sit quietly for a moment. When you feel calm simply ask for something to come forward within you which knows how to interpret dreams. You may or may not get a sense of a different feeling within you. Just take what you get. It does require practice, so now is a good time for you to start.

The opening sequence of Carl's dream is very indicative of the material which is going to be developed. " Something is missing." This is a straightforward statement that essential information, material or connection is not present. The nature of the missing something is indicated by the setting of the dim, large church. The setting of a dream sequence always tells us something. This setting tells us that the theme of the dream will have to do with the spiritual area of this man's consciousness.

The lighting is another clue. The dimness emphasizes the hidden nature of the material. This is something which is not clearly seen. After all, his mind could have presented a church brightly lit, but this would not be consistent with the theme of something hidden which is expressed in the dream. The lighting is an important detail.

How did I arrive at this interpretation? This is where the second level kicks in. I think about the image of a church. What is a church? A church is a place of religious worship; a church is where people go to honor God and Spirit; a church is a building where spiritual areas are important; a church is a place which people recognize as being focused on spiritual areas. A church is also a community center; a place where weddings and funerals, baptisms and other ceremonies take place; a place for different personal and community functions. The common element in all activities which take place in a church is the spiritual, even if the event is a picnic or a garage sale! In other words, the church is a context. Anything which happens there is under the umbrella of spiritual connection.

What do you think a church represents? A church is not merely a place where one goes to practice one's religion, or participate in activities of a spiritual or religious nature. A church is also a building, a structure.

What is a church/structure? This is the kind of question we must ask to get to the heart of the dream. The church represents an area of consciousness which is concerned with spiritual pursuits. A second level reading emphasizes church as structure. Church = structure = spiritual beliefs, held in form.

KEY POINT

Dreams may be understood on several different "levels," each level going somewhat deeper than the one before. New information is found on each level. To fully and successfully interpret a dream, we must take the time to search out the deeper meanings which may always be found.

It is a large church. We might be looking at a well developed and established belief system regarding spirit and God. This is a logical, second level deduction. Formal religious structure is a way of containing, understanding and setting boundaries on the spiritual. It is in essence a masculine approach. It is an attempt to define through structure something which is not understandable in linear terms. In this way humans try to understand and experience the mystery of Spirit and Universal Consciousness. We will explore feminine and masculine context later on in the book.

Based on this way of looking at the church symbol in the dream, what can we discover? Remember that Carl is searching for something in the church which is hidden from him. The theme to be developed in this dream will concern the dreamer's search for something which he feels he needs and does not possess. This will be within the boundaries of Carl's well developed belief system and representation of spirit and the spiritual.

How are you doing so far? Do you begin to get a feel for how even the simplest beginning contains a wealth of symbolic information for the dreamer? Does the interpretation feel "right" to you? We need to look at each detail of the dream to attempt to come to an understanding of the meaning of each symbol. When we think of "church" we might be tempted to rush on by. We might briefly dismiss the symbol as mere setting so that we can get on to the rest of the dream. Or we might be satisfied with an initial level of interpretation as "spiritual area," and thus miss a few more clues.

KEY POINT

To successfully interpret a dream, you must be patient and examine carefully every detail. It is always worthwhile to think again about familiar items and situations to see if you are really feeling into the potential the images hold. The church in the above dream section is an example of this point.

As the dream continues, the dreamer turns to leave the church, unable to find that which is sought. This indicates a part of his consciousness which is discouraged with the approach which he has been taking. In his outer life, Carl at this time was indeed feeling at something of a dead end in his work. He was feeling a need for new stimulus, and a certain disillusionment with what he had accomplished so far.

Suddenly Carl realizes (in the dream) that what he has been looking for is a paper hidden behind the altar. He also realizes that he has been "listening" in order to find it, but that there is a flaw in what he has heard.

Now the dream is beginning to present an elaboration on the material. A paper contains information of some sort. There was a sense by Carl when he related the dream of something written on the paper. This is the information he has been seeking. "Paper" and "information," like "church," are words/images/thoughts which needs to be examined. Paper = information = knowing. The paper symbolizes a knowledge the dreamer does not yet possess consciously.

Do you see how we arrive at this interpretation?

The "listening" which is flawed means Carl has been incorrectly interpreting that which he has "heard." What he has "heard" is the information/knowing/experience which he has been building up (church again!) about the spiritual for many years. The dream then tells Carl that since he knows this, he can now find the missing paper, which is hidden behind the altar.

The altar represents the essential mystery of Spirit. The altar is the heart of every church/temple. Carl has to somehow approach this mystery in order to find the knowledge he seeks. He now knows that something has been flawed in his perception. The implication is that recognizing the flaw will lead to that which is at present hidden from him in the area he seeks. This is the practical advice for the real world which this section contains. Find the flaw in perception which you now know exists and the knowledge will be revealed to you.

We are now moving to a deeper level, a "third level" of interpretation. On this level intuitive deductions and leaps of understanding are made. This is the level which holds the true message of the dream. It is the level which gives practical advice for the conscious mind to work with. This is usually not stated directly in the dream but is implied by the images the dream offers.

KEY POINT

Much of the information for change contained in a dream is understood by implication, rather than direct advice. A dream will present the current state of affairs and sometimes show a direction to be followed, if action is necessary. Just as often, what is not shown or stated is as important as what is shown. This is one reason dreams are difficult to understand.

I want to make another "Key Point" here which we need to consider. I will explain this more thoroughly in the chapter about the Unconscious Mind. For now, please consider it as a working context for looking at dreams.

KEY POINT

Dreams ALWAYS tell the truth about what is really going on within you. This is a fundamental perception which

must be held to successfully interpret dreams. Dreams NEVER lie to you. Confusion comes not from the dream but from the outer mind's attempts to understand.

Now comes a very interesting part, because it reveals honestly certain areas of Carl's psyche which he might otherwise wish to ignore. This is the section of statements, almost shouted "I can use it! I know what to do! I won't abuse it!" Abuse what? When I asked Carl about this, his uncomfortable response was the "power" which this information might give him. He was uncomfortable because he recognized the less enlightened side of the "spiritual quest." This is the part which is motivated not by the desire to serve Spirit or be useful as an instrument of Spirit but to have power for its own sake. He thinks that in real life he might be unable to use power without abusing it. Carl is caught between the desire for spiritual knowledge and his uncertainty that he could use it wisely. This is a self judgement which emerges when dialoging with him about the dream.

When statements are shouted or images in some way appear to stand out from the rest of the dream it is an emphasis by the psyche on the material.

KEY POINT

When you take on a dream for understanding, you must be willing to be absolutely as honest as possible with yourself and how you feel.

KEY POINT

When something is emphasized in a dream through sound, color, or repetition it is important. When this happens we need to pay extra attention.

Are you still with me? If this were your dream, would you be able to feel honestly into the symbols and situations being presented? It was uncomfortable for Carl to notice that he had self serving motivations for his spiritual work. This is developed in the next sequence.

Carl is even willing in the dream to go back into the church and interrupt the "service" in order to get what he wants! He is stopped from doing this in the dream by David. In order to discover David's symbolic meaning in the dream, I asked Carl what he thought about David in real life. This is what emerged.

In waking life, David is a friend of Carl's who has become very successful by conducting a popular weekend "self discovery" training. The training features an elaborate belief system about Spirit and God. It emphasizes a set of techniques and practices which are designed to encourage self healing of the psychological woundings of life, particularly during childhood. There is also a focus on service to humanity and the world which is taught during the training. At one time Carl was deeply involved in this training and committed to its belief system.

Just as Carl sees that all is not as it seems in his outer motivations regarding spiritual power, he also sees the darker side of his involvement with this particular training. This side is concerned with being right about what the training teaches and not about what is "right" for the students who are being trained. The reward for Carl was a position of personal power within the training community. The "power" came with the position, so to speak. However, the "power" was dependent on maintaining the belief system which the training presented. As Carl matured in his understanding a conflict developed. It became more and more difficult for him to reconcile his new understanding and the belief system which he taught in order to preserve his power and position within the community. Eventually he left because he could no longer feel in integrity with himself if he stayed.

The training elevates the child part of self to a position of prominence. This sets up a teaching dynamic which is parental in nature, establishing a set of rules for the spirit which the good child will follow. In turn this leads to dependence on the community and teaching which the training represents. It sets up dependence on the leaders of the community at the expense of authorizing self. Carl is no longer willing to do this.

The figure of David represents all of this to Carl, and especially a belief about life and Spirit which is not consistent with

Carl's current understanding and teachings. Yet, in the dream, it is David who stops him from going to the altar where the information is hidden.

What does this mean? Can you take a moment, now and feel into what the message of this symbol means to Carl?

If you thought that David represents an area within Carl's own consciousness active in its beliefs and dogma, you are right. Within Carl a piece is alive and well which holds to the old viewpoints. On the negative side of things, this aspect is concerned with authority and power over others. It is concerned with a belief about Spirit and being right about that. Moreover, this aspect is inconsistent with what it teaches and what it does to maintain its position of authority. Carl needs to recognize how this powerful but self serving and dogmatic area within himself is somehow capable of blocking access to the dream altar and that which is hidden there. What is hidden represents a more essential truth or connection to Spirit. This is what is missing.

KEY POINT

The people who appear in your dreams whom you know in real life symbolize not only past or present associations, but also ways of perceiving life and reality. Because they are in your dream, they represent aspects of you which may also perceive life in that way.

As Carl's dream continues the next sequence emphasizes the information already presented. Carl dreams that he is relating the dream analyzed above to John. John is a teacher and friend of Carl's, a person who has come to symbolize many things in Carl's consciousness. One of these things is wisdom in the spiritual sense. John is interested in the story about the hidden paper. This indicates further its symbolic importance to Carl. Carl again repeats the theme (in the dream) of "something missing or incomplete in all my dreams lately." John, the symbol of spiritual knowledge, then puts a symbolic capper on the importance of the dream by agreeing that this is true.

We have now completed a fairly deep analysis of the dream. The message can be summed up. If Carl were to receive a telegram from someplace with this message, it might read as follows:

Dear Carl: You need to pay attention to the following. STOP. You are not seeing clearly what needs to be done. STOP. You have not understood correctly the information you have received. STOP. The information you seek is contained within the structure of Spirit you have created but is still hidden from you. STOP. You must pay attention to self serving areas within you which are still seeking power from the position of "spiritual authority." STOP. You should review past ideas and perceptions of what constitutes "spiritual" and discover if you are still holding on to ideas which serve self primarily. STOP. The information you seek is not available to you until you have done this work. STOP. You feel incomplete because you have not yet connected with the heart of this information. STOP. This is true. STOP. End message.

No wonder Carl feels uncomfortable about this dream! Wouldn't you feel uneasy getting a message like that?

I'd like to briefly review the key points presented so far before we look at another dream. We have covered quite a bit of material already.

1. Dreams are an interface with a source of wisdom and knowledge not usually available to us in our waking consciousness.
2. The images of our dreams always contain deeper levels of meaning which may have little to do with the outer appearance of the symbol.
3. The symbols which appear as dream images are almost always personal in nature; therefore only you can ultimately interpret the correct meaning each image holds for you.
4. Dreams are a way for the Unconscious mind to bring information to us as needed.
5. Dreams may be a way by which we can connect to a greater awareness.
6. Our Unconscious mind is connected to powerful intuitive/wisdom areas which exist independently of

our "normal" awareness and experience.

7. The first step to working with dreams is recording everything you can remember.

8. The state of consciousness between wakefulness and sleep is a powerful time for helping you remember your dreams.

9. A series of dreams over time may present you with different but similar pieces of information about the issue within your psyche.

10. Something within you brought you the dream, knows the meaning of the images and knows how to interpret the dream to your conscious mind.

11. ASK your unconscious to help you understand the dream.

12. All the images and details of a dream are important.

13. The differences and similarities between how you feel in the dream and how you feel when awake give you valuable clues and information about the real content of the dream.

14. The first part of a dream establishes the theme and symbolic message of the entire dream. If you can understand this you can understand the rest of the dream more easily.

15. Even if your first interpretation turns out to be accurate you must seek a fresh perspective which views the dream anew.

16. The interpretations given in this book are brought forward by the "Dreamer Within." Even though this aspect speaks with certainty about the meaning of symbols, this does not mean that these symbols always represent the same thing.

17. Dreams may be understood on several different levels, each level going somewhat deeper than the one before. To fully understand a dream we must take the time to search out the deeper meanings which may always be found.

18. To successfully interpret a dream you must be patient and examine fully every detail.

19. Much of the information for change contained within a dream is understood by implication rather than direct advice.
20. Dreams always tell the truth about what is going on within you.
21. When you take on a dream for understanding you must be willing to be absolutely as honest as possible with yourself and how you feel.
22. The people who appear in your dreams whom you know in real life symbolize not only past and present associations but also ways of perceiving life and reality. They may represent aspects of you which also perceive life in that way.

This is a framework for your exploration. With practice you will be able to determine if what I have stated above is true for you. Please, don't just take my word for it. Apply the ideas expressed above and make them work for you.

Let's look at another, longer dream. This dream was related by a woman in her early forties who has been attempting to reach a deeper understanding of herself and her life, which has not always been a happy one for her. We will look at the dream in sections and see how the theme and information is developed.

You can begin to utilize the previous key points which have been given to discover what the dream means as you go along. By breaking a dream down into obvious sections we can discover many interesting things which are often overlooked when viewing the dream as a whole. This is a very effective way to work with interpreting any dream.

Mary's Dream: Section One.

I was standing at a corner. A sidewalk ran in from the corner toward a magnificent old oak tree. The tree trunk was very thick and the canopy was a rich, Summer green with no dead leaves or branches. I spent some time with this tree, placing myself on different branches. The sidewalk circled the tree and led on to the corner of a building.

This is a good example of how the opening sequence of a dream states the theme to be worked with. Take a moment, now, to feel into the images which have been presented, especially the large, magnificent oak tree.

The tree is the central image in this section. This is one of those images which is seen again and again in mythology and stories of humankind's search for conscious interaction with God. The image of the "tree" can be found in almost every culture and time. It often occurs in stories of the quest for understanding and communion with God and Spirit. It appears as the "tree of life" in these stories, and symbolizes an essential and primal life force and energy, something Divine and central to not only our being but the being of all life in the universe. In one's relationship to the tree and the appearance of the tree much can be determined about one's relationship to life and the Transpersonal forces.

Transpersonal means "beyond the personal." A Transpersonal energy or force is something which is far greater than any one individual. A Transpersonal force, by definition, is not concerned with the personal agendas of our "egos." However we are deeply involved on a very personal level with these forces. When such an image appears in a dream, we know that the dreamer is being shown something fundamental about the dreamer's self. One of the great challenges we face as humans in a vast and impersonal universe is to discover our own personal and unique relationship to these larger forces.

Mary is first standing at a corner, that is, a place where one has a choice of direction. From here a sidewalk leads to the tree. This is significant, because it could just as easily have been a path or a thicket! Remember, the dreaming mind can choose any symbol it wants. A sidewalk is neat, orderly and man-made. It is a clear path, but it also has the qualities of the logical mind inherent in its nature. Mary is able to walk to the tree on this sidewalk. This shows that she has built up a mental area of logic and order which she uses as a path through life. One might say this is a more masculine side of her psyche, if we generalize and say that the masculine is more concerned with order and logic. By contrast, the feminine areas would be less concerned with control and order and more involved with feeling areas. The tree indicates powerful and natural forces of life present in her consciousness, available to her and accessible through the work she has done which has established the "sidewalk."

Mary explores the tree, placing herself on different branches. She puts herself in different relationships with the central symbol of life in its full Summer maturity. This is an excellent omen for her outer life, and her participation with life. As we shall see, though, there is more to come. The sidewalk circles the tree and leads on to the corner of a building.

Mary's Dream: Section Two.

The building was quite large and was of heavily carved stone. It reminded me of old court houses which were built by communities more as a statement about themselves than the function of the building. It was four complete stories with a smaller fifth floor situated on the roof of the fourth floor. The fifth floor had a domed roof which was supported by a series of columns. There were large columns at each corner of the building which ran the full height of the four floors and smaller columns supporting the curved archway over the entrance.

What do you think is meant by the thought Mary has in the dream about "communities" ? What does the symbol of the large building mean? This is the way her psyche presents information to her about what she has already built within. The "community" is the community within, composed of all the myriad aspects which make up who she is, known and unknown. It is indeed a statement by the "community" about self, and tells her that she has built a solid, strong structure within.

It reminds her, not accidentally, of a courthouse. A courthouse is a place where records are kept, administration is focused, and where "court" is held; where law is administered, where judgement is pronounced. What a powerful symbol for the mind and its view of the world! Judgement is implicit in the symbol of "courthouse," and an ordered, logical approach to life. This is what Mary has tried to create in her life, perhaps at the expense of something else. If that is so, then a later section of the dream may reveal what is lacking or needs to be corrected.

Numbers begin to appear here, and numbers can be confusing in dreams. The study of numbers as symbols is called numerology. In numerology all numbers have meaning, since they are symbols. All multiple numbers can be reduced to a single number, by adding all the digits together. For example, $27 = 2 + 7 = 9$. $3582 = 3 + 5 + 8 + 2 = 18 = 9$.

The building has four main stories which support a fifth, domed structure. The columns suggest strength and the domed structure, if you can see it in your mind's eye, might resemble a temple. You do actually see such temple-like top stories on older official buildings, which reflect the classical influence of Greece and Rome and the Italian Renaissance. On a deeper level, these architectural designs are suggesting the influence of the gods or the Divine, temples of power and mystery, graced and authorized by the Divine presence. So it is in Mary's dream.

Four is a number associated with foundational energies. The square or rectangle, with four sides, is fundamental in design. There are four winds, four seasons, four directions, four corners of the Earth in old mythologies. On a metaphysical and also tangible level the heart energy of Divine and unconditional love is located at the "fourth" chakra, or energy center.

The fifth and domed or rounded level represents a different area of this structure which Mary's psyche has created within. It is clearly part of but different from the rest of the building. Five has been called the number of man, and can be taken to represent the human condition, in life. Five is the area of the throat center. Thus it may be associated with expression of self and an externalization of that which is within.

It is not necessary to know anything about centers of energy or traditional interpretations of numbers to understand that the fifth floor in this dream symbolizes something different from the rest of the building.

KEY POINT

It is not necessary to be familiar with previous interpretations of symbols or their meanings in order to get a full understanding of the dream. Each symbol within a dream carries its own message, inherent in itself. If you take the time to feel into the image presented, the essential meaning of the image may be made clear to you.

The fifth level is resting on all the levels below it. The entrance, a curved archway in a square structure, suggests contrast. The contrast is between what the structure represents within Mary's psyche and a different area within her which allows access to this strong and spacious building.

Mary's Dream: Section Three.

The entrance was located in the corner and seemed small when compared with the scale of the building. Over the entrance was an inscription and the building's address, "12345."

The path from the tree leads to the corner of the building (a corner again) and to the entrance. It is not the grand entrance one might expect in such a building. This is saying that a certain humility may be called for in order to gain access. Mary needs to re-evaluate her ego involvement with the material of the dream. The numbers again state a progression, 1 through 5, suggesting a sequence and also a possibility of movement from one level or floor to the next. What do you think the numbers mean?

"12345" adds up to fifteen. $15 = 1 + 5 = 6$. Remember, in looking at numbers, one always reduces the total to a single digit. What does six sound like? To the unconscious "six" and "sex" could be the same! This is not a dream about only physical sex, which does not occur in the dream. Sex is about relationship, the relationship of energies. Six is a number of relationship. The relationship that is meant in the dream is the relationship within Mary of masculine and feminine energies and their expression. This is shown more clearly later on in the dream. For now, we are working with the "feeling" of curved, square, nature and man-made. All of this has been presented in the dream at this point.

Mary's Dream: Section Four.

I found myself on the second floor sitting in an overstuffed chair of rich purple velvet. The chair was placed in the center of the room with its back against a small yellow supporting wall. There were square support columns at each end of the wall. The chair was very comfortable and I sat there simply enjoying the room.

This section marks a transition in the dream to material which will begin to elaborate on what has already come before. The theme will be developed. The second floor is reached somehow through the entrance on the first floor. This is a step in the progression, and actually the rest of the dream will take place in this room. Therefore we can make the assumption that further progress through the building and what it symbolizes will depend on using whatever information is presented in this setting during the rest of the dream.

Close your eyes, and see if you can picture the setting . See the colors and try to feel into the energy and images of the dream.

The chair is set exactly in the center of the room. This is the seat of experience for Mary in her dream and is central to her understanding. It is backed by a supporting wall of yellow, and the square columns emphasize strength. The yellow color is traditionally a color of the mental areas. It is also a color of life and radiance, the color of the sun. These associations with yellow suggest a strong supporting system in Mary's psyche which backs her up in the symbolic events of the dream. The purple suggests a royal color, like a throne, a place of security and strength. All of this tells her that she has the support and comfort she needs within to deal with whatever the dream is about.

Mary's Dream: Section Five.

There was brilliant sunlight streaming in from floor to ceiling windows, but the room felt cool and pleasant. The floor was a golden oak covered by a rose carpet with green ivy vined around the edge. The walls were a pink which when struck by the sunlight turned a golden peach. The high, arched ceiling was deeply carved to present a pattern of leaves and branches. The furniture seemed antique, but wasn't worn or faded. The furnishings had been well cared for and the wood was oiled to a soft luster. Small conversational groupings had been made which conveyed a sense of coziness despite the room's size. There were flowers in vases placed throughout the room.

This is quite a room! The emphasis is on quality, comfort, spaciousness and beauty. The colors are pleasing, feminine, a setting for discovery and conversation, arranged for pleasant usage. The flowers in vases again emphasize the feminine touch adding color and life. The room is brilliantly lit, indicating a willingness on an unconscious level within to literally see and understand the material which is presenting itself in the dream. Overhead, the ceiling again picks up the theme of the tree outside, the emphasis on nature and natural energies. So does the rug with its twining vines of green. Rose is a color of life energy, a soft and comforting but vital color. The room is really very spacious, which indicates a lot of potential for expansion and discovery.

In metaphysical approaches, the second level or center (chakra) is associated with life forces — sexuality, reproduction, the energy which drives and births new areas, and the balancing of masculine and feminine forces within. This dream is dealing with this very fundamental material, an area not well resolved in Mary's outer levels of consciousness. This is referred to in the number sequence as presented earlier.

Mary's Dream: Section Six.

I was reading a newspaper supplement which contained the history of the building and acted as a tour guide. I noticed a small piece of furniture beside me. It had gears, a wooden wheel, and a piece which was flat, possibly a seat.

Have you remembered to ask something within you to come forward, something which knows how to interpret dreams? It really is necessary to ask for this, if you wish to understand. You will know it is present because you will get "hits" of understanding and distinct feelings about the dream.

A newspaper presents news. This is a supplement, therefore "news" is being presented which is in addition to that which she already knows. Although she doesn't consciously remember what the supplement contained, within Mary's consciousness is the information she needs about the entire image of the building and all it represents. There is even a tour guide for the exploration. She contains all the necessary information within her.

The piece of furniture is interesting. It is mechanical in nature, perhaps one can sit on it. She is not sitting on it, and that is important, since the chair suggests some kind of mechanical involvement with this material of the dream. It is present and could perhaps be used. Mary would need to determine if she has in the past approached these issues of femininity and sexuality, life and vital force, from a mechanistic standpoint. In fact, she has sometimes done this, as most of us do.

Mary's Dream: Section Seven.

A man approached me and began to address me in a familiar manner; but I didn't feel I knew him. I thought this was odd; however, he was quite pleasant, and we began a conversation. He brought over the one piece of furniture which had been neglected. It was a small, delicate chair which had three legs. One of the legs had been dried out and drawn in under the chair. He showed me it was unsteady and wobbled.

This is a crucial section of the dream. Once again, a chair image is presented. There have been three; the chair in which Mary sits, the mechanical piece of furniture on which she might sit, and now a third, neglected, delicate chair. Remember that in the beginning of the dream she sits in different places in the tree. All of these images are related in some way. Do you think that these separate and different images of "a place to sit" might be important?

KEY POINT

Important symbolic images within a dream may be presented with variation for emphasis.

In Mary's dream the chair is one example. Another is the motif of nature and natural forces presented first in the tree, then in the rug and on the ceiling. The place where one sits is the place from which one acts and has one's being. In this dream Mary is being shown the current options and possibilities of her entire viewpoint about herself. She is being shown her relationship to powerful life forces, especially in regard to her natural beingness as a woman. This includes sexuality and her expression of self as feminine.

The man who approaches is part of Mary herself. Remember, it is always wise when first attempting to interpret a dream to assume that all characters and activities in the dream represent something personal within the self. Although there are dreams which are related to impersonal and collective areas, or to prophetic and clairvoyant areas, most dreams will be giving information about the dreamer's own psyche and relationship to life internally and externally.

This man is friendly although not recognized. This means that the aspect of Mary which is represented is a masculine area not consciously appreciated by her but one which supports her. A masculine area acts in ways which are different from the feminine. This is something which each of us needs to discover for ourselves. It is one of the rich discoveries awaiting each of us as we begin to feel and appreciate the differences between these energies within us.

The man shows her the one neglected chair. Three legs might suggest many things. How about Mind, Body and Spirit? It might also represent the physical, the emotional and the mental. It could be referring to the first three chakras and be saying that one of these is unbalanced or needs attention. This would imply expressing the energies of the unbalanced center differently. Chakras will be discussed briefly in a later section of the book.

One leg of the triad is not functioning correctly. The implication of the image is to pay attention to that part which has been neglected. The triad or "trinity" is a metaphor for the wholeness of Spirit and the expression, in real terms, of Spirit.

Mary's Dream: Section Eight.

The man and I were standing by a large, thick, curved table that was of dark wood. I was trying to find something in the newspaper supplement that was of interest to him. The corners of the paper were covered with fabric shields and as I turned the pages, I caught whiffs of my perfume. I hoped he could smell it and would find it as pleasant as I.

He said, "Do you get the sense of what is meant?"

This is the final section of the dream. Mary has moved out of the chair and this implies movement within about this dream material. She wants to please this man and find something which is contained in the history of the building, the supplement, which interests him. The feminine is again emphasized, by the fabric shields and by the perfume. "Shield" is an interesting word here, as Mary has spent much time protecting herself from men and from the powerful issues men arouse for her.

Perfume is meant to appeal to the senses and is usually associated with feminine areas. A woman's perfume is a statement she makes about herself, an essential statement. Mary wants this man to find the perfume as pleasant as she does, that is, she wants him to approve of who she is and the statement to the senses, through essence, of who she is. This is a very fundamental image of self which her unconscious has presented to her.

The man's question, "Do you get the sense of what is meant?" is a powerful summation of the dream. Something within Mary wishes her to understand. Something is telling her that she needs to appreciate self. The dream's images of nature, the feminine, and the places from which Mary views the various actions of the dream all indicate a deep internal shift. This may express as self appreciation as a feminine being, a mature woman.

The question is also a humorous emphasis by Mary's psyche. The "sense of what is meant" is like "scents" (perfume) and "essence" (perfume). Sense, senses, essence, scents — all related to the images and the message of self. The dreaming consciousness is sometimes very fond of puns and plays on words. Do you get the sense of what I mean?

Maturity and the quality of aging has been indicated in the setting of the dream. This is a woman who holds a deep inner potential for the richness and appreciation of life, something which has often been difficult for her to connect with in her past. She has a wonderful combination of feminine and supportive masculine forces. These forces support and enhance each other. She is being asked to pay more attention to the feminine side of herself, recognizing and appreciating the strong masculine structure which she has already established for the exploration.

The domed temple on top of the building in the dream will be reached, and that which it symbolizes realized, when Mary accepts this message. She first must do whatever work necessary to integrate and act upon the information given in this dream.

One other point which needs to be mentioned. The grandeur and size of the building and the room inside could be an indication of ego enhancement and a distortion of perception regarding the entire issue of how Mary sees herself and her relationship to the feminine and masculine. I feel that the small entrance to the building bears this out and is a reminder to her to pay attention to the down to earth humility which we all need to bring to these areas. We are, after all, humans living a human life with all the ups and downs which this means. It is wonderful to contain a richness and grandeur within and to allow ourselves to feel comfortable with our own inner quality. It is wonderful and appropriate to elevate our ideas of Spirit and the essential mystery of the forces of life. It is also well to remember how easily we can let these ideas come between us and the reality of the simple presence of Spirit in our lives and in all that we do.

Please take the time to review the step by step process by which we worked with the dream. In my experience, the best way to learn how to interpret dreams is through the observation of the way in which it is done. We can use the mind's deep ability to associate images and actions with thoughts and ideas, with the help of an aspect within us which really knows how to do it. There will be many dreams given in the following chapters and you will have plenty of opportunities to practice.

4
HEALING DREAMS AND
DREAMS OF HEALTH

Dreams are particularly valuable when there is a question of health. If we pay attention, our dreaming consciousness will forewarn and advise us about the health of our bodies and the course of any disease process with which we are involved. It may be something simple, like advice about what we are eating, or an allergy we might have. In case of very serious illness, such as cancer, the dreams will keep us informed of the progress of the disease and will tell us if we are on the road to recovery or moving towards death.

Healing does not always mean curing. If we look at Native American cultures, for example, we find that the primary emphasis is on the restoration or establishment of inner harmony. Curing may take place or it may not, in the sense that the disease process is halted or reversed. Healing is to make whole, to bring about a sense of connection and harmony with the forces of life. These forces include disease.

The Navaho culture has several beautiful and powerful ceremonies which are meant to restore the ill person to this harmony. The phrase which sums this idea up succinctly is "To walk in beauty." The idea is to bring the patient into a renewed sense of their connection to Spirit/life, and the harmony with life which is seen as the natural heritage of being human.

When harmony has been restored it is possible that curing will take place. Dreams tell us when the inner harmony is disturbed. If we can in some way restore that harmony healing has taken place. In our modern culture we see this idea gaining strength with the hospice work that is done with the terminally ill. It is not expected that the patient will "get better" and be cured of the disease. This important work focuses on establishing a sense of harmony for the patient. If this is done the process of moving towards death is changed dramatically and all benefit. Dream work can be an important tool in this difficult situation.

Here is a short dream which I had not too long ago which is an example of simple and helpful advice for my personal health and spiritual well-being.

I am standing in front of the kitchen sink. The sink seems to be blocked up, and water cannot go out through the drain. I see that the drain is blocked by a coffee filter, full of old grounds. I clear away the debris of the old coffee and the water rushes in a spiral down the drain.

What advice do you think is being given here? If you had this dream, assuming you drink coffee, or if someone related the dream to you, what would you feel it meant?

At the time that I had this dream I was basically addicted to coffee, always drinking at least one pot of strong coffee each day, often more. I had always liked coffee, and liked the "wake-up" effect. I awoke from this dream with a strong feeling that I ought to pay attention.

Everyone has a different tolerance level for substances such as caffeine, and for the other elements which are found in coffee. I took this dream to mean that in effect the residue of coffee which I had been drinking was starting to block the effective elimination of these substances and by-products and the clear flow of energy through my body, symbolized by the water. Coffee has to be processed by several different organs of the body and can affect the adrenals, intestinal system, kidneys and liver, among others. In fact, I had been experiencing some symptoms of let down from coffee after the initial rush, and in general vague feelings that something was not at its best within me.

Much as I regretted giving up coffee, I decided that this was what the dream was calling for. To my surprise I found that it was really rather easy to stop, and I began to feel much better within days. The dream was clearly telling me something my conscious mind would have ignored, and gave me the incentive to shift. This was all the more interesting to me because I am not a person who believes all that is said about substances such as coffee and all the other things which we are told are " not good for us." I do believe, however, in honoring what the body tells us is not good for us, even though this may not be easy for the outer mind to accept.

Remember the **"KEY POINT"** given earlier about "levels" in dreams? All dreams have levels which contain progressively deeper meaning and new information. The initial interpretation given above is a first level interpretation. There is a "second level" to this dream as well. Do you have any sense as to what that might be?

What we have so far is useful. It brought advice which resulted in feeling better on a physical level. That has been the result of not drinking coffee. The second level has to do with health which is not simply physical. It is about the energy of Spirit and the healthy, free flow of that energy. We are a configuration of energies. It can be said that we are nothing more nor less than energy, existing on various levels of manifestation in the world. Taking this viewpoint, the dream suggests that spiritual health is involved here as well.

Every substance carries its own patterning of energy. This dream is saying that for me coffee is a substance which has become counter-productive. The old coffee grounds and filter block the flow. When I remove this in the dream, the sink drains quickly and clearly with a strong, spiral flow. Spirals are fundamental patterns of energy on every level which humans are able to perceive in nature.

The kitchen sink is a symbol to be looked at on this second level. The kitchen is the place where food is prepared. Food is washed at the kitchen sink, cleansed. Food = nourishment = nurturing at very fundamental and essential levels. Therefore, removing whatever is involved with the symbol of the coffee grounds and the "old filter" will have something to do with nourishment on many levels, not just the physical. Filter = something through which something else is strained so that a part of the original thing is left out. Filters block light, for example. We "filter" information selectively and unconsciously. The dream is stating that free flow is blocked by an older way of seeing things or responding to things, and the residue in the psyche which this creates. What exact older viewpoint is not stated directly.

We could go deeper, a "third level." On this level we have to reach for an understanding which is not only deductive or associative. The key image is the old coffee which blocks the flow. What does coffee represent, aside from the actual substance? Coffee in the dream becomes a symbol for something else. The first level sees that coffee as a substance needs to be eliminated; the second level associates removal of the actual physical substance and restoration of energy flow and health, physical and spiritual; the third level sees coffee as representing addictive patterns of behavior. What patterns of behavior am I addicted to which might hinder a free flow of energy and, perhaps, Spirit? How do these patterns affect me? The dream indicates that I have the ability to remove such restrictions and restore the flow. That is surely food for thought.

Here is another dream, a powerful example of someone with serious illness being presented with information about his disease. This person was diagnosed with a massive brain tumor which was rapidly causing deterioration of his life. The tumor was inoperable and he was given about six weeks to live.

George's Dream.

I am walking through a large house with many rooms. Some of the rooms are disused and empty, and there is an air of neglect. Some of them seem familiar. I enter the living room and I see a large television set standing in the center of the room. The set is not working and smoke and sparks are coming out of it. The repairman is there. Other people are present also, looking at the smoking TV.

This is an example of a dream which indicates the real possibility of physical death. The TV set in the "living room" is disordered and not working properly. We already know there is a brain tumor, but if we didn't the TV would make it clear. Like the brain, a TV is something which presents picture and sound and information. It is a good symbol for our device (organ) which processes information from life and the outer world. The repairman represents the energy within which presumably might be able to "fix" the set, but in the dream he is not doing anything. However, the presence of the repairman is the sign that healing is possible. The dream thus indicates that there is a very serious problem (which George already knows) and also that the energies of "repair" or healing may possibly be activated, since they are present.

What is harder to see is what this disease process may be about. What is the disharmony which has brought about this fatal process? One clue is the large house with neglected rooms. The house is a metaphor for the totality of George's self, his inner "living space." I have seen this image before, with variation, in the dreams of people who are terminally ill or threatened with death.

The neglected rooms suggest that there is a large area of life activity which is not being utilized and has been abandoned or neglected. This in turn would suggest that the dreamer was narrowly focused and not making use of the many different possibilities which he contained within. In fact this was the case. George in real life was a "workaholic," who took little time for himself or his family aside from his work. This was becoming more of a problem, as he had newly married some time before and his wife was now expecting a child.

George was caught in a classic conflict between what his feelings demanded and his mind decided. He had not been able to resolve this dilemma. He was no longer able to completely control the situation as his workaholic pattern demanded. The conflict of inner feelings and overriding mental demands was literally killing him.

This particular story has a happy ending. George had come to a friend of mine for a consultation about his illness. I was invited to assist with whatever work we might be able to do with George, including psychological work and the focusing of transformational, healing energies. During the course of the work with George he told us his dream. We then did what we could to assist him and hopefully stimulate his own energies of healing. This included some of the observations I have shared with you above. About a month later George had the following dream:

> *I am walking in an underground cavern, with many winding tunnels. I come to a heavy door. I know that there is a monster locked behind the door and that it can not get out. I know it can't get me. There is water on the floor of the tunnel, perhaps six or eight inches deep. I am digging for treasure, which I sense is buried beneath the water.*

This is a dream which clearly and unequivocally states that the problem has been handled. The monster locked away behind the door is the death process which had manifested as the tumor. Something new has been initiated in George's psyche, because he is now seeking the "treasure" hidden within himself and covered by the water on the floor of the tunnel. The water could be many things; I feel it is the water of the flowing unconscious and that on an inner level the dream says that George is now beginning to look more deeply within himself for the treasures of life and consciousness which were almost lost to him.

There is, however, a potentially disturbing aspect to this dream. Can you see what it is?

If you zeroed in on the monster being locked away, you have accurately put your finger on the problem. The monster is not dead, or permanently gone. Even though George feels that it is now safely locked up and can't "get him" it is still present somewhere within his psyche. It represents not only his physical death, but all of the inner and hidden components of his psyche which led to the disease process in the first place, all of the ways of being in life which do not support George in a truly nurturing and life-sustaining way. These patterns of behavior and perception are still present. George will have to be careful in the future not to slip back into older ways of relating to life and especially his workaholic patterns, or he may see the "monster" return.

The only way we would know for certain that this second dream was actually stating what I have indicated would be through medical confirmation that healing had indeed taken place. It follows that if the "monster" has been locked away and that this is symbolic of a healing process, we should see results in the real world which bear out the interpretation. That is what actually happened. After this second dream George had a new C.A.T. scan which showed no signs of the tumor, a tumor which had been so blatantly obvious and large that it was apparent even to my untrained eye when viewing the films which he had brought with him to his consultation. All his symptoms, including pain and the beginnings of paralysis, had disappeared. Four years later, as of this writing, the tumor has not returned.

KEY POINT

If you take the trouble to learn to interpret dreams and learn to read your own dreams with reasonable accuracy, you may be able to take steps to avoid potential health problems. If you are ill, you may be able to accurately monitor the real course of your illness and the effect of whatever treatment you are receiving.

It is also true in my experience that seeing the inner material which may be involved with the illness is usually not enough. Action is required. Information received is useless if it is not in some way integrated and used. Sometimes the unconscious material is so powerful that the ill person can not muster the strength and inner resources necessary to confront the self and change on the level which is needed for a cure to come forward. Usually the change will have to be as great as if the person had literally died to be effective. If we think about this it is easy to see why it might be difficult to make that kind of change.

You can see from the above that I consider the inner psyche to be deeply involved in any illness or problem of health. This is because that has been my observation and personal experience. It has also been my observation that dreams can be very helpful in working with illness of any kind, although one must go slowly and carefully, and with great respect for the being who is ill. This is particularly true in cases of terminal disease. In all dream work we must remember that the people who share a dream with us are exposing themselves on the very deepest levels. They are vulnerable and we must lovingly respect that vulnerability.

5

WORKING WITH
SOMEONE ELSE'S DREAM

The guidelines for working with someone else's dream are basically the same as those you would use for your own dream. There are several important differences which you need to bear in mind. Because this is not your dream, the meaning of the dream images the dreamer gives you will not often be the same as yours. For example, suppose you had a dream which showed a mountain lake. When you analyze your dream you arrive at a feeling about what that lake means to you. If someone else dreams of a mountain lake it can mean something entirely different for them. Your mission, should you choose to accept, is to find out what that lake means for the person with whom you are working. You and they will both know when you've got it right because it will feel right in your bodies.

As the person relates the dream to you, it will be difficult at first to not jump into interpretation. The most important step when working with another is to listen very carefully. Allow the images of the dream to flow through you, as if you were dreaming the dream with them. See if you can feel and see the images they are telling you.

It is an interesting task to take on the interpretation of another's dream, and one which is not to be approached lightly. When I began to work with Dr. Joy, I was impressed with his ability to guide the dreamer into his or her own interpretation. From him I learned the important skills of listening and allowing the images of the dreamer to pass freely through me. Joy talked about what amounted to an almost telepathic experience when attuning to the dreamer's dream, and emphasized the need to let the dreamer tell the dream as it was without any attempt at interpretation. Later, as I became more familiar with the work of Carl Jung, I again saw this echoed when Jung described what he thought was the correct way for the therapist to work with a patient during dream analysis. Jung also recognized the possibility of a telepathic component. If you are interested in Jung's ideas about the relationship between dreamer and interpreter, please see the excellent book by Jung *Dreams*, published by Princeton University Press, 1974. There are many relevant sections, particularly the chapter on the practical use of dream analysis.

Both Joy and Jung draw attention to the fact that we must be aware of our own unconscious material when looking at someone else's dream. We all have a lot of unconscious material which can get in the way of successful dream interpretation. There is a chapter in this book which talks more about the conscious and unconscious and how these areas interact. For now, make the assumption that you do indeed have unconscious areas which may interfere with clear understanding. Don't take my word for it! Rather, use this as a working framework for exploration. Pay attention to how you feel and over time the truth or untruth of what I am saying will become clearer to you.

KEY POINT

When you work with another to interpret their dreams, assume that dream images familiar to you do not necessarily have the same meaning for them. You must try not to impose your own meanings on their images. Ask them to tell you the dream without any interpretation on their part.

It is important for you to hear the dream as they dreamed it without their ideas about what that means. After they have told you the dream, the next step is to ask them for their interpretation. Even if they are confused by the dream, let them make the first attempt.

This is simply good therapeutic practice as it encourages their own ability to understand dreams and empowers them. You will be helping them take responsibility for their own growth and understanding.

At this point you would begin a dialogue with them to see what the images might mean to them. You may already have a good feeling level within you of what the dream is about. This is something which you will develop with practice and which you will learn to trust over a period of time.

I find it helpful to ask how the person feels about any interpretation that I am bringing forward. If you are close or accurate, there will usually be a corresponding feeling of "rightness" in the person who is telling you the dream. Sometimes you may be very accurate, but the dream material is too loaded with meaning for the dreamer to easily accept or look at. Then they may deny that the interpretation is valid. You will need to practice and relax, and let go of any "investment" you might have about being right. You can only do the best you can. If you have a good heart and a good intention, that is good enough.

Your intention when working with someone else's dream will make a big difference in the result of your work. When I take on the task of interpretation, my intention is to discover what the dream means for them, not what I think the dream means to me. This is a crucial distinction. I set my intention to get out of the way and let the "Dreamer Within" come forward and interpret the dream. This is my best shot at arriving at an interpretation which is not badly skewed by my own unconscious material, whatever that may be. My good ideas about the dream are not important. What is important is attuning to the energy of the images which the dreamer is sharing and allowing something to tell me on a feeling level what those images may mean for the dreamer.

When working with dreams, either our own or another's, we must set our intention to support the inner process which is being revealed to us through the dream images. We must be willing to stand aside and let the images speak to us. We must be willing to be wrong. We must learn to recognize that our mind, no matter how brilliant or developed, how experienced or practiced, does not have the ability to perceive accurately the truth of a dream unless we are able to shift to another state of awareness which does have the ability. We are capable of doing this.

KEY POINT

When we take on another's dream for interpretation, we must set our intention to discover the true meaning of that dream for the other being. By coupling our desire for this result with our will to have the truth of the dream revealed we can set the stage for an interaction with the dream material which leads to accurate interpretation. We must try to hold our intention within a context of heart felt appreciation for the mystery of dreams, life and consciousness.

I have already mentioned the vulnerability of people who share a dream with you. Because the unconscious does not lie when it presents dream images it means that truth is being revealed. If you become adept at interpreting dreams you will become adept at seeing the innermost thoughts and feelings which the dreamer has. We must be very careful to respect the privacy and confidentiality of dream material. If we are not willing to do this, then we should not work with other people's dreams.

6
TOOL BOX

A tool box contains the tools you need for the job. That is the purpose of this chapter, to place in one convenient place the main tools you will need for the job of dream interpretation. The same tools apply whether it is your dream or another's.

Like any complex task of work, there are several things it is helpful to do before you tackle the job. First you may want to organize your workspace. A lot of that is internal, and some of us are pretty disorganized! But there are things you can do to assist yourself and make it easier.

Your dream work environment is important. It is very helpful to create a pleasant place where you can do your inner work with dreams. Light, space and privacy are good to have if it is possible. Have some green and flowering plants around you when you work with your dreams. See if you can create a space where there is a feeling of calm and restfulness, a place for meditation, relaxation and focused attention.

It is quite possible to create such a space in your home, no matter how crowded it may be. It may be only a corner with a comfortable cushion or chair. You can separate this space from the rest of the room with a few plants and add a small, colorful rug to define the area. If you are fortunate enough to have a separate room which can be dedicated to inner work, so much the better.

There are several major tools provided within this book, and others which are available. Some you may already have, in the physical sense. These would include a tape recorder, paper, pens, perhaps a blank book for dreams, and anything else you can think of which might help you work with your dreams. Others are tools for the mind, which grow familiar to you with practice.

One of the tools is the audio cassette, *Dream Mysteries*. You may have purchased this cassette when you bought the book, but if not information is included at the end of the book which will tell you where to get it. Aside from my natural bias towards my own creation, *Dream Mysteries* is a very effective aid for working with your dreams. This is based on feedback from people who have used the tape.

Other tools discussed in this section are meditation, a worksheet which has proven itself useful, and a nine step guide for interpretation. We have already covered a simple approach to help you remember dreams and we have discussed keeping a dream journal. You could say that we have already taken these two tools out of the box and laid them on our workbench. In addition you will find throughout the entire book pointers on working with the dreams. Add these to your mental "Tool Box" as seems appropriate to you.

Using the Audio Cassette *Dream Mysteries* as a Guide for Understanding Your Dreams

Dream Mysteries is an audio cassette guide which I created in order to help people understand their dreams. It contains two beautifully recorded meditations with music and the sounds of nature. This tape can help you practice changing levels of awareness. Repeated use will make it easier for you to shift levels. It may give you the ability, with practice, to move to the area of consciousness which understands and appreciates dreams. It can be used to work with specific questions about the content of your dreams. As with all dream related work, it will reward you to the degree that you choose to use it and make the material your own. The music and meditations are specifically designed to induct you into a centered level of awareness.

Side One takes the listener on a guided journey to meet the energy which I call "The Dreamer Within," an energy which can give YOU more information about a dream. This meditation does not attempt to interpret your dream for you. Rather, you will be guided to a place of deep relaxation and then images will be presented to you. During the meditation you are brought before a mirror, the "mirror of your dreams." In the mirror, you may see something which relates directly to the dream which you wish to understand. Because, as you now know, the language of dreams is symbolic, you will be presented with information in a symbolic form. It is a dream about your dream which you will see.

Using the material presented in this book, you can work with the images shown to you during the meditation and get further information about your dream.

Side Two contains a deeply restful meditation which has proven very effective in helping people remember their dreams. It can be listened to while you are drifting off to sleep. This side requires only that you relax and listen, and your consciousness will do the rest.

The tape contains no subliminal messages or material of any kind. It is recommended that you listen to the tape when you are sure that you will not be disturbed and with the aid of a good pair of earphones. Because it is a powerful relaxation/meditation, it is not a good idea to listen to the tape while you are driving or working.

If you would like to order a copy of *Dream Mysteries*, please see the "Resources" section at the end of the book.

A Meditation for Understanding Your Dreams

Here is a meditation which may help you set your intention for interpreting your dreams or the dreams of another. When you practice this meditation, please be sure that you will not be interrupted. It is always helpful to set aside a quiet time and place for just this purpose of meditating. It does not matter if you are experienced in meditation or not. Anyone can learn to quiet themselves and if you achieve nothing else, at least you will feel refreshed and calmer after doing this meditation.

Begin by making yourself comfortable. Unless you are physically unable to sit up, it is best to meditate in an upright position, comfortably supported. A chair is fine, or you may prefer a pillow on the floor or a small bench.

Begin to breathe easily and fully. I use a long count of seven and a pause of one. You inhale through the nose for the count of seven. Then you hold the breath for a beat of one count. When you exhale, place the tip of the tongue gently against the roof of your mouth, just behind the front teeth. Breathe out through the mouth with a soft sound. Repeat this pattern for some minutes; in through the nose for a count of seven, pause one count, out through the mouth for a count of seven, pause one count, and repeat. Do this for as long as it feels comfortable to you.

This is a very old breathing technique and it is very effective for calming the mind and body. It is also energizing at the same time. I often use it to begin a meditation, as it helps me still the "chatter" which is usually present internally.

When you have steadied yourself and feel calm and centered, ask for the part of you which knows how to interpret dreams to come forward. Focus on these statements at the beginning of your meditation:

I ASK FOR THE CO-OPERATION OF ALL THOSE BEINGS ON THE INNER AND OUTER PLANES CONCERNED WITH MY DEVELOPMENTAL SEQUENCE.
I OPEN TO THE ENERGY OF UNCONDITIONAL LOVE.
I ASK FOR THE CO-OPERATION OF THAT WITHIN ME WHICH KNOWS HOW TO UNDERSTAND DREAMS. I ASK THAT THIS ASPECT COME FORWARD WITHIN ME AT THIS TIME.

These are actual statements which you make within yourself as you deepen into the meditation. You may also say them out loud if you wish. After making these statements, simply sit quietly and see if you can feel a response within. If you are centered and relaxed, you may actually feel a physical response to these powerful statements. Take what you get and honor your experience. You may also choose to make up your own statements which emphasize the idea of inner co-operation and the opening to a heart-felt energy of unconditional love.

After you have made these statements and noticed whatever you may notice within you, shift your attention to the dream you are attempting to understand. Let the images of the dream play through your mind's eye. In your mind's eye, see the dream unfold before you. As you do so, you may have thoughts about what the images mean, or even clear intuitive flashes which carry a sense of certainty about the meaning of a particular image or sequence. These flashes are often accompanied by a physical feeling in the body, a feeling which tells you that you are on the right track. Learn to trust these feelings and act upon them.

This part of the meditation takes as long as it takes. When it is time to end the meditation, you will know it because your attention will be pulled back to the place where you are sitting and your environment. At this time, end the meditation. A good way to end is to simply acknowledge whatever help you have received from within with a simple feeling and statement of gratitude. "Thank You" is enough. It doesn't really matter who or what you think you are thanking. What matters is the energy of gratitude to self and whatever you have been working with.

Don't be discouraged if you have some difficulty with this at first. Remember, it takes time and practice to develop the skills that reveal the meaning of dreams. If you work consistently you will achieve results.

If you are working with another, you may want to take the time with them to meditate together on the dream, using the suggestions above. This can be a very powerful way in which to arrive at a good interpretation of their dream. Not everyone will want to do this, so it is really up to you to take the time to prepare yourself when you know that you will be taking on another's dream for interpretation.

Nine Steps

Let's review the approach to interpretation, step by step. There are nine steps to follow.

STEP ONE:
REMEMBER AND RECORD THE DREAM.

STEP TWO:
ASK FOR SOMETHING WITHIN YOU TO COME FORWARD WHICH KNOWS HOW TO INTERPRET DREAMS.

STEP THREE:
FEEL INTO THE IMAGES WHICH ARE PRESENTED AND WRITE DOWN ANY THOUGHTS AND FEELINGS WHICH YOU HAVE ABOUT THEM.

STEP FOUR:
WRITE DOWN YOUR FIRST INTERPRETATION OF THE DREAM, WHATEVER IT IS.

STEP FIVE:
PRETEND YOU ARE WATCHING A MOVIE...WHAT DOES THE SETTING TELL YOU? WHAT IS THE THEME YOU FEEL FROM THE IMAGES?

STEP SIX:
LET YOUR MIND FREE ASSOCIATE WITH THE IMAGES.

STEP SEVEN:
SEE IF YOU CAN FIND A NEW PERSPECTIVE OR POINT OF VIEW ABOUT THE DREAM.

STEP EIGHT:
WRITE DOWN YOUR DEEPER INTERPRETATION AND WHATEVER NEW IDEAS YOU HAVE DISCOVERED.

STEP NINE:
REVIEW YOUR INTERPRETATION AND ASK YOURSELF IF IT FEELS RIGHT TO YOU. IF IT DOES NOT, GO THROUGH THE NINE STEPS AGAIN.

Remember that honesty is required. You may be uncomfortable with what you begin to see about the dream. Be careful not to avoid this feeling. Sometimes people fool around with an interpretation until they get what they think they want to hear. This is useless.

A Dream Worksheet

Here is a sample worksheet which you may want to copy and work with. You can use this format to give yourself a consistent framework for the exploration of dreams. It will work equally well with your dream or someone else's. Consistency in your approach is especially valuable at first as you are learning how to do it. I have found this worksheet well worth the time it takes. It will be demonstrated throughout the book.

1. Write down and re-view the dream.
2. The images or events in the dream that I feel are most powerful are:
3. I feel that the most important event or image is:
4. The way I feel about this image is:
5. This image reminds me of: (put down anything, no matter how unrelated it appears, which comes to mind)
6. The next image or event I feel is important in the dream is:
7. The way I feel about this image is:
8. This image reminds me of:
(Continue to do this with all the images and events in the dream, down to the least important detail)
9. Any other details I now remember are:
10. I feel that the dream is about:
11. Another thing that the dream is about is:
12. The way I feel about this dream is:
13. Some other thoughts that occur when I review the images of the dream are:
14. Review what you have written in response to all the questions above. You may already have a strong feeling about what the dream means.

15. When I ask for help from within about this dream, I sense that the dream is about:

16. My interpretation of the dream is:

You can use this question and answer format to help you understand the dream. When working with another, use this as a guideline for determining how that person feels about his or her dream. When you also work with the meditation you will quickly discover that you can develop the capacity to understand. If you follow the "Nine Steps" as well, you will soon determine the best approach for you when you begin to look at a dream. Remember, ASK for help from your unconscious in understanding the dream.

You may create another approach which is helpful for you. The key here is to use what works for you. If you work with the suggested tools I have given you may find another approach which is better, or you may modify what I have presented to suit yourself. The most important thing is to remember and trust that something within you knows how to interpret dreams. Anything which is helpful for you as a way to access that something is valuable.

7

THE UNCONSCIOUS MIND

Earlier in the book I stated that we could simplify psychology for our purpose and divide the mind into two parts, conscious and unconscious. That could get me into a lot of trouble with some, because the mind isn't really that simple! Trying to understand the unconscious is like trying to read a book in a pitch black closet. It presents problems of perception. When we move into the world of dreams, whether we are dreaming or remembering a dream, we enter a world where the unconscious is King.

Our so called "conscious" mind is deeply influenced and programmed from the unconscious. This means that we often have no idea what we're doing! Perhaps you have noticed this from time to time in your own life. All is not hopeless, however, since we can learn to recognize areas of behavior and life experience which are influenced by our unconscious. This is one of the challenges of life, and dreams are a readily available source of information that we can use to take up the challenge.

The unconscious has its own rules. The rules are: There Are No Rules! If you don't think this is true, just recall a dream you've had where you did things which you would never think of doing in your waking life. In the dreaming interface with the unconscious, anything goes. Please pay attention to what I am about to say, as it is crucial to understanding dreams and to understanding self on a deeper level.

KEY POINT

The unconscious mind is not concerned with issues of morality, ethics or cultural imperatives. Because the unconscious does not concern itself with these issues, it does not need to present itself as anything other than what it actually is. This means that the unconscious NEVER needs to lie to you. The unconscious is what it is and it will present accurately, in dreams, what it contains.

What it contains is within you. Although the contents of the unconscious may sometimes shock and horrify you, denial of the material will not make it go away. This does not mean that it has to be acted out. Working with what is presented in dreams can lead to a deeper acceptance of self. The key to acceptance is to appreciate the richness and mystery of our life experience in its totality.

There is a difficult problem when working with dreams which has to do with all this unconscious material which we contain. This is a phenomenon called projection . Projection means just what it sounds like. We "project" our unconscious material onto events, people and things outside of our selves. They become a screen for the movie our unconscious is showing.

What does this mean practically? What does it have to do with dreams? It means that we do not see events, people or things (including dreams) clearly because our unconscious movie is superimposed over whatever it is we are looking at. When we look at a dream we immediately begin to lay down a layer of judgement and ideas about things over whatever the dream was actually about.

For example, suppose you have a dream of violence and doing harm to others. This may not present a problem for you if you live a violent life and frequently harm others! If you are a "peaceful" person and you have such a dream, you may be very upset by the images. Your natural inclination might be to try to rationalize the images or even dismiss them as "just a dream," a form of denial. Your judgments and ideas about violence will immediately be activated upon waking, and may even be present within the dream. If you view the dream from the perspective of these judgments (violence is wrong, I don't like hurting people, that's sick, etc., etc.)

you will never arrive at an accurate interpretation of what the dream is actually about. In order to understand the dream the judgmental state, based on your personal beliefs and ideas about life, must be set aside.

It is at first difficult to experience the concept of projection as a reality. This is one of the most important challenges for doing successful dream work. Once we get an experience of how we overlay reality with our own material it becomes easier to see.

It is an ongoing and lifetime work to separate what we think is there from what is really there. Dream work is one way to practice noticing the overlay and identifying what is you and what is not. Practically speaking this in turn can lead you to a new and deeper perspective of life. Wouldn't you like to base your life on what is really going on instead of an illusion?

There is an area of our lives which will immediately benefit from taking the time to notice how we may be projecting our unconscious material. That is our personal relationships. We do not usually see the person we are with. We see instead an illusion of our unconscious projected upon the person, like a movie on a screen. This always leads to trouble and disappointment. After all, the other person is not a screen, they are a unique and independent being who is not created by us. If we are relating to them out of our illusions, there is bound to be upheaval in the relationship when the illusion finally breaks down. Their reality as a being will eventually emerge. If we are caught in our illusion of unconscious projection, it will be a shock to see what we didn't know was there.

KEY POINT

Regardless of your personal value system and ethical standard of life, you must set this aside when viewing a dream. Because the unconscious is not concerned with issues of right and wrong, it is a fundamental mistake to impose these issues upon the unconscious images presented in a dream. This point cannot be emphasized too strongly.

Please notice that I am not advocating setting aside your personal value judgments and beliefs permanently! I am saying that these must be set aside for accurate dream interpretation. Only then will the true meaning of the images become clear to you. Dreams are successfully understood from a perspective which is appreciative and nonjudgmental. This is why the phrase "Unconditional Love" appears in the meditation given earlier for understanding dreams. An energy of unconditionality must be cultivated for good dream work.

Why would we want to take the trouble to set aside our value systems in order to understand a dream? Because once we understand what the unconscious is trying to communicate to us, we then have more options for harmonious behavior in life available to us.

If we have begun the task of recognizing what our unconscious is "working with" we have a much better chance of seeing how that spills over into our waking life. By paying attention to the unconscious as shown in dreams, we discover what we really think and feel about things. This reflects in all our daily activity, whether we know it or not.

Sometimes we discover that some of the things which we think and feel result in activities which do not serve us and others. We may discover patterns of behavior which we were unaware of, based on the unconscious material. If we don't like the results we are getting in our life, we can take steps to activate a different pattern of behavior which is more satisfactory to us. We'll look more deeply at patterns later, after we have studied some more dreams and kinds of dreams.

When we take the time to look more deeply into our unconscious through the window of dreaming, we discover more of who we are. What is certain is that sooner or later we are going to come across material which we would like to deny. Denial is one of the most powerful and most insidious forces within our psyche. Because life often presents us with uncomfortable or difficult situations, we have all developed ways to avoid, deny or ignore things which do not fit with how we would like life to be. Yet these things don't cease to exist because we ignore them.

I never thought much about denial, much less as a factor when looking at dreams, until 1975. That was a difficult year for me.

Things were not going well, I was in a dead end job, my relationships were lousy and my primary relationship was awful. My health was shaky, and I was drinking heavily. I was at a turning point, without joy of life and feeling at the end of my rope. In desparation and with an attitude of nothing left to lose I took Werner Erhard's est training, then building to a peak of popularity.

Although I have many reservations about popular psychological trainings and the belief systems which they teach, there is certainly much of value contained within them. One of the principle themes which these trainings seem to have in common is the necessity for beginning to tell the truth to oneself about how one really feels. Although true understanding and resolution of painful feelings and self destructive behavior may not be achieved, what can happen is the beginnings of a process which leads to the recognition of denial. Once denial is acknowledged, acceptance and integration of the denied material becomes possible. One begins to accept and include what was previously and unconsciously pushed away. The recognition within myself that I was caught in a powerful web of denial which was of my own creation was revelatory. It initiated an internal process of reclamation which continues to this day.

As I began to work with Dr. Joy I again heard the message of inclusivity as opposed to exclusivity. One of the main thrusts of Joy's work with the unconscious is based on this balanced and inclusive approach, and it has influenced my own work to a great degree.

The idea of inclusivity may also be seen in so called primitive societies and in the Eastern religious traditions, where the balance of negative and positive aspects is recognized and appreciated. For example, in Bali there are representations of adult figures whose feet rest on dark and light aspects symbolically presented. This is an indication to the Balinese of the mature stages of life which recognize the totality of life as being more than just the "good" things. It is assumed that only an adult can appreciate this balance, and it is thus seen that denial is innappropriate to the adult. Denial is a function of a less mature stage of development.

This is fundamental to the understanding of dreams and of the unconscious psyche.

One of the marvelous things about the unconscious is that it is a rich and endless resource which we can learn to tap. Because it is mysterious and for all practical purposes infinite in depth, we will never run out of the potential which lies within waiting to be discovered. When we embark upon an exploration of the unconscious we are embarking on an adventure into unknown territory. Like all adventures worth the name there will be trials and difficulties, thrills and spills, exciting and new possibilities, and times when we wish we had never left home. In the end we will have mapped out new territory and discovered something about ourselves which would not have been possible without undertaking the journey. Dreams are our passport to adventure.

8

FEAR ABOUT DREAMS

Sometimes people are reluctant to look closely at their dreams. You are probably not like this since you are reading this book. If you have been following the material about the unconscious in the last chapter, you can see how it might be unnerving or even frightening to look at your dreams. If you have ever had an unpleasant dream, you may have wanted to quickly forget it. Many people have reported dreams to me which seemed to foreshadow some unpleasant or tragic event, such as an accident or illness involving a friend or loved one. Naturally we tend to avoid things we don't like.

I feel that the main reason people fear the material which comes forward in dreams is not because of the kinds of examples cited above. When we are dealing with the unconscious we are dealing with the unknown. Remember that by definition we don't know what the unconscious contains. How many of us feel comfortable with the unknown? Indiana Jones aside (and we all know how much trouble he gets into), most of us would prefer to stick with what we know, and only occasionally cross the boundaries into unfamiliar territory. Even then, we try to control the unknown factors as much as possible, through planning and preparation. Something usually happens, though, that could not have been anticipated.

Have you ever travelled in a foreign country? Did everything go exactly as you had planned? Were you comfortable with the strange language, the different food, the hot water being in a different place if it was there at all? You may have found the experience stimulating or fun, but was it comfortable? Did you ever experience a little twinge of fear during your journeys? That could be a big twinge of fear in some situations!

I could go on, but you probably get my point. That which is unknown to us is fearful, simply because we don't know what it is.

KEY POINT

Since dreams are unpredictable by our normal awareness and present unknown material from the unconscious, it is predictable that we might experience fear when we set out to explore our dreams. This may not occur at first, but an unpleasant or terrifying dream could activate the fear response and cause us to retreat. At this time it is important to re-affirm our intention for self discovery. We can re-center and remember to move our awareness to a place of unconditional love and acceptance of self, as best we know how. From this point of center and unconditionality, we can safely and accurately explore any difficult material which may emerge.

We learn through experience and often through difficult experience. This is a constant path of initiation into the mystery of life. Life would be terribly boring if everything were always easy and perfect, and there would be no need for us to stretch our awareness and learn anything! Dreams provide us with the raw material of personal change and growth. It is only human to occasionally fear the change that such growth might bring. We intuitively know when the unknown is making its presence felt, and our human reaction is usually denial and avoidance, accompanied by differing degrees of fear. Acknowledge the fear and step forward.

Dreams can give us information which leads to new discoveries about ourselves. Part of the fear we may sometimes experience working with dreams is the fear of what a discovery might bring. Often discovery brings change, which is uncomfortable. We are afraid of how others might react to us if we should institute change. At this point we may go into all sorts of unconscious avoidance symptoms. Those can include everything from boredom, listlessness, nervousness, anxiety attacks and sleepiness to chocolate binges.Perhaps you have an experience of what I am talking about.

One of the best ways to overcome any fear about dreams is to start working with them and observe how other people have done it. Through years of working with people I have discovered that the best teaching comes through example. This is why so many different dreams will be presented in this book. You can see how the dream reveals its secrets when approached systematically and you will have as many opportunities as you like to make your own interpretation before you come to mine.

Have you ever noticed that it is often easier to see what is going on with someone else? Of course you have. This does not mean that you would reach the same conclusion about what is going on for yourself in a similar situation or that you would act on it if you did. Humans are like that. Nonetheless, looking at someone else's material often gives us insight into our own, and sometimes deep recognition. It is like that when we are learning to work with dreams. The more we see how it works for others the more we can see about how it might work for us.

This chapter concludes the first section of What Your Dreams Can Teach You. The following chapters examine different and specific kinds of dreams. In these dreams you may recognize yourself or some piece of yourself. At this point you now have enough information to begin to successfully work with your dreams. It's time to see if we can put this into action.

From time to time I will suggest that you do a worksheet for a dream before you have looked at the interpretation. Of course you may choose not to do this and that will be OK. On the other hand, if you begin to practice as we go along you will be that much further ahead when you begin to look at your own dreams. It's up to you.

Section Two

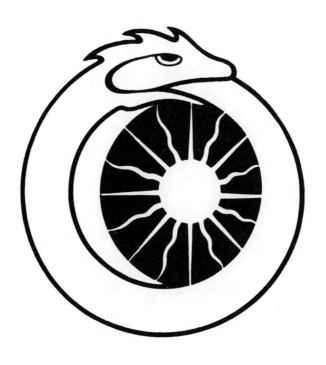

CHAPTER 9:
THE MASCULINE AND FEMININE
IN DREAMS

This is really an ambitious heading for a chapter! An entire book could be written about either the masculine of feminine in dreams, and probably will be. It would be impossible to present an in-depth analysis on this subject in a chapter, and I'm not going to try. My purpose is to introduce you to a framework of exploration which may be helpful. It has been my experience that this is one of the most confusing aspects of dream work. That feels appropriate to me, since it is one of the most confusing aspects of our self understanding and our human experience.

I want to remind you here that a good, general approach to dream figures is personal. The working assumption is that all figures in a dream represent aspects of yourself. They are the characters of your play, acted out on the stage of your dreaming consciousness.

It is also true that some of these characters may carry energies and display attributes which are not entirely personal. In this case we are tapping into symbols which are more universal in nature. We have some relationship with them because they appear in our dreams, but they represent energies which are not necessarily created by us and which exist outside of our personal sphere. This can be very apparent when we are looking at certain masculine and feminine figures which appear in our dreams.

This isn't really so difficult to understand. If you stop and think for a moment, what could be more personal and impersonal at the same time than gender? Differentiation by sex is an impersonal process. Men and women exist as a life reality regardless of our personal existence. When we're gone, men and women will roll on. Yet our personal experience of life is deeply intertwined with the gender we carry. There are qualities of masculine and feminine which have nothing to do with our personal thoughts about these things; there are also personal qualities of expression which we bring to the experience of man or woman in our life.

In our dreams this personal/impersonal reality will be faithfully mirrored. An example is the figure of "mother" or "father." These are individuals in the personal sense and we have a personal, individual history with each figure. This is true even if the parents are not present or are unknown. We have a personal relationship with the physical parents. On the other hand there is the impersonal life energy of masculine and feminine which for humans becomes personified as Father and Mother. These are the separate processes which combine to initiate and gestate life and move it from potential to manifestation. This is true whether we are talking about people or plants.

In sum there are energies of the life process which have different functions regarding the development and evolution, continuation and expansion of life. Life is the important word here. Life is an impersonal process which we take very personally!

When we get past the fundamental process of conception and reproduction we begin to get involved with the personal expression of what feminine and masculine are. This expression is for all purposes infinite in variety. Certain expressions such as mother and father take on collective and cultural values. The roles, over time, become powerfully defined. Any one definition, however, cannot possibly take in all the possible variations of role expression. In our effort to understand what is going on we make judgments and create categories which further define the mask of the feminine or masculine which we are seeing. We say, "She is a good mother" or "He is a bad father." Immediately a list of criteria for these judgments is flashed before our consciousness, based on the belief systems held by our culture and society.

In our unconscious are contained, perhaps, all of the possible energetic variations on the theme of masculine and feminine. It is like the representations of the gods and goddesses in

Eastern religion. We see these powerful dualistic forces presented as demonic or angelic, nurturing or destroying, sincere or full of falsehood and trickery. They appear as ugly or handsome, young and old, beautiful or deformed, and in every conceivable timing of life personal and impersonal. So, too, with our dreams. The figures of men and women, boys and girls, young and old, demonic and angelic, nurturing and destroying, wise and foolish appear again and again. Each figure represents some aspect within us which carries a particular quality. The message of the figure comes through the understanding of our relationship with that quality within.

KEY POINT

The male and female figures which appear in our dreams represent aspects of ourselves which are symbolically presented by the dream image. We contain the qualities represented by these images within ourselves. These qualities may or may not be based on our personal experience of life. Since we contain these qualities within ourselves, we may be able to see them in our outward expression as man or woman. Our expression as man or woman reflects both personal and impersonal qualities of consciousness. It is important for us to learn to distinguish the difference.

I want to spend a little time with this, because it is a very important part of our self understanding. I am saying that we are involved with both personal and impersonal areas of consciousness. It is not beginner's work to discover the difference. By presenting this idea to you in a chapter about masculine and feminine, I am hoping to plant a seed which may in some way bear fruit for you now or in the future.

If what I am saying is true it follows that we must often confuse personal and impersonal energies in our lives. We do not see the energies for what they are because of our personal involvement. In the case of masculine and feminine energies this leads to mistakes in relationships with other men and women. This has to follow logically if we are unable to see the difference between personal and impersonal areas. We will react to something on our personal level which was not an expression of the other's personal areas. Hurt, blame, arguments, anger and violence may easily follow.

Working with dreams can teach us something about this personal and impersonal dichotomy. We contain both masculine and feminine forces. As we begin to identify the many faces of the feminine and masculine within us, we begin to identify those faces in others. More importantly, we begin to see our projection of inner material upon others and pull it back to ourselves. We begin to see more of who the other person really is rather than the illusion we have unconsciously created about them.

This is not an easy process! It is not for everyone to do. If we do take on the challenge we may be rewarded with richer and deeper relationships which reach beyond our usual ideas of self and other.

Many dreams show us the progress, or lack of it, which we are making in the task of conscious integration of our masculine and feminine energies. The dreams show us different qualities of masculine and feminine and our inner relationship to those qualities.

I feel that one of our most important challenges for personal discovery and the development of heightened awareness is the discovery and ongoing integration of masculine and feminine within. The more we are able to accept and appreciate these very different energies the fuller our life becomes. Life begins to reveal new possibilities and excitement. Here is a dream which illustrates some of the things I have been talking about.

Faye's Dream.

I dreamed of understanding, groking, that birds, plants, animals and humans are all different energy forms. God communicates to me clearly and says to trust Him and do as He says — all will be well. I dress as He says, with wings. I cross a bridge. I get sucked up into God's protection in heaven. I know birds are safe (protected).

My friend Phyllis decided she didn't want Bill, her husband, any more and wanted to go on to husband number three. I am next in line for a relationship, so she introduced him to me on the condition that I find the natural fulfillment of my body...be willing to receive love. Bill and I had always been attracted to each other, so this was OK with us. We hang around getting used to the idea, and someone tells us that we need cups to make it official. We head for a ceremony and grab some brownies along the way.

At first glance the two sections of the dream may appear unrelated. Faye is shown somehow that all forms are different expressions of some universal energy. This includes her as well. She is then instructed by God. This exemplifies impersonal, masculine, Father energy — "God," whom Faye sees as masculine in this dream. This supreme authority is reassuring and protective. Following God's instructions she dresses in wings. She then crosses a "bridge" and is taken up into heaven where birds are safe and protected.

Crossing the bridge is very important as it represents a transition within Faye's psyche. This is a bridge of trust. The action of crossing leads to the ascent to heaven. If we remember that this is all inner material which Faye contains, we can see that she is being shown something about her own masculine energies within. This will be amplified in the second section. The dream says that she can trust and respond to her inner masculine authority. This is safe to do. In the dream she knows birds are safe; birds have wings; she has wings like a bird; therefore she is safe.

So far Faye is being told that she contains wise, nurturing and powerful masculine forces which can allow her to soar into "heaven," where she will be protected. The action of surrender to the advice and guidance of these forces will lead to the protection and safety. Then the dream goes on.

The next section clearly states the necessary conditions for success and fulfillment. Faye must be willing "to receive love." This means to let herself be receptive to the nurturing and supporting masculine. Since all these energies occur in her dream, she is being told that she must love herself on a fundamental level, and that this level will have to do with her relationship to masculine energies within. It is like the first section; trust in the masculine and you will be fine, you will be fulfilled.

You can imagine how this might be difficult! If you are a woman reading this book, you can instantly relate to the problems involved in trusting the masculine. If you are a man, you can also quickly see that this might not be easy for someone to do. We have taken up some very rigid positions about man and woman in our society which are not easy to shift. We fail to see that much of what we think men and women are about is an illusion created by our inner material. Faye's dream represents the potential for an inner healing of this conflict, a conflict which she carries within but which she experiences without.

A third level interpretation of this dream will relate to Faye's outer life. In real life Faye has unresolved issues about her real father. She is also in an executive work position where she uses masculine modalities to succeed and where she frequently runs into conflicts of authority with male co-workers and bosses. This conflict is partially an expression of the inner dynamics which are being worked with in the dream. Resolution on some inner level of trust and interaction with the masculine will change relationships on the outer level. This will be true even if her bosses and co-workers are difficult and chauvinistic in their relationship with her. Faye can relate to them in a different way if she has come to a level of integration within.

This is one of the most powerful and fulfilling benefits of dream work and the understanding which comes out of it; as we accept and integrate the material within, our relationship to outer life changes dramatically. We handle things differently, because we perceive them differently.

Shortly after she had this dream, Faye realized that something was changing in her relationship with her real father. This is something she has been trying to achieve for a long time. The change is for the better as far as Faye is concerned. Her work situation is also undergoing dramatic change, which excites her.

There is a key image yet to be looked at in the dream. This is the need for "cups" to "make it official." What will be made official is the union, the relationship of "Bill" and Faye. The cup is an ancient symbol of the feminine. It appears over many centuries. A good example is the Holy Grail of the Arthurian legends. The Holy Grail represents that which contains Spirit and life, mystery and God. It is that which is sought to bring life back to the wasted and desolate kingdom of the myth. It is a complete symbol of the union of masculine and feminine. The masculine structure or form of the cup provides a context for the formless, life giving feminine Spirit. The cup allows the contents to be held in form. The form in turn is an image of the feminine.

This image tells Faye that the union with the masculine (Bill) will be consummated through the feminine (the cups). Getting the cups in order to make the ceremony of the union official means recognizing this co-creative interaction. In other words, there is no conflict here but rather a mutuality and blending of energies which will result in fulfillment. This requires Faye's conscious acceptance of the conditions.

There is something about the brownies which requires attention. Brownies are something which usually relates to a more childlike part of the consciousness. There is a suggestion of the child in the image of grabbing the brownies. Childlike is different from childish. Childlike suggests the freshness of viewpoint and experience which a child brings to its life; childish is quite different, the negative side of the child which emphasizes the undeveloped ego levels and immaturity. I feel that this symbol is telling Faye to open to a fresh and new perspective which will nourish her. It is a subtle directive to allow a childlike newness to come forward in her perception of masculine/feminine relationship.

This dream illustrates the relationship of masculine and feminine energies within. On the deepest levels it implies a possibility of resolution and fulfillment. Integration of the material will lead to better relationships with the men in Faye's life. It will also change her work relationships and her relationship with her father. In her waking life Faye has deeply ambivalent feelings about her goal oriented and logical masculine side and her feeling level feminine side. This dream holds the promise of resolution on this level as well.

Just a little dream, which may portend a major shift in Faye's life!

Here's another dream about feminine and masculine. In this dream, the "sister" who appears does not actually exist in the dreamer's life. She represents an important aspect of the dreamer which has been unavailable to him until the time of this dream. See what you think.

Kevin's Dream.

I dreamed that I was at my parents', in my old bedroom that I shared with my brothers. Only my younger brother is present. I am crying because my brother has just told me that we have a sister whom our parents have kept secret from us. Then in come our parents, as it is the last day of my visit, and they have come to say goodbye. I hug my father and say, "I am glad to have had the chance to see you." He responded with, "No you're not, you're crying." My response to myself is, " Well, that's just how he is." I am mildly surprised by this.

He then vanishes from the scene which changes to another room. My brother and I are talking with mother, asking about our sister. My parents had kept her away at a private school or the like, and thought not telling my brothers and I about her was inconsequential.

I then meet my sister, who is only one year younger. We catch up on the years, and I am filled with a feeling of completion, and how so much suddenly fits together on a feeling level, as if something that had been long missing was suddenly found.

Kevin's dream contains both personal and impersonal elements mixed together in the symbols of his family members and the sister who does not exist in real life. The dream begins with a powerful emotional content. Kevin is crying because of all the feelings he has about the separation from his sister. Whatever she represents must be very important to him, and this is borne out and balanced at the end of the dream when he experiences a feeling of completion and reunion with the sister.

Who is to blame for this separation? In the dream it is the parents, whom Kevin is visiting. In real life, Kevin blames his parents for a lot of things, especially his mother. Symbolically in the dream it is their fault Kevin has not known he even had a sister. On an inward level the parents represent energies of authority and rule making. For Kevin they represent suppression and criticism and having to do what they want at the expense of his own desires. This information emerges when talking with Kevin.

In Kevin's dreaming mind it is not his fault that he never knew the "sister." This is the kind of dream information which can be overlooked easily, because the excuse is the action of the dream parents, who never told Kevin he had a sister. That would be a mistake when interpreting the dream, because it is important. The first level doesn't really know what to do with this because Kevin doesn't really have a sister in waking life.

The second level of interpretation makes an association with feminine, feeling levels and says, "Aha! Because my parents rejected me I have suppressed my feminine areas. It's their fault for not being sensitive to my needs." The third level message for his outer life which the dream is immediately pointing out is that he is going to have to look at this more deeply and take back the responsibility for what he feels is missing.

Like many of us, Kevin also has strong unfulfilled feelings towards his parents of love and affection, which also reflect the lack of love and affection he felt when he was a child. If you had a childhood like this you may have had a personal experience of what I mean. There is a lot of unrecognized feeling here on Kevin's part. This is indicated when he hugs his father.

It seems that Kevin doesn't really care very much when his father invalidates him in the dream. The father is essentially telling Kevin that he is lying. To whom is he lying? It's Kevin's dream, so he must be lying to himself! Do you see this? The father is saying that Kevin is lying because Kevin is crying. The action of Kevin in the dream is not consistent with his statement of gladness. Something's going on here! The something is that Kevin has blocked off a lot of feeling about his real father with a "that's just how he is" approach.

Kevin dismisses an entire powerful and emotionally loaded aspect, inner and outer with that statement. This is what he does in real life also. When I asked him what he thought about this section of the dream his response was that he felt he had "handled" his feelings about his father and that these no longer were a strong factor for him. This is not so, but it was one of those times when pushing for a deeper recognition of what the dream contains was not going to be productive. Sometimes the material is so loaded for the dreamer that even a very accurate reading of the dream can not be accepted.

In negating the father image and suppressing his real feelings Kevin is negating himself. A double whammy, because he does this on an inner and an outer level. This leads to deep problems in Kevin's expression of mature masculininity.

The mother figure explains that it wasn't important for Kevin to know about the sister. There is not a lot of direct information in the dream about Kevin's mother, but what we do see is the invalidation of Kevin by this energy. It simply was inconsequential to her whether Kevin knew about his sister or not.

This mother figure does not care at all about Kevin's relationship to the inner feminine which is represented by the sister. This is quite true in Kevin's real life as well. The only person Kevin's mother seems to care about is herself. We have to be careful here. It would be easy to let Kevin's unconscious "stuff" jump out and land on the mother where we could agree with it. Not so! Whatever his mother is really like, she is not responsible for how Kevin thinks and feels about the feminine. If we give her that power, we disempower Kevin and make him his mother's victim. Kevin is responsible. Unless we take on this approach we do a disservice to ourselves and others.

KEY POINT

Responsibility does not mean fault, blame or guilt. To be responsible means to accept the possibility that in some way, conscious or not, we influence and participate in the situations which we feel are not under our control. This does not mean that we created the situation. It does mean that we must develop our ability to respond to ourselves and our feelings about the situation by being aware of them and accepting them.

It may take a while for us to recognize that we are responsible for ourselves and that we are not the victims we think we are. I was first consciously exposed to the idea of personal responsibility for one's feelings in 1975, and I began to make changes in my life based on validating those feelings. I spent several years studying different approaches which worked with feelings, including Gestalt work and Reichian approaches, breathing techniques and release through working with the physical body.

In the fifteen years which have passed since I finally realized that I could do something about the feelings I had and could work with them in a way which was not suppressive or manipulative, it has become a very "mainstream" concept that working with one's feelings and honoring them is beneficial. It is sometimes hard to recall that this was not well accepted prior to the emergence of the Human Potential movement of the sixties and seventies.

Even though I had worked extensively for years to attempt to integrate the difficult feelings which I had regarding important events and relationships in my life, the possibilities of resolving feelings of victimization on the deepest levels did not become apparent to me until 1984 during a conference with Dr. Joy. Joy teaches the art of self appreciation in the context of a metaphysical but tangible experience of energy. When this is combined with the psychological recognition of unconscious material projected outward onto other, a new potential of resolution becomes available.

At this point I would like simply to introduce the thought that since we are the ones who are having the disturbing feelings, we are the only ones who can do anything about those feelings. We are responsible for how we feel, not others. This is really the subject for another book! For now, see if you can consider this as possibly true.

There is good news in the dream, as Kevin does get to meet and share with the sister. This is a dream of resolution on some level. Communication and meeting is established with the sister. She is younger than he, meaning this is not a mature aspect of the feminine. The sister represents energies of the feminine in Kevin which have not been available to for him in the past. The dream shows that something is opening within him which has been long hidden but is now available. Kevin has accessed another dimension within himself which will add to his masculine perspective. This can only mean good things for the future.

In the two dreams we have looked at so far we have seen examples of the dreamers' inner relationship with their feminine and masculine aspects. In these dreams a new energy is introduced which is symbolized by the new relationship in Faye's dream and the sister in Kevin's. Here is another dream which shows a different kind of relationship.

Eric's Dream.

I am a warrior/knight, dressed in soft clothes and a cape. I am offered all that I need in the way of money and food. The catch is that I have to serve some authority (I'm not sure what). At first it is appealing, but something within me is suspicious and I do not accept. Because I do not accept, I suddenly find myself being controlled. My will is not my own. There is another heroic figure who is in charge. He is stern, blond, and wears a blue cape. He carries a sword. I also carry a sword, but because my will is being controlled I can not use it well as I once did. I am not completely under control, but it is only a question of time unless I escape. I am forced to take a sword exercise with others but the swordplay is clumsy, since everyone is under control. I am struggling inside not to succumb to the influence of the heroic figure.

Then it is dusk in the dream. I am sitting with a female figure, also heroic with cape and sword. She too is being controlled and we are talking about escape. She is in the same position as I. We are sitting in some sort of courtyard and we are not supposed to be there. If whoever controls us sees us there we will be in trouble. We are trying to think how we can escape. All the time I am fighting the control impulses. I am tired of fighting and almost at the limit of resistance. Once I succumb I will not be able to break free. The woman is also my lover, and part of the control issue is to separate us.

There is another section to the dream but let's stop here for a moment. Please take a few minutes to look at the dream and see what you feel about it....

It is very clear that the dominant issue of the dream is control. Control of what? This dream is talking about the way in which Eric sees the masculine/feminine within and how he deals with it on an unconscious level.

The heroic figures, man and woman, are warriors, fighters. He is also a knight, a noble warrior. Knights, good or bad, fight for Lords and Kings. They are in service to these higher authorities. The blond knight is a mythic figure. He is an embodiment of energy which is concerned only with war; he is compassionless and stern. He is an energy of the masculine which is not concerned with life. It is the energy idealized in the Nazi mythology of the Teutonic knight. This figure does not support joy or love in life, but dedicates itself to ideals of loyalty and war.

Eric and his woman companion are also warriors and this shows a correlation between them and the blond knight. But they are different and Eric does not want to succumb to this authoritative energy of the masculine, even though it offers him money (energy) and food (nourishment). As a result, the battle of will is joined. Eric is in a deep inner struggle which will determine much of how he expresses himself and manifests his masculinity in the outer world.

Can you see and feel this?

Part of the control issue is to split Eric off from the feminine counterpart of warrior within himself. "Warrior" is an honorable profession and in this case a noble one. With the feminine energy within which mirrors and complements the masculine Eric has come this far: but now he's in trouble. She and he are trapped, losing the battle, afraid of defeat and weary. Eric is fighting to maintain a connection with the feminine within himself. Something more is needed if Eric is to recover his will.

The masculine symbol of the sword is also very revealing. This is a representation of Eric's ability to survive in the world using his masculine strengths. There is trouble here as well. Because of the conflict of direction and will within, Eric can no longer wield the sword well as he once could. He is becoming disempowered and ineffective in his masculine expression.

All of this adds up to an important dream and a crisis in Eric's life. You can be sure that this inner struggle and dis-empowerment was reflected at this time in Eric's outer world. He was ineffective, self doubting, angry and confused. Things were not going well for him.

The dream has shown the problem; now it will bring forward a potential of resolution.

Eric's Dream (Continued)

There is another female figure there, sitting across from me. She is dark haired, fair skinned. She is a friend, and I want her to help us. She would like to but is unable to help because of being watched or controlled by whatever the controlling force is. I feel like crying. Heroes such as I are not supposed to cry, yet something tells me in the dream that if I cry it will help me escape. I resist crying momentarily, but I am so tired of fighting and I know that there is little I can do. I begin to cry, deeply. Then I wake up.

This new female figure is another aspect of the feminine. She is dark haired, contrasting with the blond warrior and Eric's blond lover. This symbol is emphasizing that she carries a different kind of energy. She is willing to help but cannot as long as she is being watched or controlled by the force Eric is fighting. The issue of control for Eric is also about suppressing what this energy represents. It's his dream, and his psyche.

What is being controlled will now be made clear in a general sense. The control is an issue of suppressing deep feeling and emotional levels, although we are not shown what they are about. If Eric will cry, he may yet escape. Resisting at first, he finally surrenders, tired of the long and hopeless battle to escape the force which is overwhelming him. The messenger of salvation is the feminine, and he will have to surrender to feeling levels in order to survive.

This dream presents the classic battle between what are generally though inaccurately perceived as "Feminine" and "Masculine." In this limited view the masculine is not concerned with feelings and is essentially locked into competitive and mental relationships with life which will lead it to dominance. The Feminine is perceived as emotional and internal, not interested in dominance, and supportive of feeling. In Eric's psyche, on the level he is working with, these old ideas and perceptions must be broken down. Although the perception may be limited, the results are true for Eric as long as he holds the viewpoint.

The problem with traditional and limiting viewpoints of what masculine and feminine are is that the viewpoint determines the experience. Eric holds this viewpoint within himself on a very deep level, or he would not have had this dream. He has now come to a point in his development as a man where the conflict between what he thinks and what he feels is interfering with his life. He faces a challenge of maturation as a human being. The key to a successful resolution lies in his potential surrender to the feeling levels and the discovery of new options which that surrender can lead to. His old viewpoint must go and this must be accomplished through allowing the experience of his deep feeling, feminine levels to guide him.

In each of these three dreams we see a situation of change for the dreamer. In each case a new relationship is being initiated and called for, a relationship of masculine and feminine energies within. In each case a conscious effort to integrate and work with the change will bring a different experience of life for the dreamer. The dreams point the way for the conscious mind to expand and explore a different potential of life.

One of the mistakes which we commonly make when looking at masculine/feminine, man/woman dichotomies is to assume that the mask which we see is the totality of what we are observing. It takes only a moment's reflection to realize that any man or woman we look at is an immensely complex being, with many different ways of expressing self. The expression of self which we see in the moment is not necessarily what we will see tomorrow or what we saw yesterday. How many possibilities do you contain, for example?

Each of us seems to be a multiplicity of being and possibility, but we forget this. As man or woman we express our personal and impersonal selves in any given moment. That expression will be the result of the complex tapestry of masculine and feminine which our psyche has woven. Our dreams will show us which threads of the tapestry are in need of repair, which colors are dominant and which parts are unfinished or still on the loom. This helps us not only to appreciate our own complexity but to see the tapestry which others have woven in a new light of understanding.

The interaction of the masculine and feminine forces in our lives has infinite expression. One of those expressions is sexuality. That is what we shall explore in the next chapter.

10
SEXUALITY IN DREAMS

Whenever I conduct workshops in self discovery and personal growth dreams are an important part of the work. Sooner or later, someone will always share a dream which contains strong sexual imagery. When I ask participants if there is anyone in the room who has not at sometime had a powerful sexual dream, no one ever raises their hand. Sexuality is so fundamental to our human existence that it would be inconceivable to not have dreams which were sexual in nature. Problems arise only when one attempts to understand them.

Sex and sexuality is one of those areas which precipitates strong unconscious material which will immediately overlay the actual dream material. No one escapes confusion when it comes to sex! This is a loaded area within us. If you have any objections to considering sexually oriented material, you may skip this section and move on to the next chapter. Dreams are often quite explicit when it comes to sex and the images must be looked at in order to understand the dream content.

Before we consider individual dreams, I would like to share some thoughts with you. If we are going to understand sexuality in dreams, we have to remember that the images are symbolic, like any other dream image. Therefore by definition an image of sex or sexuality within a dream must mean more than is immediately apparent. Because of our unconscious material we usually are thrown into a reaction based on the surface image which is presented to us, and all our attitudes about sex come into play. If, however, we treat the dream image as symbol rather than substance, we immediately open a whole new range of possibility for understanding the meaning of what is presented.

What is sex? It is fundamentally a relationship of forces. Sex is about relationship. By relationship I mean that there is some correspondence of force and energy which interacts on a fundamental level. There is an exchange of some sort, a blending and fusing of forces which then holds a potential for something different to manifest. This is true whether or not an actual potential for procreation exists. It is the forces and energies which are carrying out the interaction.

At this level of perception the very Creation of the Universe may be seen as a sexual interplay of forces. If we are to really understand a dream with sexual content, we need to keep deepening our level of perspective until we arrive at this fundamental observation of the dance of energies.

KEY POINT

Sexuality in dreams must be viewed symbolically in order to fully understand the meaning. The deepest levels of any dream which contains sexuality will not be found through an interpretation which limits itself to the physical, sexual action seen in the dream.

It is not possible to give a standard interpretation for a sexual image which appears in a dream. For example, it would be superficial and often misleading to interpret a dream about having an affair with someone else's mate as indicating a wish on the dreamer's part to really have such an affair. This kind of interpretation can get everyone in a lot of trouble! Even if the person confided in you that they were attracted to the other in real life, this would still not be the level of interpretation which we are looking for.

What does this desired person represent to the dreamer? What qualities does he or she possess that beckon? Because we now know that the unconscious projects itself onto others, what is it within ourself that we are seeking to fulfill with the other?

Right here I want to acknowledge the simplicity (if that is the right word!) of pure physical desire, sometimes called Lust. There is a fundamental biological desire to further the species, triggered by many different stimuli. There is also an addiction to pleasure which is possible in the physical sense. Many books have already been written about this. When we consider sex in dreams, however, we can assume that something else besides instinctual physical desire to further the species or simple physical desire is present. That is the approach which I wish to offer to you.

It would be impossible to talk about sexuality in dreams without talking about feminine and masculine energies. We contain all energies within us. This will be a controversial statement for you only if you are locked into a perception of sexuality which is based on gender. One of the ways by which the human mind seems to perceive and learn is through the experience of comparison and duality. We perceive the world dualisticly. For example, you would not know what "hot" was unless you had an experience of "cold" or "not hot" to compare it with. Everything we see in our world is ultimately filed away in our psyche in dualistic terms. Think of all the "opposites" we perceive. Up/Down, Black/White, Young/Old, Right/Left, etc. The list is infinite and includes "Masculine/Feminine."

When our cultural value systems and beliefs are confronted with an apparent contradiction of what opposites are "supposed" to be, confusion results. A good example would be the wide range of attitudes and reactions that occur when men display feminine characteristics and women masculine ones. If this is carried on into the sexual area there is liable to be a polarization based on judgement and disapproval by the majority, which is in turn based on unconscious and unrecognized material.

This carries over into the interpretation of dreams. If a "heterosexual" man has a "homosexual" dream, he is likely to be so activated by the material of the dream that the entire point of the dream message is lost, particularly if he has taken on a feminine role in the dream activity. The problem, as always, is the superimposing of the outer mind's beliefs about life and "right behavior" onto the unconscious, which could not care less.

KEY POINT

The unconscious mind does not make any distinctions based on learned belief systems and value judgments about sexuality and sexual behavior.

This statement also holds true for any other kind of behavior. I want to reiterate that the unconscious is not bound by the behavioral values we have adopted, whatever they may be.

If this statement is true, then we can see how the sexual material presented in our dreams is a symbolic message from our unconscious to our conscious, showing us something we are working with on an internal level. This may or may not require action externally. It does require internal contemplation if any value is to come from the message.

The message of any dream may always be read on several different levels, as we have seen. When we look at dreams with sexual content there may be a first level which has to do with physical desire. One dreams of having sex with another, actual person and on a real level does want to do that. This might not be consciously recognized or it might be well known to the dreamer. That is valuable to know and can be useful information. On a deeper level much more is going on and that is the tricky part when it comes to the interpretation. All our ideas regarding masculine and feminine, as well as our value judgments about sex and sexuality must be looked at if we are to get to the real meaning of the dream.

Let's look at some dreams and see if we can get a better idea of how it works.

Bill's Dream.

I was in a place like a department store, and I was like a manager. I had been interviewing vendors, people bringing me merchandise (selling). A tall woman came in and asked to speak with me. She had dark hair and was wearing a flowered dress, not particularly attractive. Another man came in and the woman faced him and ran her fingers down her body and said, "Hello there. Are you ministering to Carol?" She was not attractive or sexy and I felt some revulsion.

A woman security guard came in and attempted to eject the woman in the flowered dress, apologizing for letting her slip by her (the guard). The woman said to me, " I guess we can't do business, but thank you for being nice to me." I said, " What is it you are trying to sell?" She said, " Why, myself, of course."

Before we go through the dream you may want to try an interpretation for yourself. Even though you don't know the dreamer, there is enough information presented for you to do a good job when it comes to understanding his dream. One piece of information for you: "Carol" is not an actual person that the dreamer knows, so you don't need to know anything about her in order to fill out details of the dream images.

This dream illustrates some of the ideas I have been sharing with you in this chapter. The sexual content is mild in appearance but powerfully present.

The setting of a department store tells us a lot about Bill. A "department" store has many different departments which carry different items or inventory. This is an analogy for departments or compartments of the consciousness of the dreamer. Bill is the manager of the store, meaning he is the one in charge of all the departments/compartments. The first useful piece of information for him is that he is in charge of what goes on here. He is responsible for interviewing the "vendors" who will provide the items for the different departments. He chooses what will be added to the stock and what will not. That is his job in the dream — to select what the store will purchase. The dream is showing him that he gets to choose what his consciousness will stock and offer, like a department store.

Now the tall, dark haired woman enters the scene. She wants to speak with Bill, meaning she has a message for him. A dream character who asks to speak with you is always an interesting figure. If we assume that this figure represents some part of Bill, then whatever she has to say must be important to him. She represents a piece of an inner dialogue, a character in Bill's inner play. The dream is a stage, so to speak, to present the characters in this inner play.

Another man briefly appears, an unknown figure to Bill. This represents another part of self, a masculine aspect which is apparently more approachable by the dark haired woman than Bill. This is born out by Bill's feeling of revulsion towards the tall woman. The woman runs her hands down her body in a provocative and sexual gesture. Haven't you seen this gesture at some time or other?

It is usually seen as a gesture of invitation and in our culture is most often associated with "loose" or "wanton" women.

She greets the man and asks him if he is "ministering" to Carol. This is puzzling because "Carol" is a name which means nothing to the dreamer. We are looking at a hidden part of the inner play. "Ministering" is clear enough — to minister to someone is to care for their needs. The name "Carol" is a play on words, like the word care. Care/Carol. The dream is asking Bill if he is taking care of some feminine aspect of himself. This is one of those times when the psyche presents a message through the sound of a word or words.

KEY POINT

The dreaming unconscious will often present information through a play on words. This could be a written image, the name of a person, a word which sounds like something else or any image which when spoken aloud sounds by association like something else.

Bill does not find any of this very attractive. In the dream he does not see her as "sexy," which means that he does not want to engage in any exchange of energies with her that would be on an intimate level. In fact, he feels revulsion.

Revulsion towards what or whom? In the dream it is towards this female figure/messenger. Bill's revulsion means that he does not really want to have anything to do with her or what she represents, and he is not really interested in Care/Carol. He does not want to deal with the issue of caring for or nurturing the feminine side of self.

In comes a woman security guard. What a wonderful symbol! A female aspect which "guards" security. A watchdog of the feminine which is itself feminine. This is an authoritative feminine energy within which is on the lookout for other aspects which might bring disturbing news. Just the appearance of this figure tells Bill that he should watch out for an energy like this in his life, not so much externally but as an inner manifestation.

Who is the principal authoritative feminine energy in our lives? Would all the people who thought "Mother" please raise their hands? In Bill's case there were many other figures, including his first wife. This dream is now telling Bill that he has a way of seeing life which is based on the ideas of a feminine "guard" which is in charge of his "security." This might not be of value to him in his present, adult life.

Are you following the interpretation so far? The difficulty most people have with this work is the idea of parts of self which carry different "energies" and have different agendas and points of view. We tend to think of ourselves as single beings with a viewpoint which is "ours." In reality, we are many beings within which combine to make up our totality. Just think of all the times you have been inconsistent or have changed your mind about something because you find yourself in a new situation. Dreams show us the many facets of ourselves which we contain within. By seeing what those pieces are like we learn more about who we really are.

Bill's security guard represents an energy he has carried for a long time, a well established authority which guards the access to the "manager." To sell something to the manager, the vendor must get past the guard. We might wonder what has been turned away by this guard in the past.

The guard apologizes and tries to throw out the intruder. The woman then says, "I guess we can't do business, but thank you for being nice to me." This means that the timing is not right for Bill to get the message or to understand what she represents. Being nice to her means that something within Bill has allowed her and what she represents to get past the guard. At least Bill has now seen her.

The ending is classic. When Bill asks her what it is that she's trying to sell she says it is herself. Remember that Bill is the buyer and gets to choose what the store will stock. Do you think that this means she is a prostitute?

This dream illustrates how we contain within us both masculine and feminine energies. We have definite ideas of what is masculine and what is feminine. We cannot get very far into dreamwork without looking at these ideas.

Anyone who has paid attention to current events knows that there is a great deal of social upheaval and debate going on regarding the roles men and women are supposed to be playing in society. This upheaval is world wide. Change is in the wind and it is not often welcomed by many. Each society deals with the change in its own way. On the one hand we see conscientious acceptance, with the usual resistance, as is found in Scandinavian culture. On the other the change is met with rigid repression as we see in a country like Iran.

The traditional ideas of how each gender is supposed to behave have been embedded deeply in our psyche by whatever culture we happen to belong to. The unconscious, however, rolls merrily along with a full range of possibility inherent to it. Our struggle in consciousness is to bring forward as full a balance as possible, so that we may reap the reward of a life which lives up to its inner potential. To do that we must honor as much of ourselves as we can see.

The masculine provides a context for the feminine. Masculine energies define form and produce action in the external. Masculine energy without the breath of the feminine is sterile and in essence anti-life.

The feminine provides content and direction for the masculine. Feminine energies allow inspiration. Creation requires a nurturing by the feminine which then leads to form. Feminine energy without the masculine is unable to take form and remains potential rather than manifested.

In life it is not so simple as this. Everything is a continuous dance of these forces we label masculine and feminine. These forces appear to us in dreams as the characters, male and female, of our inner play. Androgynous figures, those which seem a fused energy of both, represent certain integrated aspects within our psyche.

When we view sexual activity within our dreams we are viewing this dance within. We are attempting to bring into balance and harmony these powerful forces. The dreams show us what is actually going on within and how we feel about it. They will accurately reflect to us our fears and successes, our triumphs and defeats, our progress or regression in terms of achieving harmony.

Here's another dream. This was a difficult dream for the dreamer to share, because she felt so vulnerable by what was revealed by the images. She said she was scared and felt ashamed by the dream. She said she was ashamed because of the images in the dream and also because of what she thought the dream meant.

The words people use to describe their feelings are very revealing. The choice of words, as well as the quality of their voice, can tell you which of the many aspects within them is doing the talking. If you pay attention to your own choice of words and your feelings, you can discover what I mean. This is valuable information when working with oneself or with another.

This dream occurred during a ten day residential conference which I was conducting. During the conference there is always a period of silence and fasting. This period of inner work is always a very powerful experience for the people attending. Dreams tend to intensify and present material which might not be as readily available in a different state of consciousness.

Debra's Dream; Section One.

The dream starts when I am in the fasting and silence period. It seems as though there is a lot of commotion going on. In the other room Gloria and Fay have a radio alarm which goes off. They don't shut off the radio. I can hear the news on the radio. I was annoyed that they didn't turn off the radio. I left and came down the mountain and back to what felt like my home.

The setting is present time for Debra, so what is going to happen in the dream is likely to be related to what is going on for her right now. Gloria and Fay are two women who are somewhat older than Debra, although not "elders." They both have authoritative positions in the outer world and carry a sense of maturity in dealing with life that Debra admires.

The alarm is exactly that; an alarm, something which demands your attention. After the alarm, the radio presents the "news." This is something Debra needs to hear and the information, which is new to her conscious mind, will be presented to her. She doesn't really want to hear it though! She leaves the conference and goes "home," to the place where she lives. "Where she lives," "home," is a symbol for the way she relates to life. It is the place where she connects to herself. It is a context from which everything is explored. Can you feel this? Feel into the meaning that "home" has for you, and then go deeper to the level which is symbolic.

Debra's Dream; Section Two.

I come to my old home. This is my mother and father's home. There is a lot of commotion here, and I forget to maintain the silence and fasting. Then I remember, but it's really hard. I can't seem to communicate to them about the silence and fasting, so I end up breaking it.

Now we have more information. The "home" Debra goes back to is the home of her parents. If you were interpreting, what do you think this means?

This section tells us that the dream is about something that was established during her childhood. There is something in Debra's consciousness which is connected to that earlier time. The appearance of parents and/or their home in the dream signals that the material contained in the dream is in some way related to early stages of development.

When I asked Debra what the silence and fasting meant to her she answered that it was her "true self." To her the silence and fasting are a way for her to get in touch with her authentic self. Somehow this is not something she can maintain around her parents' energy.

Does this sound familiar to you? How many of you have difficulty maintaining your normal sense of self around your parents?

For the second time in the dream there is a lot of commotion going on. The commotion is within Debra. Something has been very stirred up in her and she cannot maintain her sense of self amidst the turmoil. Debra said that it was her mother with whom she was unable to communicate in the dream. It is her mother who cannot understand Debra when she tries to communicate her sense of self.

If the dream had ended here, Debra would have a lot to work with. How do you think Debra feels inside when she recognizes that her mother cannot relate to her as she really is? Before any kind of authentic relationship can be established we have to first acknowledge to ourselves how we really feel within that relationship. Many people have trouble with this.

We have not yet gone very deeply into the dream. This is the kind of dream which so far contains a good deal of useful information on the first level of interpretation. It says a lot about

Debra's relationship with her mother and how she feels about that. It tells her that she has some unresolved issues that need attention. Deeper interpretation would take Debra to a place where she could recognize that her own internal and parenting energies are not in accord with her self expression.

Debra's Dream; Section Three.

There is a feast going on. It feels like a big family ceremony. Like a wedding or a big family reunion. Then I forget to keep the fast going. At that point I realize that I will have to leave. I start to go back up the mountain. I even leave without telling my mother because I just can't communicate with her. I go back and as I am going back I see a bunch of people being led blindfolded by a leader. I think it's from the Dharma center. It's some kind of initiation or test for students and the leader is guiding them through. They have to cross a stream blindfolded. I overhear some of the words that the leader is speaking but it doesn't seem right to me, it doesn't seem true.

At this point we have not moved into the sexual areas of this long dream. When we do get there, it will be better understood if we have the entire dream to look at. Dreams are often sequential in their presentation, so that each section follows upon that which has come before. The more that is remembered, the more we can see the relationships between each section.

The feast at "home" proves too much for Debra's desire to keep fasting. The fasting, like the silence, represents something Debra wants badly, a sense of self which is authentic and true to self. This cannot be maintained in the energy of the family. She realizes she will have to leave and does so, also recognizing that it is useless to tell her mother.

So far the dream has told her that she has deep and unresolved issues. These issues are about establishing her independence as an adult on an inner level. Although she is married and long past physical childhood, she is still caught in some childhood dynamic which is affecting her present life.

She heads back to the mountain, back to the conference, which affirms her desire to back herself up. This is a good sign in the dream, and shows that she is committed to her own growth and independence.

As she walks she sees the leader with the blindfolded students. These students represent part of her which literally does not see what's going on. She does not trust the leader. What he says sounds wrong to her, and this indicates that the path of teaching he represents is not the correct one for her. The Dharma Center is Buddhist. In the past Debra has spent some time there, but it feels rigid and incorrect to her. The students have to cross a stream. Debra feels that the stream represents some kind of feminine energy (this came from the dialogue with her about the dream). She is not comfortable with this blind crossing.

Debra's Dream: Section Four.

Then I am in a bedroom in a big house. It's an old 2 or 3 story farmhouse. I'm in the bedroom with Jack. We're going to have a private session to work on the blockage of my second chakra and the womb area. Jack is working with his hands, doing energy work and massage. We look into each other's eyes and discover that there is a sexual attraction and that it is mutual. There is a sense of release in knowing that we have both been feeling these energies but didn't know it was mutual.

We start to kiss passionately and roll off the bed. Jack doesn't look like himself, he is thin faced and looks more like the red figure on the tarot card, The Wheel of Fortune, demonic, more that look.

Part of Debra's feelings of shame when relating the dream have to do with Jack as a real person. Debra's first reaction is to confuse the actual person with the dream figure. Jack represents a lot of things to Debra, including teacher and healer. She has done a lot of work with Jack in waking life. When talking about the dream she said she had a sense that the work "Jack" was doing in the dream was necessary for some inner healing, and that this required a masculine energy.

The second chakra is often associated with sexual energies. In real life Debra is unresolved regarding the issue of having children and was experiencing some frustration in her sexual activity. The dream states that there is a "blockage" of energy in these areas. The symbol of Jack, if correctly interpreted, may offer a clue to the source of that blockage within her.

The Tarot card which she mentions shows a central figure of a mystical wheel. On the bottom of the wheel is a somewhat demonic looking figure, red, with semi human features. For Debra this is a "Demon Lover." The Demon Lover is an ancient figure in myth and story. Psychologically it can often be related to the father. For an excellent presentation of this relationship, please refer to the book *Addiction To Perfection* by Marion Woodman, published by Inner City Books.

The changed appearance of Jack in the dream tells us that the dream is not really about Debra's attraction to Jack the person. It is true that she is attracted to the real person, which disturbs her in real life, but that attraction is based on the unconscious material which is being addressed in the dream. Jack carries certain qualities which trigger the unconscious associations Debra contains.

Debra's Dream; Section Five.

Jack's body was very skinny and his penis was very small. It seemed like there was a large hole that I could see at the end of it. Jack got up and said that he would go and relieve himself first, so that he wouldn't come too soon and it would all be for me.

Jack comes back and we start making love. We're on the bed now. I notice that there are two girls sitting outside the window on the roof. They're between eight and twelve years old. Pre-adolescent. I don't want them to see me. They feel like tattle-tales. I go to shut the window, pull the curtains. I go back to bed and then the curtains open. I go back to the window, shut the curtains, go back to bed, the curtains open again. This goes on and we keep getting interrupted.

Then one of the girls is inside the room. She's watching. I open the window and stick her outside the window. I close it up and lock it. Then it starts to rain outside. I go downstairs to lock the front and back door so they can't get in again.

This section is taking Debra deeper into her unconscious. The size of the penis is contrasted with the large hole at the end of the organ. Something in her wants to diminish the power of this figure, yet the large opening indicates just the opposite. There is also something in Debra which wants total involvement with this figure, "it would all be for me." All of the sexual energy and "essence" of this figure will be hers.

But there is something interfering here. The two young girls are watching, and no matter what she does, Debra cannot keep them from seeing what is going on. She's afraid they'll tell on her. These represent younger aspects of Debra and this section tells her that the key aspects of whatever she is working with will have something to do with this pre-adolescent stage of her development.

Finally she locks the window and shuts them out. She goes downstairs to make sure they can't get in. Going downstairs in a dream is often a signal that one is going deeper into the material with which the dream is involved. More information will be presented. The second and third stories of the house where she is having this sexual interaction with Jack are analogous to sexual/emotional levels.

Debra's Dream: Section Six.

When I go down into the kitchen there are all these people. Women and children, all these people running around. I have a robe on. I'm shocked to see all these people and I ask one of the women if it's usual to have so many people here. She says, "Oh, yeah, there's always lot's of people here."

It's a really big kitchen, enough room for communal cooking, a big center. There is another woman there who does not feel like one of my relatives and she is pointing out her kids. I have a feeling that some of the people are my more distant relatives, cousins and aunts. I say, "I didn't realize, I haven't been home for so long."

Then I walk back to the parlor/living room area and there are two men sitting dressed in dark suits discussing worldly affairs, smoking. Then Jack is there on the couch. Now he is much fuller, more handsome — he has a robe on, silky, a silvery color. His legs are open and his penis and organs are showing. His penis is real large.

I'm shocked and say, "What are you doing down here? Cover yourself up; they'll know what we're doing." Jack just sits there with a smirk on his face. I know that we're not going back upstairs. I feel so embarrassed and shameful.

This is the end of the dream. The kitchen feels to Debra like the place where all the women's work is done. It is full of people from whom she feels distant, although they are relatives. She is in some way removed from these busy women and children within herself. They represent a whole cycle of maturity as woman, including the process of children and mother. This can be related to the beginning of the dream and the estrangement which she feels from her mother.

The parlor/living room, on the other hand, is the domain of the men. This is how Debra was brought up. Here is the authoritative, worldly masculine piece, talking and smoking. It is Victorian in concept. There is a distinct separation between the men(man) and the women(woman). Here is Jack again, shockingly displaying his huge phallus and smirking at her. And now she is terribly embarrassed and ashamed, as everyone will know what they (she) have (has) been doing.

Please take a moment here to pause and think about what the dream may be saying. This is a powerful message for Debra. Although the dream material is highly charged and difficult for her to deal with, the message is crucial to her if she is to move into another level of maturity as a woman and as a sexual being. What do you think the message is? What is the dream mainly about? You have all the clues before you to make a good stab at the correct interpretation.

If we look at the dream as a whole, several key points jump out at us. Here's a list. Before you read it you may want to make a list of your own of the most important images or events.

A LIST OF IMAGES/EVENTS/THOUGHTS

Jack is an authority figure and teacher
Sexual interaction; Debra's feelings about it in the dream
    and when telling it
    a. starts passionately
    b. interrupted and frustrated
    c. embarrassed and ashamed at end of dream
Goes back to parents' home
Can't communicate

Feels like she can't maintain sense of self
Lover is somewhat demonic
Wants it "all for her"
Confusion and commotion with all the women in the kitchen
Young girls interrupt her
Embarrassed by sexual display in the parlor where the older men are

The main clues are that there is childhood association, she cannot communicate with the mother, the sexual display is embarrassing when the older men might know about it and it is the young girls who interrupt her with Jack. It is also important that she sees Jack as an authority figure. When you put these together, what do you get?

This is a dream of incest and the frustrated sexual energies in relationship to the father which are bound up in the childish part of her psyche. It is also a dream of the fundamental way Debra sees herself and her relationship to her mother, although this is not as obvious at first.

For incestuous energies to be active and present does not necessarily mean that the incest is acted out on a physical level. No human escapes the conflict which arises within the psyche over the sexual attraction to the parent. Without getting too deeply into the psychology of this, let's keep it simple and say that we are all attracted to the parent in this way, although this may not be obvious or consciously realized. This is human and natural. Children are sexual beings.

Problems arise because in many ways the deeper levels of our psyche cannot recognize the difference between mate or lover and parent. We bring our unfulfilled expectations and wants that we experienced with our parent to our intimate relationships. This is not a new idea, although it is not always a popular one. We unconsciously project an impossible situation onto our sexual partner. On this level we are in deep conflict because of the taboos placed on incest. This can lead to very unsatisfying and frustrating relationships with no apparent cause.

The resolution of such a problem demands the honest recognition of the incestuous attraction. You can see how this might not be easy to do! More than the recognition is required also. Healing cannot take place unless we can come to the appreciation without judgement of the very energy which brings up those feelings of shame and embarrassment. In other words, we have to stop blaming ourselves for having taboo feelings and thoughts, appreciate that this is simply part of being human and move on. Not easy to do, but it can be done.

Debra's dream is showing her the problem. The solution is not shown except by implication. Since she now knows she has a problem with this area, she can take steps to do something about it, if she wants to.

When Debra first told me the dream, she said that she felt somehow it was about incest. She had not yet analyzed the dream, and was caught in her embarrassment about the sexual material. Debra can remember only two times in her life when she felt she had her father's full and loving attention. He was essentially unavailable to her. This is deeply painful to her. Jack is a strong male authority figure who is "safe" — that is, he is supportive of her and he will not take advantage of her sexual feelings towards him. This creates the freedom for Debra to look at the material in the dream more deeply, once she sees that it is not a simple matter of physical attraction towards a man who is not her husband.

Debra's mother taught her that genitals were "dirty" and should be hidden. Debra is "imprinted" with her mother's attitudes towards sexuality through her experience of her mother, the prime matrix for her. She is full of ambivalent feelings about her sexuality and role as a woman. She is angry at her mother and is only beginning to really recognize this. She is caught in a classic conflict between physical desire and sexuality and the thought that this is wrong, dirty, and forbidden. The main object of her early desire, her father, is unavailable to fulfill these needs. She is stuck in an endless loop of frustration unless she has the courage to take on the understanding, acceptance and forgiveness of herself.

You might need a mental break after this! Remember that the title of this book is *What Your Dreams Can Teach You*." Superficial readings of dreams may be fun but they don't teach you much. What dreams can teach you is more of who you are. As you learn more about who you are, you have more options for life and living life available to you. Since dreams are an interface with the unconscious, it is impossible to do meaningful work with dreams without entering the psychological areas. You don't need to be a psychologist to understand your dreams. You only need a willingness to feel honestly into what the images mean for you and to trust your intuition. Your connection to your intuitive levels grows steadily, and this will spill over into other areas of your life as well.

Now we'll take a short dream with strong sexual content and using the worksheet approach presented earlier we'll see if we can understand what it's about.

Gloria's Dream.

The scene is a bedroom. Two Mexicans are raping another smaller male Mexican. I don't like what's going on. Someone comes into the room and talks to the smaller one. He keeps saying he doesn't mind what the other two are doing to him. There is blood on the sheets. I watch the scene and feel sick.

Here is how we might use the worksheet with this. You may want to go ahead and do this on your own before reading what I have written.

1. Write down and review the dream (as above).
2. The images or events in the dream which I feel are the mostr powerful are:
   a. Two Mexicans raping a smaller one.
   b. blood on the sheets
3. I feel that the most important image is:
   a. the rape scene
   b. smaller man says it's ok with him
4. The way I feel about this image is:
   a. sick
   b. unable to do anything
   c. somehow want to watch
5. This image reminds me of: (put down anything, no matter how unrelated it appears, which comes to mind)
   a. men are cruel
   b. looks very painful
   c. violation

    d. sex is painful

    e. men are animals

    f. I wonder how that feels

    g. why doesn't he complain

    h. I don't like it

6. The next image I feel is important in the dream is:
    blood on the sheets

7. The way I feel about this image is:

    a. frightened

    b. messy

    c. something about this is important

    d. I don't like blood

8. This image reminds me of:

    a. women have periods

    b. women are vulnerable

    c. sex is messy and violent

9. Another image I feel is important is:
    the small Mexican telling another man that he doesn't
    mind what is being done to him

10. The way I feel about this image is:

    a. doesn't make sense

    b. he must like it

    c. disturbs me

    d. how can he like it

11. Any other details I now remember are;
    no others

12. I feel that the dream is about:

    a. something about sex

    b. how I feel about men

    c. how I feel about sex and men

13. Another thing about the dream is:

    a. I want to watch even when I feel sick

    b. The dream is saying that the way things appear isn't
    what I think is going on

14. The way I feel about this dream is:
    the dream is important for me to understand but I
    don't want to look at it

15. Some other thoughts that occur when I review the
    images of the dream are:

a. I feel both attracted and repelled by the images
b. I'm very ambivalent about sex
16. Review what you have written.
17. When I ask for help from within about this dream, I
sense that the dream is about:
My feelings towards sex and men and some
inward conflict about men and masculinity.
18. My interpretation of the dream is: (brought forward by
the Dreamer Within)

The dream is about conflicts of sexuality in the dreamer's consciousness. She has deep feelings of distaste and fear about expressing sexuality. She feels that men are uncaring and unfeeling and violent, and that sexual penetration by a man is a violation. At the same time, she knows that this is not the only viewpoint. In fact, because it is a masculine figure being violated in the dream, she can assume that there is a conflict within her about surrender to sexual energies and actions which is based in a masculine perspective.

The dreamer carries strong masculine energies of control and dominance. To surrender this role in the sexual act is very difficult for her. She is being told in the dream that it is possible and that no harm is done by this surrender.

The blood on the sheets represents an energy of life and sacrifice. The sacrifice is the act of surrender to the strong masculine and sexual energies. The Mexican figures indicate that this is an area which is somewhat foreign to her; from another country, so to speak. This means she is not really consciously aware of how this conflict arises within her.

Problems which she may experience in expressing herself sexually will have roots in this masculine orientation towards life which she has adopted. This will hinder her full expression as a woman. Because the material is not well recognized by the conscious mind, she will have a strong tendency to blame men for her frustrations. This will carry over into all areas of her life and is a result of the projection of the unconscious material.

How did you do? This is very confrontive material for Gloria. If the interpretation is correct it reveals a fundamental relationship with sexuality which is neither satisfying nor fulfilling. It does point the way towards a change if Gloria can shift her viewpoint. That won't be easy because it demands an acceptance and appreciation of masculine energies within her. On the one hand she has identified with these energies very strongly and uses them to achieve success in the outer world. On the other hand, she intensely dislikes those very same energies as they are reflected back to her in the outer world.

From a dream like this or like Debra's we can see how it is essential to move to a centered and appreciative state of awareness when looking at the revealed consciousness of the dreamer. This is true whether it is your dream or another's. Be gentle and non-judgmental with yourself and others, for we all contain vulnerable and difficult areas within. Dreams of sexuality show the deepest levels of our psyche.

11
SERIAL DREAMS

Serial dreams are distinct from what I call "progressive" dreams. Progressive dreams work over a long period of time, sometimes years, with the same material. They show a progression within the dreamer's consciousness and present periodic updates on the subject. Serial dreams are like the old serials that used to be shown at the movies. They present a complete section of the story, with each new dream picking up exactly where the previous dream left off.

I don't know many people who have had this kind of dream. If you are a dreamer who has had this experience, I would like to hear from you. You can find contact information at the end of the book.

This kind of dream is particularly interesting to me. Serial dreams show the complexity of the psyche in a different way. Something within the dreamer has a coherent and long tale to tell. It decides that the best way to present the material is over a period of several days, in a consistent sequence which is exactly like the presentation of a story teller. Sometimes, like the old serials, the dreamer is left with the knowledge that more is to come and that the present sequence is finished for now but will pick up again at some undetermined future date. You know how the trailers in the movies say, "COMING SOON TO THIS THEATER . . ."? Serial dreams are sometimes like this.

I feel that serial dreams are particularly important for the dreamer. Why else would the consciousness take the time to elaborately play out the message with such detail? The following dream occurred over a period of two weeks. There is often a day or two between segments of a serial dream. The woman who had this dream is an "experienced" dreamer in that she has been consciously recording and working with her dreams for years. She remembers her dreams in great detail. She is also psychically sensitive, and has had difficulty in her outer life with integrating this aspect of herself.

This dream presents some very interesting material. You will have to watch out for any traps your unconscious springs on you regarding the content. Remember that a fundamental rule of interpretation is that you must watch out for any placement of your own unconscious material upon the dream. Ready? Here is the dream.

Cassandra's Dream; Episode One.

When the dream begins, I find myself in the central marketplace of a small village. The village looks like one you might find in Egypt or Morocco. The people are dark-skinned and are wearing long, loose robes. People from all the surrounding countryside have gathered for marketday and the central square is very crowded and noisy. I'm there because I'm on a trip led by a male teacher and a woman teacher. There are about twenty people in the group I'm traveling with and we are exploring the market.

It's very sunny and hot, and the air is filled with dust and spicy smells. Everyone seems to be moving around the square in the same direction as they look and barter for things. I join the flow of people.

Then I see coming towards me a tall, thin, dark-skinned man dressed in white. He and a smaller group of people are moving in the opposite direction to the other people in the market. As he comes abreast of me he turns and stops and looks directly at me. In this moment I feel a compulsion to turn and follow this man. In fact, I feel that I am meant to go with him. But I hesitate. I'm afraid that if I go with him I won't be able to rejoin my tour group. The crowd pushes against me and carries me away from the man.

There is enough within this first segment of the serial dream to provide plenty of information by itself. The setting is a central square and marketplace. This shows that this is a "central" issue within her consciousness. A marketplace is many things. One can pick and choose between many items, objects and foods. It is a place of option and choice. She is touring under the guidance of a male teacher who is in real life a well known and respected leader in metaphysical areas. There is also a co-leader, a woman present. The woman is not identified. She represents a balancing, feminine, teaching aspect. These figures symbolize the path Cassandra has been following in her personal, spiritual development up to this time.

The "path" aspect is emphasized by the way everyone is moving around the square, all in the same direction. The hot, foreign scene says that she is in an area of herself which is not familiar to her. There is a lot of commotion about her, a press of people. These are symbolic of the multitude of ideas and viewpoints within her. We do not yet know exactly what this is about, though.

A strange and commanding figure appears on the scene, dressed in white and followed by a much smaller group of people. This figure is moving in exactly the opposite direction as the rest. He represents, among other things, an energy which follows its own path and does not move "with the crowd."

The figure stops before her and she feels strongly that she should go with him. Although she wants to go, she fears losing the group she is with. This means that if she is to follow whatever this figure represents within her, she will not be able to continue on as before. This is a figure of transformation and change. Then, in her hesitation, she is carried away by the crush of people (her ideas/viewpoints/agendas/older ways of seeing/ways that do not relate well to this figure). This shows the current, dominant way she relates to this new energy at this time (The time of the dream).

This is a figure which would be described in Jungian terms as "archetypal." It is called "The Messiah." The "Messiah" and other kinds of archetypal images will be discussed later on. For now, think of archetypal figures as representing energies and patterns of behavior which seem to be universal in human experience and consciousness. These figures occur, in various guises, in all human cultures. When such a figure appears in a dream, we know that the dreamer is dealing with very powerful and basic energies within.

Something in the dreamer resonates deeply with what the figure represents. Such dreams are particularly important.

The segment ends here. It is introducing the dreamer to a new and disturbing energy. Future sections of the dream should take her into a deeper interaction and relationship with the unconscious material and develop the symbolic story. That is actually what happens, as we shall see.

The messiah in human culture is the figure who brings the true and Divine word to man. If one follows the messiah, everything will change. The messiah brings the call to God and Spirit. If Cassandra heeds this figure she cannot go on as before, and her psyche knows this. So she hesitates.

Cassandra's Dream; Episode Two.

In the next dream I find myself walking through the back streets of the village. The streets are very twisting and narrow and the earthen walls of the homes are close around me. I come to an opening in the wall to my right which opens into an inner courtyard. The courtyard is small and square with a bare, earth floor. Opposite me is a wooden door set into the wall and beside it a bell cord.

I step into the courtyard and I sense that behind me the male and the woman teacher from my tour group are standing in the doorway. At this moment something compels me to reach up toward the sky. As I look up I am looking directly into the brilliant sun and I can't see what I'm reaching for. But my hand grasps something and I find that I am holding a white feather. I know that this is a sign that I have come to the right place and that the man whom I am meant to follow is waiting for me on the other side of the door.

I go forward and pull the bell rope and hear the bell ring. Then a small panel in the door is flung open and a very strange character peers out. He is small and hunched, and one eye is scarred. He's dressed in a dirty white robe and a turban. He squints at me and says, "What?" There is about him the feeling of a trickster or a magician and I hesitate. But I know that what I seek is on the other side of the door, so I say, "I've come to talk to him." I feel almost breathless as he pulls the creaking door open.

Let's take a look at this dream using the techniques we now have available for interpretation which have been presented so far.

If we use the worksheet approach with this section we can get a good sense of what is meant.

1. Write down and review the dream (as above).
2. The images or events in the dream that I feel are most powerful are:
   a. the blinding sun
   b. the man with the turban
   c. the inner courtyard
   d. the white feather
   e. teachers behind me
3. I feel that the most important image is:
   the man with the turban
4. The way I feel about this image is:
   a. surprised
   b. unsettled
   c. I have the right to go by him
   d. he's a guardian of the door
   e. he's not trustworthy
5. This image reminds me of:
   a. Sinbad the sailor
   b. magical
   c. old movies about strange people in secret places
   d. Ali Baba and the 40 thieves
   e. a guard
6. The next image I feel is important in the dream is:
   teachers behind me
7. The way I feel about this image is:
   a. like parents
   b. support me
   c. surprised they're there
   d. they're behind me
   e. good about it
8. This image reminds me of:
   a. parents again
   b. something in back of me

The next image I feel is important is:
   The blinding sun
The way I feel about this is:

a. very bright
b. warm
c. attracted
d. right to go for it
e. lots of energy
f. can't see what's there
g. overpowering

This image reminds me of:
1. Religious painting
2. nature
3. Greece in Summer
4. good place
5. powerful energy
6. God

The next image I feel is most powerful is:
The inner courtyard

The way I feel about this image is:
a. secret place
b. hard to find
c. comfortable but strange
d. like the simplicity
e. feels right
f. hidden

This image reminds me of:
a. mysterious
b. calm and centered
c. an entryway

The next image I feel is important is:
the white feather

The way I feel about this image is:
a. don't know
b. it means something
c. strange thing
d. pretty

This image reminds me of:
a. birds
b. white dove
c. spirit symbol
d. a message

e. a key

9. Any other details I now remember are:

no others

10. I feel that the dream is about:

Finding something inside me which knows a secret. Something about this I want to know. This man is important to me. There is something which guards the way and it's not trustworthy, but I can pass.

11. Another thing that the dream is about is:

Search for connection to God.

12. The way I feel about this dream is:

I feel excited and like there is more to come. I feel good about the dream. I feel special.

13. Some other thoughts that occur when I review the images of the dream are:

a. this is an important dream

b. I am excited

c. I am a little worried

d. the guard bothers me

14. Review what you have written.

15. When I ask for help from within about this dream, I sense that the dream is about:

Something about the spiritual quest and my choices to pursue it.

16. My interpretation of the dream is: (brought forward by the dreamer within — the dreamer within is impersonal and often presents the interpretation in the third person.)

The dreamer is ready to begin the exploration of a new energy within her. This energy represents a powerful, spiritual guidance and has knowledge she has been seeking. She must watch out for the kind of illusions which her mind can place between her and this energy, but she knows how to gain access to it. She is supported in this task by the work she has done before, represented by the teachers she has travelled with in the past.

The key to the new guidance will be found in her willingness to feel into the energies of life and creation.

Although she cannot see how this is to be done, this is only a problem to her outer awareness. If she will find the place within her which is protected, simple and still she will be in the right place to feel into the energies which are here represented.

She must trust her abilities and hold firm to her intention to be with this inner guidance.

Did the worksheet help clarify the dream for you?

Cassandra's Dream; Episode Three.

In the next dream I find myself walking along a dusty country road outside the village. I am with my travel group but they are far in front of me. There are trees along the side of the road that offer some shade. It is early morning and still quite cool. Again, walking towards me I see the tall man with his small group of followers. They are talking and laughing. I stop in the middle of the road, directly in front of the man. He has an interesting, angular face and dark eyes that are full of life. As I look into these eyes, I instantly know that this man is something beyond the merely human. I say, " You're the one." By this I mean that he is one of the great teachers of all time and that his teachings are a translation of the Divine to the level of human understanding and that because of the impact of these teachings history will be changed. People will learn to live in new ways, but people will also die and whole nations will be swept away. I see in his eyes the knowledge of all these possibilities and I also see that this will not alter his course. I turn and follow him..

So far the dream has taken Cassandra progressively deeper into her involvement with this teaching figure. First she saw him, going a different way, in the crowded marketplace. She hesitated and was swept along by the "crowd ". Then she found a quiet, hidden place where he could be found. She was shown that she has the support and way of access to this energy within her. Now the dream takes her to the next step: recognition of the importance of this energy for her. Now she is far from the village and the crowd; something within her is taking her out of her old ways of seeing things and placing her into confrontive and direct relationship. She has become separated from the "travel group ", the energies of a different teaching. The "travel group" also emphasizes teaching as exploration. The group coming toward her is happy and laughing. They represent a new possibility which is appealing and welcoming.

She now sees that this is a connection to the Divine. She is also made aware that this is an energy of upheaval for her. "People will die and whole nations will be swept away ". This is the kind of statement which fits with the commitment to the messenger of Spirit. This means nothing short of total change. Nothing will be the same. In keeping with the quality of this energy, this result is inevitable. It is inherent in the process. Now she recognizes that following this energy will lead to transformation.

Cassandra's Dream; Episode Four.

I find myself sitting by a campfire somewhere in the desert. The teacher is sitting directly across from me on the other side of the flames. Around the fire his group of followers is sitting in a circle. It is night and the sky is full of brilliant stars. The air is cool, but there is a soft, warm, almost magical breeze blowing from behind the teacher. The group is talking and laughing softly.

Suddenly the teacher looks directly across the fire at me and it is as if no one else is there. He asks, " Are not the stars beautiful, the air full of promise, the desert ever changing and yet still perfect?" This description is so wonderfully apt that all I can say is " Yes." He touches the fingers of one hand gently to the earth and the other hand gestures toward the sky. He says, " You have created all this. Pay attention.."

Time has progressed in the dream. When she met the teacher on the road it was morning; now it is night. This is another symbol of progression within the psyche. Now the old group is completely gone and she is with the new energy. The fire is a change of form for the energy represented by the sun in the earlier segment. It has been brought down to a human level, a friendly and serving level. The circle represents wholeness and completion. There are no more squares, as there were in the earlier segments. A square can represent the logical processes of the mind; a circle carries a completely different feeling. The circle is also a symbol of feminine, inspirational energies.

Now we arrive at the essential teaching of the dream. What is it that this numinous messenger of Spirit has to teach her? What is the message which he brings that can sweep away nations?

The teacher tells her that she is responsible for creation, the earth, the sky, the stars, all the beauty of creation which surrounds her. He is affirming the Divinity within her. At the same time he is reminding her that she must pay attention. This is an injunction to pay attention to the way she sees life. It is saying that she creates life through her perception and that this will determine her experience. The implication is that she has not been paying attention, or might forget to do so. She is being told to affirm the Divine perception of life and creation. She is reminded that this is her task.

If any of us actually do this on the true and meaningful feeling levels, it will create a vast upheaval in the way in which we relate to the world. It is not enough to pay lip service to the idea that one carries the spark of Divinity within, nor is it enough to say we love life. Only a shift to the level which knows that this is so will make it true on a conscious level. With consciousness comes responsibility in a more expanded sense. With the consciousness of the Divine within comes a deep change in our relationship with life. Certainly, nothing can be the same after that.

When Cassandra related this dream, she was caught up in her own unconscious desires to have a real, physical Messiah appear and guide her safely home. Her inclination, because of the unconscious material, was to see the dream as prophetic in nature. She was just about ready to fly off to Egypt or Morocco! If you had this dream, what would you think?

The desire for the appearance of the Messiah is one of the great collective streams of the human consciousness, particularly in our Western tradition. We can learn to identify these powerful energies and interact with them in a way which is conscious and expansive.

There is a trap here for the unwary. Dreams of powerful figures which bring Divine messages must be looked at very carefully. There is an element, perhaps, of compensation present. Some dreams will present ego enhancing material in order to strike a compensatory balance with an outer life which is not satisfactory. When we have a dream which singles us out for Divine attention, such as this one, we need to go slowly.

This does not mean the message of the dream is invalid. It does mean that we have to take the time to notice if such a dream makes us feel special and important. Cassandra, in her waking life, is uncomfortably aware of a desire to be powerful and "special ". She is attracted to Shamanistic work and the specialness of initiated and mystical states. Her dreams frequently have her interacting with strange and mythical figures. She has practically a full range of Jungian archetypal figures appearing from time to time in her dreams!

Cassandra needs to pay heed to the very powerful message which the dream presents. At the same time she needs to watch how her unconscious will trick her into misinterpreting that message and distorting it. This is what is symbolized by the figure with the turban who guards the door.

If you have a serial dream, treat each section separately and arrive at an interpretation which is unique for each segment. When you piece it together it will make sense to you, just like a movie. Sometimes the editing can be a little rough, but the story is there, nonetheless.

12

DREAMS OF CATASTROPHE AND WAR

As we move more deeply into looking at different kinds of dreams it is predictable that "neat" classifications begin to break down. Our outer mind would be happy to have all dreams nicely compartmentalized so that we could determine right away what it is we are dealing with when we have a dream. This is the approach often taken in books about dreams. One looks for a key image and then consults a list which says that the dream is about x and z. The mind is satisfied on the outer level by this logical approach.

If you have been following along with me in our exploration you know by now that nothing is ever that clear or simple in the unconscious. A dream always contains material that is deeply inter-related within us. This is why we work with dreams; to begin to see what is going on within us so that we may have a better understanding of self. As we see more about ourselves we gain the possibility of more freedom and options for our personal expression. We develop the ability to choose how we will relate to life on a deeper level with more satisfaction than we had before.

A dream of natural or man-made catastrophe or war never means just one thing. It would be simplistic to say that the dreamer is experiencing an inner conflict, for example. One can be sure that there is an inner conflict, but what is that really about? There may be elements of conflict with authority, sexuality, denied emotion, family history, compensation for feelings of disempowerment, unexpressed rage, fear of life and a desire for inner change, just to mention a few possibilities.

This chapter takes the theme of catastrophe and war in dreams and develops it in an attempt to provide some guidance about these kinds of dreams. The material might as easily fall into another category, such as death and transformation. At this point in our journey the categories begin to break down.

I am often struck by the ease with which people who have these kind of dreams slip into the trap of projection onto their outer reality. A woman dreams of a dam bursting above the town where she lives, and makes real plans to move away so that she will not be caught in the flood. This is a true example from my experience. She made the unconscious mistake of confusing her inner world with the outer, and saw the dream as prophetic. It was indeed prophetic, but not in the sense that she saw. The dream portended a major shift within and the release of powerful, repressed emotional material which she had literally "dammed up" for years.

Dreams of nuclear holocaust are sometimes seen in this way. The primal fear of annihilation which is activated by such powerful dreams is readily supported by the evening news and the genuine danger which exists in our world of such an event. The dreamer then begins to act out of that fear, seen by the outer mind as an immediate threat which has been brought to its attention by the dream. This leads to a skewed relationship with life and reality.

The error of interpretation is always the same; we impose the values and beliefs of our outer mind on the rich symbolism of the unconscious. This has been pointed out previously, but bears repeating. My experience has been that we need to be constantly reminded of this ever present trap when we are working with dreams. I have been working with dreams for many years. I still get caught by my own material time and again, especially when the subject is "loaded" for me.

It is always dangerous to make generalizations about dreams, but I will risk it here, as long as you remember that there are many exceptions to any generalization which can be made. When we dream of war and disaster we are looking at a time of upheaval within. The actions we take or experience in the dream will tell us how we are dealing with this upheaval and will tell us what the upset is about. War is an instrument of change, as is flood or famine. There is always a change being called for in some way when we dream of these disasters. Usually we do not welcome change and we will tend to resist it on all levels.

We feel threatened in the external world when something looks like it will go against our will to have things the way we think we want them. This can be a person, group, collective event, an act of nature, or anything else which offers a challenge to the status quo of our personalities. Internally our dreams will reflect the confrontation with whatever energies of change are being called for, whether from within or without. Dreaming of war is to dream of the conflict with life within, and of the destruction of something which represents an older, established way of viewing life. If we can interpret the meaning of the dream, we may be able to identify the conflict with accuracy. Once the inner conflict is identified there may be steps which can be taken to resolve it.

The following dream is a good example of imagery which shows both war and natural catastrophe as symbols for the inner conflicts of the dreamer.

Barbara's Dream; Section One.

I am in a parking lot of a shopping center and I'm walking between two cars when a huge airplane flies over (very low) making a loud, terrifying sound. I crouch between the cars and watch it fly away. As it does, it drops bombs. I look around and in the distance other planes are dropping bombs. Fires are starting. The man I am with yells for me to get in the car and we take off down the street. The streets are full of cars by now and people are fleeing, just as we are. Accidents are happening all over.

This section presents several key images. The rest of the dream will develop the meaning, symbolically, of what is shown here, and it will give Barbara specific information.

The first thing that is apparent is that the threat and confusion is general. Whatever this dream is about, it will have to do with Barbara's whole being. Her psyche could just as easily drop bombs on her, but leave everything else intact and normal! That is not the case. Bombs are falling everywhere, above and in the distance. Fires and confusion break out. The entire community is fleeing and this causes accidents. This is a message in itself.

It reads: FLEEING FROM THE SITUATION IN PANIC LEADS TO ACCIDENTS! Accidents are random and uncontrollable events with negative consequences. This is what she can expect if she does not pay attention. It also tells her that she is currently fleeing in response to the problem. She is not able to deal calmly with the situation. That is consistent if she feels threatened on a very deep level.

The airplane is a huge, impersonal and terrifying force. She is clearly not in control here. It swoops suddenly upon her, which indicates that this is an unexpected event for her. Something has been activated within her which now comes to her attention by way of this dream. Barbara at this time was doing a lot of personal exploration and was beginning to get glimpses of deeply held feelings which had not been allowed expression for many years. Mostly these were feelings of loss, anger and frustration, involving her early childhood and adolescence and her passage towards womanhood.

The energy which "yells" at her and tells her what to do to escape is masculine. Perhaps there will be more information about this later in the dream.

Barbara's Dream; Section Two.

We somehow manage to get through the traffic and we head into the mountains. When we get to the mountains my companion knows of a house we can go to. He shows it to me but we don't go right in. He says we need to see the neighbor first. We are talking outside with the neighbor when something drives us into the house. There is a husband, wife, small child, the man and me. We are in their house in a corridor that is lit by a bare lightbulb and we are discussing what to do. I have a feeling we ran inside because of looters and people running through this residential area.

While we're talking, I produce a newspaper that tells of the coming tidal wave — a result of the heavy bombing. The map in the paper shows that the coast will be inundated, as well as a great deal of the inland areas. My companion grasps the implication at once and tells me we must leave.

Pull out your worksheets and let's see what comes up. You do yours and I'll do mine. See if we come to a similar conclusion or reading for what we have so far. Here's mine:

1. Write down and review the dream (as above).
2. The images or events in the dream that I feel are the most powerful are:
   a. head into the mountains
   b. house of refuge
   c. nuclear family in house with dreamer and companion
   d. newspaper about tidal wave
3. I feel that the most important image is:
   the newspaper
4. The way I feel about this image is:
   a. wonderful image of "news" and event
   b. tells her something she needs to know
   c. warning
5. This newspaper reminds me of: (put down anything, no matter how unrelated it appears, which comes to mind)
   a. Edgar Cayce prophecies
   b. a dream I had years ago
   c. overwhelming event
6. The next image I feel is most important is:
   the family group
7. The way I feel about this image is:
   a. no safety
   b. nuclear family; family equals nuclear, nuclear war, disaster;
   c. vulnerable
8. This image reminds me of:
   a. *Night of the Living Dead* (movie); all vulnerable to unstoppable and dangerous forces
   b. must be important to dreamer
   c. my own thoughts about family

The next image I feel is important is:
   house of refuge

The way I feel about this image is:
   a. not really safe — only temporary
   b. something about the neighbor first

This image reminds me of:
   a. not sure
The next most important image is:
   head into the mountains
The way I feel about this image is:
   a. mountains are masculine
   b. mountains are higher up
   c. mountains are more difficult to live in

This image reminds me of:
   a. place to get away
9. Any other details I remember are:
   none
10. I feel that the dream is about:
   The dreamer's way of dealing with the problem; big change coming for her; change already initiated and beyond her control; something about family and parents.
11. Another thing the dream is about is:
   The dreamer's relationship with the masculine.
12. The way I feel about this dream is:
   Very important dream.
13. Some other thoughts that occur when I review the images of the dream are:
   a. She's got a problem here.
   b. she can't go back
14. Review what you have written in response to the questions above.
15. When I ask for help from within about this dream I sense that the dream is about:
   The dreamer's way of dealing with change; a need to see something about the way she relates to life. She is on the run.
16. My interpretation of the dream is:
   This section of the dream shows that the dreamer relies on masculine modalities for dealing with crisis. She seeks a place of refuge which needs to be recognized from a new perspective (the neighbor) before it is accessible, but she is driven to it without understanding

by the force of events. This refuge is a configuration of energies which revolves around her childhood and family. This is the significance of the family grouping within the house. Responses for dealing with life which were established during this time of childhood are inappropriate for her present situation. She needs to discover what this is about.

The newspaper tells her that it is too late to avoid the upheaval which is coming, and that she must take steps to prepare for it. Her strong masculine aspects have an ability to handle the situation. This energy of direct action shows that she must leave the "family" home if she is to survive. However, she is too much under the influence of these masculine properties. Balance with the feminine is not yet indicated in the dream.

Did we come up with something similar? If you did not, remember that we are practicing here. It is OK not to understand dreams! Also, you may have a different insight and perhaps a deeper interpretation than I do. Trust what you get and take it all with several grains of salt. Eventually, if you keep working, you will develop a feeling of certainty about dream work. You will know when you are right in your interpretation, when you are doubtful, and when you can't do it at all.

It was interesting for me when I did the worksheet to see the associations which surfaced; the *Night of the Living Dead*, the Edgar Cayce material and a dream I had many years ago, which I had forgotten.

The movie mentioned is a grade "B" horror film which you may have seen. Much of the action takes place in a house which is being attacked by zombie creatures which have been brought back from death and who are uniformly hostile towards the living. There is a relentless pressure by these creatures as they attack the house. The association in my mind is one of "no safety" in the home. The worksheet reveals as much about my psyche, perhaps, as it does of the dreamer's!

The Edgar Cayce prophecies have to do with a widespread inundation of the United States and the world, causing great change and upheaval of the established order. In my dream I was aboard a ship during this great flood and was shown a map of the devastated areas. The Rocky Mountains had become islands, and the West Coast was now somewhere in Kansas.

Although the dream has to do with personal material for me, it also seems to be one of those collective images which appears to many different people in dreams and intuitions. I do not consider this flood to be imminent in the physical sense, if indeed it is ever to happen. We will talk about collective and personal images later in the book.

Perhaps you have realized by now that the worksheet is more than just a tool for working with dreams. It is a mirror of your self. The associations which occur to you and which you write down may have to do with the dream; they may also have to do with your own unconscious material. Your attitudes, conscious and unconscious, will be revealed about any subject which is suggested by the dream images. In the section of Barbara's dream which we looked at above, my personal material about home and parents must be taken into account when I assess the accuracy of my interpretation. If I know what that material is or at least know it's there, I can then separate that which is mine from that which is the dreamer's.

Do you follow me on this? In other words, if I have done the work on myself which at least allows me to see that I do have unconscious issues about parents and safety I have a chance to recognize when that might get in the way of a successful interpretation. I have a better shot at seeing Barbara's dream clearly.

Most of the time when people interpret dreams they have not done this work of observing self. The result is a very inaccurate interpretation. This principle also holds true in other areas, such as "psychic" readings, tarot readings, interpretation of the I Ching, and other approaches designed to attune to intuitive levels of information. The principles of dream interpretation as presented in this book may also be applied to these other areas.

Barbara's Dream: Section Three.

The next thing I know, I'm at the bottom of the mountain. I don't know how I got there. Chaos is raging about me and I begin my ascent back up the mountain. There is a stairway hewn out of the rock and I am able to get up the mountain easily. When I get back to the residential area I find the house and my companion. He has a boat — a very small boat — and he says the only way to safety is to get in the river and go. We get in the boat and he accompanies me for a short distance. Then, he gets out of the boat and into the water. He tells me to go ahead, that he'll catch up with me later.

In this section we are getting some emphasis and some advice. Barbara is told by her male companion in the last section that she must leave the house and then suddenly she is plunged back into chaos. She is being told how she really feels about leaving whatever the house and family may represent. In her mind this will lead to chaos. The mountain is masculine in feeling and offers a safer place for her. Leaving the mountain = leaving a masculine perception of how to handle challenge, stress and danger in her life. Leaving the mountain = a descent into chaos. This is the chaos of the feminine forces. It is the contrast between the two places in the dream which gives us this information, and it is a "third level" interpretation to see the contrast between mountain and chaos as masculine and feminine.

She climbs back up the mountain by way of a ready made stairway. This is how she has done it in the past — gone back to the house with the family (gone back to earlier well established patterns of perception and behavior) and the masculine "companion." The way is well established through practice and habit.

Can you feel how this represents a pattern of behavior in her psyche? This is a difficult dream and Barbara found it very confusing when she worked with it. The key here is the sequence and the image. We have to learn how to pay attention to the sequence. The sudden transition back into chaos is confusing to our outer mind, which likes orderly transitions. The sequence provides the answer; told to leave house leads to chaos leads to re-climb mountain leads back to house = established way of dealing with the situation. Barbara is then told that there is only one way to safety — via the small boat. The old pattern of behavior leads back to the same place and she will have to do something different if she is to find safety.

The small boat means that she is not very confident of success in this venture, but at least she has a vehicle for the journey. Success and safety means getting into the river. The river does not feel safe to Barbara, as we shall see. The boat is not a very large or stable vehicle. The river represents a powerful, natural force which is not under her control. She may ride it out but not anything else.

The masculine companion leaves her and she is now asked to go on. This says that she really is capable of doing whatever is called for without the help of whatever the figure may represent. She doesn't need this aspect to move to safety. She is being encouraged to develop something else from her own inner resources.

Barbara's Dream; Section Four.

The water is moving fast but it is fairly smooth. It looks like a roller coaster ride — with water where the tracks should be. There is a framework much like a trestle ahead of the boat, that I have to pass through. I become afraid that I'll catch my head on the frame and get knocked out of the boat or even killed. The first plunge comes up and I'm scared. I can see the girders ahead and I close my eyes.

I pass easily under the framework and the boat flows down the slide rapidly and easily. It's not as dangerous as I thought. I continue down the river and through additional sluices, encountering no trouble along the way.

The key images are the river and the trestle like framework which pose a danger. "Like a roller coaster ride" means just what it says. When we are dealing with powerful inner material that is just what it feels like. We experience an unsettling series of ups and downs which are not under our control. Ever ride a big roller coaster? Personally, I dislike them — they scare the heck out of me and make me feel ill! The dream image is confirming how she already knows she feels in her waking life.

The river is taking Barbara along. Ahead looms the "framework" which looks like a "trestle." A trestle is a way to cross an obstacle — it carries something across the obstacle, usually a vehicle or roadway of some sort. What do you think this means? "Framework" = "trestle" = structure for getting over obstacle ("river"); obstacle = river = uncontrollable flow which can lead to safety. This is frightening but turns out not to be as dangerous as she thought. Following the flow within her leads her to safety; but following the flow also leads her on a roller coaster journey which she fears will injure or kill her because it may lead to a collision with the "framework."

The framework/trestle is the way Barbara has done it in the past and the way she looks at things now. She has followed a path which avoids the powerful flow within. She deals with this force by staying out of it and utilizing the framework she has erected. She is terrified by the possible confrontation between the flow of self and the structure she has built to avoid self.

The river is also associated in some way with the flood predicted in the newspaper which will inundate things, inundate her psyche. This is not stated directly in the dream, but is a "third level" of interpretation. The relationship between flood and river has to do with the fact that both are uncontrollable and dangerous images of moving water.

Once she manages to get past the obstacle of the framework, Barbara encounters no trouble. Notice that the trestle/framework has become a potential hazard rather than an assistance.

Barbara's Dream: Section Five.

The scene changes to somewhere that seems to be more inland. I am reunited with the man and we are entering a town where the scenes we fled from earlier seem to be re-enacted. I am tired, fearful, and very wary.

This is the final section of the dream. Barbara is not getting resolution here. Even inland, she cannot escape the chaos. It's almost like the saying that you can run but not hide. This emphasizes the difficulty and importance of the dream material. She is faced with the entire sequence all over again, which is making the point that something needs to be done. What the dream has done is show her the problem; explain how she has dealt with it in the past; shown her how to take on the resolution; and emphasized that there is no resolution for her until she gets the message. The resolution is shown by the journey down the river.

The resolution for Barbara, if there is one, will occur in the future, not now. She is for the moment still caught in the repetition of conflict and chaos, and something in her is very tired of all this. Until she energizes whatever needs to be done in her life to make the shift which is being called for, she can expect more of the same.

Often in a dream of war the dreamer finds him or herself attacking and killing some enemy. That is the nature of war, after all. The enemy in this kind of dream may or may not be personified. In Barbara's dream the enemy is an impersonal and terrifying force, represented by the airplane. This indicates that she does not yet understand what it is that is upsetting her. If she had shot the airplane down or somehow destroyed it, this would be a different kind of relationship with the "attacking" force than is actually shown in her dream.

If you find yourself at war in your dreams, notice whatever you can about the attacking figures. Are they men or women? Are they impersonal or people you know? What is your response to the attack? How do you feel in the dream about the action you have taken in response to the attack? Were you successful in stopping the attack or were you overwhelmed? Is the war over, just beginning, or well in progress?

If an atom bomb goes off in your dream it has to mean that some very powerful force of change has been unleashed within or is at least being contemplated by you in some way. It makes sense to see if you can get a feeling for what that change is about and to notice how you feel about it. What atom bombs, floods, great storms, war and plagues have in common is that they are all impersonal and uncontrollable forces which have dangerous and life threatening elements. They are also, however, powerful instruments for growth and change. If you do not believe this is true, think of how Europe, Asia and America were changed through the cataclysm of World War I and II (one war, really, with an intermission).

If you have ever been in a great storm you know that the fear of death and the sense of overwhelming and powerful forces is certainly present; you also, perhaps, know of the exhilaration and sense of life which is stimulated. This requires passing into a different relationship with your fears so that you may be simply present during the event. That shift also allows appropriate action. The same principle applies to understanding your dreams. The challenge with these kinds of dreams is to take on the feeling of the content, whatever it may be, and honor it without getting caught in its power.

If a natural catastrophe takes place in your dream, what is its nature? Is it spontaneous or instigated by other forces, as in Barbara's dream? The kind of disaster which occurs carries lots of clues for you. A powerful storm coming or in progress tells you upheaval is on the way of some sort. This may make you nervous but does not necessarily have negative consequences. Watch out for the traps of your ideas about things like big storms.

If characters appear in your dream they will offer valuable symbolic information about the nature of the issue which is upsetting you. The first clue will be related to gender, which will give you a basic idea about the way that particular aspect relates to the overall problem. Is this masculine or feminine piece supportive, destructive, indifferent, confused, frightened, allied, an enemy, or what? How do they look? What kind of clothes are they wearing? How old/young are they? What do they say?

Always ask yourself these questions, if they are applicable. Every detail of your dream is important. Every detail contains a clue. Ask yourself, what is it that threatens me in the dream? Why do I want to flee/kill/surrender/watch/ignore/blow up; why do I want to take the action I take? The first level of interpretation relates this to the activity in the dream and whatever the familiar association is. The second level reads the symbols and derives a whole new content of information. The third level makes the intuitive leap to understanding which goes beyond logic.

Don't let the violent and often frightening material of dream wars and dream catastrophes scare you away from understanding.

13

DREAMS OF
DEATH AND TRANSFORMATION

Although it wasn't planned this way, I find I've gotten to Chapter 13 and the subject is Death and transformation. Thirteen is a number of transformation. It is the number of the death card in the Tarot, and we all know of many superstitions regarding this number. Have you ever been in an office building where there was no "thirteenth" floor? Numbers on the elevator in such a building go from 12 to 14.

If I had a dream of a building like this I would be very uneasy, because I would interpret it to mean that I was avoiding the powerful issue of inner transformation and skipping by it. It may occur to you that simply labeling the thirteenth floor number fourteen does not change the real nature of its location! It is still the thirteenth floor no matter what we call it. In addition, all other floors past that point are now inaccurately identified.

Our "conscious" mind is constantly doing things like this — attempting to change the nature of reality by labeling it as something different. We see this today on a collective level in the United States when politicians talk about the national deficit and the budget. By labeling it as something other than it is, the problem appears to be satisfactorily handled. One of the most skilled proponents of this art was Joseph Goebbels, Hitler's minister of propaganda. In the end reality destroyed the illusions he and the Nazis had created.

Reality has a habit of destroying our personal illusions also. When we are faced with a conflict between belief about reality and reality itself we are thrown into confusion. There are only three possible responses in such a situation. We may go into paralysis of action, which disempowers us and leaves us at the mercy of whatever winds of change are blowing; we may precipitate more strongly into the old belief system, in an effort to avoid the change which is called for; or we may embrace the new reality, at the expense of what we previously believed to be true.

I have been privileged in being allowed to work with people who were very ill and facing death within well defined time frames. They knew they had six weeks or sixty days or six months left in their life. They also knew, some of them, that there was a possibility of survival against the odds if they could find a key within them which would release the healing energies which were available to them on various levels. These people always had dreams which would indicate what was going on within. An example of this kind of dream has already been given.

Invariably, these terminally ill people were being asked to change some deeply held viewpoint of life and their participation in it. Their dreams often would point the way to that which needed to be changed. My experience has been that the dreamers got better when the message was received and acted upon. At the very least, their experience of the time left to them was changed dramatically for the better.

One does not have to be ill and near death to have a dream of death, nor does a dream of death necessarily mean physical death is on the way. Usually a dream of death, especially our own death or that of a loved one, throws us headlong into the reactive areas of our mind which fear annihilation and our personal extinction. In this frame of mind no accurate interpretation of the dream can be brought forward.

Death as a symbol means transformation and irrevocable change. When something dies, that's it! Whatever it is that is dead or dying, symbolically speaking, will not spring back anew. But, like the mythical Phoenix, something new may be born from the ashes of the transforming fires. That something has its origin in the death of the old form. Until the old form is swept away the new manifestation cannot occur.

Nature is full of symbols of transformation. The butterfly is one well known example. Another is the snake, which renews itself by shedding its old skin. Without the shedding new growth is impossible. You can probably think of other examples as well.

Transformation is one of those words which is sometimes taken lightly. This is a mistake, as transformation means nothing less than the death of something old so that something new may come forward. Make no mistake — if we consciously pursue transformation of self and self understanding, we will have to let go of some ideas and viewpoints which are held most dearly. These will not go easily.

As we approach transition points of transformation in our lives we will find that our dreams give us fair warning and good advice about the change. Dreaming activity may often increase considerably, or at least the number of dreams we remember. Sometimes a transformation is shown which may take years to realize, and then only in hindsight. Other dreams deal with an immediate or imminent change which is developing.

It could be said that all dreams are in some way concerned with our inner transformations, as we are constantly changing and experiencing new input and stimuli. In this chapter, though, I want to concentrate on dreams which are clearly indicating that a major change is at hand, something which will have a deep and permanent effect on us. Perhaps as we look at some dreams of this sort we can get an idea of how we might understand our own experiences of deep change.

Here are two dreams from the same dreamer, spaced some time apart.

Carl's Dream; Number One.

I am looking at a coffin. The room is lit by daylight. Somehow I know that the Feminine is in the coffin. Then I am in the coffin, which is closed over me and sealed. It is still light in the coffin, I can see perfectly. For a moment I panic, then I realize that I can get out of the coffin. I take out my little pocketknife and I begin to work it around the edge of the lid and the casket. This is how I will be able to open the lid. Somehow I can then see the outside of the coffin even though I am still inside. I can see the point of the knife coming through as I work it around the edge. It rips through the lining of the coffin from the inside. The lining is pushed out a little by the action of the knife. The lining is a lovely, pale blue, perhaps silk.

You can't ask for a better symbol of death than a coffin! But what is this about? What is contained in the coffin, what has died? Remember that death as a symbol means transformation, a change of form and perception, leading to a new reality.

Carl knows that the "Feminine" is in the coffin, with a capital "F." Whatever his ideas and beliefs about the feminine are, they are symbolically in that coffin. Then suddenly he is in the coffin. This has got to mean that there isn't any difference between the two on some fundamental level. Carl and the "Feminine" are the same, they are one. This doesn't mean Carl is a woman or that he is particularly feminine in expression. It means that the dream is about Carl's relationship internally with the feminine energetic principle.

Briefly he panics. Trapped in the coffin, the same as the feminine. To get out of the coffin he pulls out his knife and begins to work it around the lid. The knife is a masculine tool. Carl uses masculine modes to free himself and by implication the feminine energy also confined in the coffin.

He is also detached from this process, watching it from the outside while it is going on. This tells him that he is separated from the feeling levels that are involved with the whole action of being in the coffin and what it represents. A third level interpretation picks up on the association of death, the feminine and confinement in a place associated with death. Carl feels trapped by the feminine in a way that is like death to him. He uses masculine ways to escape.

The dream is a positive one, however. For one thing there is only a brief flash of panic. Carl knows how to get out. He commented that the dream was full of gentleness and light. This bodes well for the resurrection of the feminine energies within which have "died," i.e. been confined in the coffin.

We are beginning to see how many times our dream material in some way relates to the balancing of feminine and masculine energies. This is a direct connection to the integration with Spirit and expanded levels of awareness. It is not that one is better or more important than the other. It is rather that we need to appreciate and consciously incorporate these energies within ourselves so that we may experience a new dimension of wholeness and expression in our lives. Each of us will have unique challenges to bring this balance forward.

Here is the second dream which Carl had, some time later, which illustrates the theme of deep and ongoing transformation. Based on his earlier dream and others which he has had, it is probably a good assumption that this new dream also relates in some way to the integration of masculine and feminine energies. See what you think.

Carl's Dream: Number Two.

I am with a group of people in a building. It is night. I am on the second or third story in a large room. There is a large, open window, no glass, just a large, square opening. I am looking out at a dark forest with tall, old pines. It is black out, a storm is rapidly approaching. I realize that there is going to be a lightning strike, and move quickly to a different part of the room. The lightning comes with a terrific crash and rumble and strikes the base of a large tree outside. It is not far away, perhaps twenty or thirty feet. The lightning is sustained in duration and awesome in its display of purple-red-white light. It branches at the tree and seems to surround it at the bottom. It is very powerful and luminous. Awesome is the only way to describe it.

I look at the tree, which is still standing after the strike, and it is as though I can see into the heart of the tree, where there is a deep, red glow. I know that the tree is burning inside and will be destroyed. There is more very loud rumbling and crashing and I think there will be another strike.

This is a dream of transformation and the initiation of transformational energies for the dreamer. The dream takes place at night, looking out into the dark forest. This is indicating that the personal material of the dreamer which is addressed in the dream is of a deeply unconscious nature. The feeling is one of something old, ancient and primal.

This is one of those dreams which looks at a long term process. The tree is still standing after the strike, but we know it will be destroyed eventually as the fire burns within. The fire has been ignited by the energy but has not yet consumed the old growth which the tree represents. The tree is the symbol of that within the dreamer which is to be transformed/destroyed by the fire. The dreamer does not know exactly what it is that will be transformed through the energy symbolized by the lightning.

The setting is masculine in its feeling; a large room, a square window. A storm is coming. The storm represents an upheaval of beliefs and ideas for the dreamer. As with dreams of natural catastrophe we are seeing the awesome and uncontrollable power of natural forces. The storm is gathering for Carl.

The window is open and large and looks out on the dark forest. The absence of glass shows that there is no barrier between the dreamer and the events outside. Because Carl is within the room he is still somewhat removed from the ferocity of the storm, but he is not fully insulated or separated from it. If there were glass in the window it would indicate a detachment or insulation from the events, a separation. That is not the case here, and this means that Carl is in some way already involved with the material. In a way this is similar to the earlier dream where Carl was standing outside of the coffin watching himself work his way out. He was both in and out of the coffin, both detached and involved. The old, tall trees outside suggest a fundamental and natural energy present within the dreamer.

When the storm arrives, the transforming and awesomely powerful energy of the lightning blasts the tree at the very base of its growth and strength. The tree in some way symbolizes a strong, old and powerful relationship with life. It is old growth, old perspectives, well established and therefore central to Carl's viewpoint about life. It is a life symbol, a living tree. This tree is something very fundamental for Carl.

This tree could represent a masculine relationship with natural forces. If this is what is being destroyed (destroyed = transformed) by the symbolic lightning, the implication would be that a new energy will need to be called forward, and by contrast this energy could be feminine in nature. The dreamer would not know what this really meant. He does know that the tree has been destroyed. It is also clear at the end of the dream that more is to come but what that will bring is not shown. That is consistent with a long term transformational process. We usually know what has been transformed only in hindsight.

The dreamer can see into the very heart of the tree, glowing and burning deep within. This transformative energy of the lightning has gone deep to the very heart of things. This could be related to the energies of the heart chakra, which are transformative. When this energy is ignited, old beliefs and structures must inevitably be destroyed, since life does not at all look the same from the perception of heart appreciation. In my workshops and retreats I try to guide people into an experience of this transformational energy.

The people in the room represent other aspects of the dreamer's consciousness. He moves away from the strike, which indicates a reluctance and a fear of the full participation in what this energy brings to him.

To sum up, a dream such as this heralds powerful and permanent change taking place at a very deep level of the psyche. There is no indication as to where the change will lead.

The person who had this dream actively pursues self discovery and exploration in his waking life. To Carl, transformational energies are tangible realities. One thing is for sure; the dream represents something which has already happened for the dreamer and this is a process over which he has no control. He is symbolically dealing with forces far beyond his comprehension. This is emphasized by the dazzling and powerful display of energy about the base of the tree when the lightning strikes. It will take years for the full meaning of this dream to emerge for the dreamer.

KEY POINT

Sometimes dreams will present imagery which indicates the beginning of a long term process which is not fully understood by the dreamer. It can take years for the full meaning of this kind of dream to become apparent.

I have often seen dreams where the energies of change were foreshadowed by the image of a huge storm. This is one of the more common images our consciousness relates to. The storm usually indicates that the process of change is on the way or already engulfing the dreamer. If you have a dream like this, see if you can identify what ideas and ways of looking at life are being threatened.

If you seek, you will find. The key to using the information is to see it as just that: information. Once you know what the change is about you may be able to take steps to adjust to it.

None of us are comfortable with change, and frequently we hate it because things will not be the same when the transition is over. But once the process is initiated our choices become limited and ultimately come down to whether we accept the change or not. It is a good idea to surrender gracefully and get on with it. If we do not see clearly what is being called for, that's all right — something within us knows what needs to be done, and the task then is to be patient and observant and let things work out. This can be difficult but we really don't have a lot of choice about it.

The images of transformation and change which appear are often not as dramatic as the dream given above. Very frequently images of buildings and structures may be presented, in various states of repair or demolition, construction or renovation. These dream buildings are symbolic of areas within us which are undergoing the symbolic change. Sometimes the dreams will give very specific information, symbolically, of what it is that is changing. Other times the dream will show the energies which are initiating change without saying exactly what the change is about.

I remember a series of dreams I had several years ago, just before a major change in my perception. The change was principally about an entirely different experience of God and Spirit, and my relationship to the forces of life. It was a renovating and unsettling change. This was foreshadowed by the dreams, which had to do with buildings, foundations, renovations and new construction.

The first dream involved the demolition of an elaborate church. The church was a symbol of the structure of belief which I had built up over my life concerning spiritual forces. Dreams which followed, over several months, showed the clearing away of the debris left by the demolition, followed by new construction appearing as foundations were laid and walls began to be erected. These dreams were prophetic, because I had not yet had the experience which led to the collapse of my old belief system. I did feel uneasy, however, and there was certainly noticeable stress in my psyche regarding the work I was doing at the time and how that inter-related with Spirit.

After the collapse of my beliefs I could see in hindsight what the dreams had been indicating. While the dreams were going on, I only knew that this area of my psyche was undergoing some kind of change. It was not possible for me to know what exactly that change was until it happened.

Here is another dream which uses an image of a building as a central symbol for what is happening in the dreamer's psyche. As you read the dream, feel into the images and see what you feel is going on. It will probably be clear to you on the "first" level. Since you have come this far with me, by now you have absorbed quite a bit of information about working with dreams. Notice that you have already learned quite a lot about dreams and are, hopefully, better able to get the overall meaning of a dream. Once the theme is identified then time can be spent on the details which fill out the dream and give more information.

Kevin's Dream.

I am in an apartment, upstairs in a barn. There is a farmhouse nearby, and I rent from the owners. The buildings are in the midst of the land surrounding the farm, East, out near the interstate highway. I start frying a couple of hamburger patties but then leave on a trip in my car with a woman. I have a little concern that the hamburgers will burn while I'm gone. However when I return I find that they are still all right.

I have returned alone and go to the ground level of the barn which has large open doors North and South. The east wall has a large flapping section through all of which much light is entering. In the recent past I have been here rearranging the boards that are propped here and there for added structural support. There is now a sign posted to the effect that any more rearranging or addition of structural members will result in a collapse of the building. The openness and disintegration of the building suggest that it will not remain standing for long.

Take a moment now to feel again into the images. What is the first thing that you feel the dream is about? If Kevin were asking you to help him understand his dream, what would you tell him and what would you ask him?

Of course you already know that this dream must have something to do with transformation since it is placed in this chapter. But wouldn't you have known this dream was about coming change anyway?

The sign tells us right away that no matter what else the dream may be about, the collapse of something is imminent. It also tells us that although Kevin has been rearranging and propping up this structure of the barn, anything else he would do along that line isn't going to help!

A first level reading of the dream ignores most of the beginning section entirely and zeros in on the warning about collapse of the barn where he lives. Remember, Kevin has his apartment in the upstairs of the barn. If the barn goes, so does his living space. Is it getting a little clearer for you?

At this point we could stop and Kevin would have some useful information to think about. He would know that something he had shored up and rearranged was now about to collapse. If he thought about it he would probably come up with something which gave him an idea of what the issue of collapse was about. It might be a relationship, for example. He might be ready to quit his job. A project dear to his heart might be about to collapse. In dialoging with Kevin we might then see exactly what was going on. If you had this dream, you might be able to see what was going on.

Let's go a little deeper, to the second level, and see if we can get some more information. If we go back to the first section of the dream several things stand out. The apartment Kevin lives in does not belong to him. He rents it from the owners of the farmhouse. The dream is set on a farm. A farm produces food; food is a symbol for the essence of nourishment. Kevin lives in the middle of a farm which he does not own. The dream is telling him two things here; that this dream is about nourishment of Kevin on some level, and that he does not yet "own" the place where he lives or the place where nourishment is produced. Not owning the place where he lives means that he has yet to develop a deep level of self acceptance and self appreciation. For now he is "renting."

The place where we live is an expression of self on fundamental levels. It does not mean physical structure, although that will reflect our inner attitudes. It means the way in which we view life. It is the place from which we move out into life. It is our fundamental ego perception of life. It is also something which is subject to change as new ideas and experience are presented to us.

Kevin is entering a period of change which will lead to the collapse of the old perception and the potential for something new.

The theme of nourishment is seen also in the symbol of the hamburgers. Kevin is preparing food for himself, but then goes for a ride somewhere with a woman. This is a cause for concern, concern which turns out to be unfounded when Kevin returns. This part is very revealing of his inner attitudes. To Kevin, the feminine is something which may interfere with his nourishment. On an outer level Kevin does not trust women and sees them more as taking nourishment than giving it. This is a major problem for him. He has built up a long personal history of painful relationship and loss, starting with his mother. He has a worldview about women and the feminine which is ambivalent and contradictory, like many men. This is part of the structure he has erected in his life and may be part of what is on the way to transformation. Because the woman is present in the dream the feminine is a factor; because the food is still good after Kevin returns from being with the woman, he is being shown that his ideas about nourishment and the feminine/women may be inaccurate.

This is really going from second level to third level interpretation. Sometimes the distinction, which is simply a convenience created for the outer mind, becomes blurred. The second level would note that the hamburgers and the woman were in some way related, and that the issue had to do with nourishment. The third level, which I inadvertently slipped into when I was looking at the dream, is shown above.

What about the barn?

"In the recent past" Kevin has been shoring up the structure (where he lives) and rearranging the support. Now he is told that there is no more he can do in this way, or the barn will collapse. It's ready to collapse anyway. Light is streaming in, from the East. Third level interpretation notes that the East is the direction of the rising sun. A new energy has dawned in Kevin's psyche, and the light could not enter if the structure were solid.

Kevin has been involved in self growth and personal exploration for several years now. He has, in the past, taken much of the work and used it to "shore up" his confidence in himself and his way of dealing with life. He is at a point in this work where he is strong enough to take on alternative viewpoints which are in many ways very different from the way in which he looked at life in the past. The barn is a perfect symbol for this process. The dream is saying that it will no longer work in the same way. The old structure must go. The tools of self which he has discovered and used in one way to support himself in the past must now be applied elsewhere.

The dream is very positive in many ways. This barn could be collapsing into a dark pit; the light could be absent and chaos could be present. That kind of setting would indicate trouble and confusion and hard times dealing with the change. Instead, the fresh wind is blowing through and the light is streaming in. That is a very different feeling of change which is presented. The dream bodes well for Kevin's future.

We are always faced with the necessity of change. At times of crisis or at critical junctures in our inner growth, dreams will come forward to show us what is happening. Our outer mind may have no idea about what to do, or what change is being called for. There is always something within us, an inner guide and advisor which does know what's going on. This advisor is our friend. A good friend does not always tell us what we want to hear, because real friendship demands full respect and honesty. If we learn to trust our inner friend who speaks to us through our dreams we will open a door of transformation which can take us to new heights of understanding.

This next dream also deals with masculine and feminine energies.

Ellen's Dream.

Bill (my husband) and I had half buried and half covered over a dead man in our backyard. He was buried in the driveway going to our garage/shop. For some reason we had to move him to the other side. We got him partially uncovered. The dead man really stunk and Bill was gagging from the smell. I couldn't smell him that much.

Then the dead man's arm shot up in the air because of rigor mortis. Outside the fence a van with Auto-Electric painted on the side pulled up and a man got out. A friend of ours pulled up next. They both wanted to use the wood shop in the garage. Somehow we had to get rid of them.

Bill went out to tell our friend. I kept the gate closed. Our friend knew about the dead man. He would help get rid of the other guy with the van. As I held the gate it blew open partially, but I caught it and got it closed.

It would seem something smells here! That is telling Ellen to really pay attention. Notice that the masculine partner, her husband, is gagging because of the stench but she can't really smell it at all. This is saying that she is not aware of the masculine aspect, whatever it is, which she has buried in the "back yard." She doesn't know on a conscious level what she has buried. The back yard is something that is behind the house where she lives. The back yard is a symbol for hiding whatever the dead man represents in her unconscious.

The dead man is incompletely buried and now for some reason she has to dig him up and move him to "the other side." The other side = moving him from an unconscious area to a conscious one. This is a third level interpretation. Does this feel correct to you?

The arm shoots up in the air suddenly. This was a very difficult symbol for Ellen — she really couldn't get what this might mean. It is an emphasis, an exclamation point, demanding her attention.

A van arrives with the words "Auto-Electric" painted on the side. This is tricky. It is telling her that there is an automatic response that is triggered in her psyche. This must have something to do with the dead man's upraised arm (calling for attention) because it comes sequentially in the dream. It is related to the symbol of the arm. Therefore, a third level interpretation says that she goes into some kind of unconscious and automatic response pattern when the masculine aspect represented by the dead man wants her attention.

An aspect of us is only a piece of the whole, a fragment of the totality of who we are. When we speak of aspects of the feminine or masculine we are breaking down the whole into manageable pieces for our understanding. Therefore Ellen relates in many different ways to the masculine. This dream is trying to give her information about one piece of that which she sees as masculine.

We still don't know exactly what the dead man represents except in general terms. We only know he is something which needs attention within her, something she has buried and now has to bring into consciousness.

New figures enter, two men, one a friend. They want to use the workshop but that would mean discovering the dead man. One already knows about him. Ellen does not want them to see the man — she blocks the gate, blocks the access. This is a conflict of masculine forces and perceptions within herself. Part of the conflict has to do with work. This is true in her outer life, since she and her husband own their own business and create a product in the workshop. They are successful and overworked.

Her masculine allies in the dream are Bill and the friend. They symbolize aspects which are masculine in their expression and which co-operate in keeping the secret of the dead man. The man driving the Auto-Electric van is a symbol of another energy trying to bring the whole situation to light. He is the one bringing the message that Ellen is caught in some unconscious and automatic pattern of response. Ellen does not want to hear this and she does not want to open the gate to discovery of what has been buried.

Something tries to open the gate — the wind almost blows it open, but she manages to shut the gate anyway. The wind is symbolic of the energy within her which wishes to discover what all this is really about. She is not yet ready for the revelation, and that is why she gets the gate shut in the dream.

The dream, then, is telling Ellen that she has something going on in her psyche about the masculine; that she is not noticing it or paying attention; that she is in the grip of some unconscious and automatic patterning about the issue, whatever it is; and that she is not yet ready to take on the discovery of the problem or its solution. By implication this may become apparent in the future.

How do you feel about this dream? Can you see how the interpretation was arrived at? A dream like this is a little confusing on the surface, as most dreams are. A first level interpretation would give valuable information if it simply noted that something was going on about the masculine — something was buried and stinking. If Ellen thinks about it and looks for some correlation in her outer life, something may begin to emerge which makes sense. There is also a clue on this level that it has to do with her work, which is very masculine in the sense that she manufactures a product with tools, according to schedules and very linear procedures. That is indicated by the garage/workshop. Perhaps a conflict is growing within her about expressing herself in this way, through this work. That is a second level of interpretation.

All dreams which picture death will be referring to the end of something or to an unconscious patterning of suppressing and "killing off" of something within the dreamer's psyche. Sometimes a dream of death actually foreshadows a real event, but not usually. In cases of terminal illness a dream of death may or may not portend the actual event. Often in these cases the actual, physical death is presented symbolically in some other way.

I recall the dream of a young woman with cancer with whom I worked some years ago. She dreamed of a huge, dark and abandoned house. The house was Victorian, dilapidated, Gothic in feeling. The setting was dark and oppressive. Inside the house the halls and rooms were strewn with garbage. Outside, the house was surrounded by a high fence. Beyond the fence was a beautiful, lush, deep green field. She yearned to enter the field, but in the dream she was confined to the house and the yard, unable to reach the pasture beyond.

This is a dream of physical death. An otherwise healthy person might have a dream like this and it would be a powerful and deep warning of a disease process under way or about to erupt. It would still be symbolizing the real possibility of death. In this woman's situation, with advancing stages of cancer already present, I knew she would die unless something radically shifted within her consciousness.

The key image in this dream is not so much the house itself, or the yard, both littered with garbage. That is a symbol of the body and psyche ravaged by the disease and the patterns within which contributed to the cancer. This is further emphasized by the fence which confines her to the yard. The image which indicates death is the green, beautiful pasture. Originally when interpreting the dream I saw the pasture as a sign of life which could not be reached.

I worked with her intensely during a two week residential conference. During the conference, which always focuses on nourishing and healing energies, she improved. She had a second dream which seemed to me at the time to offer hope. In the second dream there was now a gate in the fence, and the garbage had been placed in bags which were stacked up by the gate, as if to be removed. Based on my reading of the green field as a sign of life, I felt that she might be able to reverse the disease process if the improvement continued which this interpretation indicated. However, she had still not left the yard and entered the field beyond.

She was caught up in powerful patterns of dependence and frustration. When she left the conference and returned to her outside life, she was unable to sustain the progress she had been making. She was not able to change the things in her life, the routines, situations and relationships, which were making her intensely unhappy and contributing to her disease process. A few months later she was gone.

The dream had indeed prophesied her physical death.

This conference took place in 1986. Since then I have worked with many hundreds of dreams, and with practice my ability to see the deeper levels of dreams has grown. I now view her dreams differently in a very important aspect. I want to share my observations with you because it exemplifies one of the key difficulties with successful dream interpretation which has already been mentioned, namely the overlay of unconscious material onto someone else's dream.

Initially when viewing this woman's dream, I was locked into the reading which saw the green, lush field as a symbol of life which could not be accessed. It seemed to me that if this were to be reached, symbolically, that there was a good chance for remission of the disease. The second dream seemed to indicate progress towards this goal, as access was now possible if not actually utilized. This was symbolized by the gate in the fence, and the stacking up of the "garbage," the ordering of the internal disorder which had previously been dominant.

My initial interpretation was correct in part, for the disease process was clearly symbolized, as stated above, and it was very clear that the first dream indicated a situation of physical death. Where I went off, because of my own unconscious agenda, was with the symbol of the green field. Later I realized that the field did not represent life but was a powerful symbol for the release from life which she unconsiously desired. Seen in this light, the second dream more clearly fortells her imminent death. Far from a "hopeful" sign of possible remission, this dream states that she is getting ready to leave physical life, after first getting things ordered and "cleaned up." In fact, this is what she did actually do, consciously taking the steps which were necessary to tie up loose ends and complete arrangements for her death. When this was done, she died.

What was the material of my own which prevented my seeing this right away? The answer, in hindsight and with the benefit of a deeper understanding of my own psyche which I now hold, rests with my desire for her to get better. More importantly, the deepest hook for me had to do with wanting to be instrumental in her healing. Because I liked her and because I wanted her to get better I made the mistake of reading her dream in a way which then allowed me to see the possibility of healing and to bring whatever assistance I could to that end. This was satisfying to the piece of my psyche which knows that it can be of service in healing, but which confuses healing with curing. It would, perhaps, have served her better to recognize that death was truly approaching. Then I might have been able to offer a different kind of assistance.

It has been a powerful lesson for me, over the years, to see the traps which my unconscious can spring. This is particularly true when it comes to working with healing approaches and energies. It has been humbling to see some of the aspects of unconscious ego involvement when taking on the role of teacher or guide to others. It has also been empowering, because seeing the material has allowed me to work more deeply and honestly with others and with myself. If you take on the work of interpreting dreams, you too will begin to see how the unconscious presents its illusions for our consideration. Dream work has taught me more about the mystery and richness of the human psyche than any other aspect of my work. Perhaps it will seem so to you as well.

14
INTERLUDE – LIFE AS A DREAM

About 300 B.C. a Chinese philosopher named Zhuang Zhu had a dream. He dreamed he was a butterfly, soaring free on the wind. When he awoke he made the observation that he had dreamed he was a butterfly, but he was not sure if Zhuang Zhu had dreamed he was a butterfly or if the butterfly had dreamed he was Zhuang Zhu.

I'd like to take a break from inner dreams and offer you a different perspective to consider. I have said that our inner world is reflected into our outer reality. It also works the other way. If there is a correlation between what goes on inside and what goes on outside, it must be a two way street. I do not mean by this that we create the totality of our external reality. I do mean that we create our perception of that reality and influence it in some way. If it is true that we are in some way interrelated with external events in a creative sense, then we could just as easily look at real events in our external reality and see those events as if they were a dream. This might tell us something we needed to know.

As I stated in the introduction, this is not a new idea on my part and you may already be familiar with it. If it is a new idea to you then you may find this chapter helpful. The concept is simple; take the daily events of your life and look at them as if they were a dream. The approach is exactly the same. You follow all the steps presented so far for recording and interpreting your dreams to the events of your life which you are considering.

This can be a very interesting experience and it can give you powerful insight about what is going on at any given time. I usually work with this approach when something disturbing or unusual happens to me, or when I feel I really need to know more about whatever happened during the particular day or days I am looking at.

This is another way in which you can take the information presented in this book and use it as a tool for self discovery and self awareness in a very practical sense.

Here is an example from my own experience. The event was an accident on the interstate which could easily have resulted in very serious injury or death for me. I have written it down as if it were a dream and then applied the principles we are studying to see if I could learn something about it.

The Crash On The Highway

I am going to Denver on the Interstate to look at an old vehicle. The car is running well and I'm feeling good. The air conditioner begins to work well, which is unusual. I am going the speed limit, 65 miles an hour. The car I am driving is my 1974 Olds station wagon, and I feel safe in this big, powerful and solid car.

As I am driving I see an entry ramp on the right and ahead of me a truck slows down to let someone in. It is a moving van kind of truck, not a big semi but a large truck nonetheless. I pull into the passing lane and start to pass the truck. Just as I come alongside, the truck suddenly veers off to the right. He strikes a large pole and sign, and then veers very quickly back to the left. It is very quick; I start to brake but I know it is too late to avoid an accident.

I try to avoid the truck but he slams into the side of my car. It sounds like an explosion as all the glass along the side of the car blows in. There is a loud crunch of metal and I feel the blow. I am still going at least 60 miles an hour. The force of the truck hitting my car drives me right off the road and onto the median which is flat and grassy. There is a huge cloud of dust behind me. I manage to stop the car and turn off the engine. The truck which hit me drives on and disappears over the next rise.

So far, if this were a dream, we'd have plenty to look at. The truck and the car become powerful symbols. The way the driver feels, the air conditioning, the speed, the accident itself and finally the disappearance of the truck all take on significant meaning. But there's more. Let me give you the rest of the "dream" before we take a look at it.

> *Immediately a young woman pulls up and stops. I get out of the car. She is concerned, helpful. Then an assistant District Attorney stops. I sit in his car and he calls the police. Then a major in the State Patrol pulls up in an unmarked car. All of this happens very quickly. I look at my car which is totally smashed in along the side. I sit in the police major's car. The major is saying on the radio that he has the "victim" in his car. I think it is very weird to be called a victim.*
>
> *Then another car pulls up behind us. It is driven by an older woman, very angry. She has been chasing the truck at 80 miles per hour. She is very indignant and gives her report to the police. Then the truck which hit me pulls up behind, and then a patrol car pulls up also. After talking to the major, the trooper is clearly on my side. The trooper is polite, friendly and efficient.*
>
> *The driver of the truck is sitting in the trooper's car with us. He doesn't seem to know what happened. He reminds me of a big, scared child. He is about fifty five or so. He said he was afraid he had killed me. The trooper gives him a citation for careless driving.*
>
> *The trooper handles all the details and helps me get my car to the other side of the road. It is still drivable although badly damaged. I go home.*
>
> *Two days later I realize that I have not yet given thanks for surviving the accident. It has taken me two days to return to my usual way of being and to calm down internally.*

Please take a few moments and review the images of the "dream." Let your mind play freely and feel into the symbolic meaning of the event. What is the message? What are the internal dynamics which are operating here? What can the "dreamer" learn from the "dream" of life?

Here is my interpretation as brought forward by the Dreamer Within. Interestingly, the Dreamer Within does not distinguish between inner and outer realities or dream/event. This is like the comment by Zhuang Zhu. To the Dreamer Within any event within the psyche, whatever its origin, may be viewed and interpreted. This is characteristic of an impersonal energy. It is not involved with the personality levels and how they perceive the event under consideration.

KEY POINT

The Dreamer Within is an impersonal energy which does not distinguish the source of any event which the consciousness experiences. To the Dreamer Within all experience is real, whether from the dreaming levels or from waking consciousness. This means that the intuitive powers this energy carries may be applied to any situation which we experience.

If you work with the Dreamer Within you will develop intuitive perception which carries over from dreams to waking reality. Once you realize this, your perception of life may deepen and change. You will have to discover for yourself exactly what I mean. Here is my interpretation.

The Crash On The Highway

The dreamer has a strong involvement with earlier patterns of behavior in his life and is often deceived by the comfort which these familiar patterns offer. This is symbolized by the purpose of the trip; to look at an old vehicle. These patterns are deceptive and will lull the dreamer into complacency if he does not pay attention.

The truck represents forces, apparently random, which are beyond the dreamer's control. He is being shown that nothing may be taken for granted and the dream carries a warning message which alerts him to his pattern of complacency.

There is much resolution in the dreamer's psyche about issues of authority and support. He is now quite capable of letting authority be supportive instead of antagonistic, and is capable of very quickly rallying the support of the collective authority if it is needed. He has also resolved many issues regarding the feminine, which is shown in a good relationship with him. A strong feminine energy resides which will go out of its way to help him. This represents an integration of energies of anger with the feminine which were a problem in the past.

The energy which is dangerous to the dreamer is further clarified by the symbol of the truck driver. He represents an unconscious and immature force, childish in origin, which creates harm through its unawareness and inattention to the consequences of its actions. Although it is not consciously destructive it is care-less and dangerous in this sense. This aspect, though originating at an earlier stage of consciousness, is well developed. The dreamer must pay attention to this force within himself and be on guard for its appearance. Otherwise severe consequences may result.

The dreamer needs to remind himself that his life is an occasion for gratitude.

When this came through I was not very comfortable with what I saw about myself, but the feeling levels within me would not let me deny the accuracy of the interpretation. There is much that is positive for me about this event. It is very true that in the past I viewed authority figures such as policemen in a wary and antagonistic light. I have had many conflicts with authority in my life, beginning with my parents and moving on from there. To experience the level of support which instantly appeared after the accident was shocking.

I disagree with the police major's assessment of me as victim. I understand the collective thinking which places this label upon someone in my situation. From my point of view I am only a victim if I cannot see how I am responsible in some way for my involvement with the energy. Because I have trained myself to look for my involvement I can usually find it. At that point victim becomes an inaccurate description. I admit that this is sometimes very, very difficult.

Any judgement I might have on myself because of the accident and my interpretation of the event would be a mistake. What is important here is to notice what has happened and move on, hopefully paying attention in the future. And if I forget to pay attention, as I almost certainly will from time to time, then my task is to pick up the thread of attention when it again becomes apparent. I sincerely hope that another close call like this one will not be necessary! It won't be, if I remember the lesson.

You also can pick up the thread of attention by looking more deeply at the life you are having as if it were a dream.

CHAPTER 15:
DREAMS OF BIRTH AND PREGNANCY

I hope that by now you are getting a deeper feeling for the themes which dreams present to us, and in the specific theme are seeing the general thrust of the meaning of the dream. Knowing the theme may not be enough to give you the interpretation. But knowing the theme will point you in the general direction.

What is birth and pregnancy about? Aside from all of our ideas about it, it is a fundamental process of the gestation and bringing forth of something new in life, something which did not exist before. This is a powerful symbol for our dreaming consciousness for the changes which we are nurturing within. It follows that if we dream of being pregnant or giving birth we are looking at an internal process which is in a stage of development. The development is not complete or is new for us.

It does not matter if you are male or female in regards to this image. Men and women do relate differently to birth and pregnancy, and that may be a factor in the dream. What is important is the fact that birth and pregnancy is a universal experience for the human race, male and female. It is experienced differently by individuals on personal levels but is fundamental to life experience. No pregnancy/birth, no life.

On a personal level in our physical bodies, pregnancy and birth is the first powerful initiation. The womb experience, whatever it may be, is embedded so strongly in our psyche that it would be impossible to discount it as a factor on the very deepest levels. Since dreams may access these deeper levels, it stands to reason that the symbol of birth/pregnancy will come forward in relationship to initiatory processes within us.

To initiate something is to begin a process which may or may not lead to a specific result. There is never a guarantee that what is initiated will be brought to fruition. This was well known in primitive societies which practiced initiatory rites. The whole point of the initiation was to bring forward the challenges necessary to move the individual to another level of personal and collective participation in life. Initiations which did not provide the very real possibility of failure fall into a slightly different category which I consider to be rites of passage. A rite of passage might or might not have the possibility of failure built in. A rite of passage also leads to a different state of being.

I make a distinction because I see rites of passage as ceremonial acknowledgements of a new phase of natural development, states of development which come if one lives long enough. An example might be ceremonies performed to acknowledge the passage from girl to woman with the onset of menstruation, or with the recognition of eldership at a certain advanced age. It is also true that this recognition of change might well entail certain conditions being met that went beyond the natural physical progression. If the ceremony contained the possibility of failure it would then blend into the initiation category. Rites of passage are initiatory and initiations are rites of passage, but for me the key factor to determine the subtle difference is the danger of failure, even death.

Dreams could produce images which deal with either initiation or rites of passage, and these factors might blend together. A man or a woman may dream of a ceremony where they are shown something which represents a passage into another level of inner development. Weddings in dreams may be like this. Birth and pregnancy, however, are initiatory in nature as it is not automatic that the pregnancy will be brought to term or that the new issuance will survive.

It is well to remember that our dreaming consciousness makes free use of imagery and events which actually exist in our waking life, such as work situations or family members. A pregnant woman may dream of pregnancy and birth and on the first level this will have to do with the actual physical process she is experiencing. The deeper meaning of the dream will be found on a symbolic level which is only partially associated with the actual pregnancy/birth.

Here is a dream which occurred to a woman who at the time of the dream was going through a major inner transition. She was being forced by external events to reconsider deeply held beliefs about her life and what she was doing with it. She could no longer ignore the conflict between what her experience was saying to her and what her belief system told her ought to be experienced. Part of her conflict had to do with developing an inner sense of direction which she could maintain in the face of criticism from authoritative, masculine forces which were consistently invalidating her.

Helen's Dream.

I was in an apartment, dimly lit, by myself. I gave birth to a baby boy. I couldn't deliver the afterbirth. I kept worrying through the whole dream about the afterbirth. I was planning to go with the baby to the doctor the next day, and I was worried the afterbirth would get infected.

Sometimes the baby would turn into a kitten that I had to restrain — it would walk out onto the window ledge and I'd have to get it. Someone in the apartment disapproved of the kitten. Then I went somewhere to the front of a movie theater. I saw Susan and some of my friends. I was hesitant about telling them I had a baby, but I did.

I was afraid to call my parents and tell them I had a baby — I was afraid of rejection and disapproval. Eventually I called my father and told him he'd had his first grandson. I realized I had delivered before my sister. I thought about putting the baby up for adoption. I didn't know how I would take care of him.

This dream is very revealing of the feelings and emotions which Helen was experiencing at this time in her life. Let's use the worksheet to look at the dream. You may already have a feeling about it.

Ask for the Dreamer Within to come forward as you work. What would you say to Helen if she asked you to help her understand the dream? How well could you feel into the vulnerable emotional levels which are being shown? Would you be able to support her in understanding the dream without telling her what it is she is supposed to understand?

1. Write down and review the dream (as above).
2. The images and events in the dream that I feel are the most powerful are:
   giving birth to baby boy
   problems with the afterbirth
   baby turns into kitten
   someone disapproves
   afraid to tell friends and parents
   considering adoption
3. I feel that the most important image is:
   giving birth to baby boy
4. The way I feel about this image is:
   worried/she is worried
   something new about masculine forces/energies/
      aspects within her
   important for her
5. This image reminds me of: (put down anything, no matter how unrelated it appears, which comes to mind)
   birth is hard
   no fun
   dangerous
6. The next image or event I feel is important in the dream is:
   problems with the afterbirth
7. The way I feel about this is:
   something which follows birth
   has to come out for success
   she will have trouble following through with this new energy
8. This image reminds me of:
   animals — something primal and basic stories about birth
   myths about birth blood
The next image or event which I feel is important is:
   someone disapproves
The way I feel about this is:
   people are like that

she has something within her which disapproves of
   the whole thing
This image reminds me of:
   parents' disapproval and non-support
The next image or event I feel is important is:
   baby turns into kitten
The way I feel about this is:
   kittens are innocent
   kittens need protection from themselves
      she's worried about the safety of the kitten/baby
      the kitten/baby is in danger
      domesticated natural force This image reminds me
         of:
      life is dangerous
      have to watch out for children and protect them
The next image or event I feel is important is:
   afraid to tell friends and parents
The way I feel about this is:
   she is very insecure
   too bad she has to worry about them
   are the friends like the parents?
   she doesn't approve/something in her doesn't
      approve
The next image or event I feel is important is:
   she's considering adoption
The way I feel about this is:
   she shouldn't do that
   she's afraid she can't handle it/support it
   the baby is difficult for her
   she's not sure she can follow through
   important for her to understand
 9. Any other details I now remember are:
      none
10. I feel that the dream is about:
      creating her own self/piece of self; her uncertainty
      about this in the face of disapproval from others,
      especially authority; something about the
      masculine; uncertainty about self–support
11. Another thing the dream is about is:

she is very uncertain if she can follow through on this without threat to herself

12. The way I feel about this dream is:

important dream for her

13. Some other thoughts which occur when I review the images of the dream are:

she's got a lot going on about people rejecting/disapproving of her; developing something new in herself confronts this

14. Review what you have written.

15. When I ask for help from within about this dream, I sense that the dream is about:

birthing something new about herself which has to do with the masculine areas of herself; the reasons why this is difficult and dangerous for her; her relationship with authority figures; her perception of herself.

16. My interpretation of the dream is:

The dreamer is attempting to establish new areas of self expression which are as yet undeveloped and in danger. These areas of expression require the emergence of new ideas about what she sees as the masculine forces within and without. The dreamer sees people as disapproving of her and needs to look at her idea that this is based in her experience of parental energies. Because she sees people as disapproving this results in disapproval of self and it is difficult for the dreamer to distinguish between self rejection and the rejection by others.

The dreamer is not confident that this energy of self can be safely delivered, due to the dynamics of disapproval already stated. She is, however, able to recognize this danger and is able to confront it to some degree. She has courage within which can take her through to completion. This is seen in her willingness to confront her friends and tell her father about the birth.

The new commitment to self is decided in the dream when she tells her father. However, the exploration and development of this new area is not yet firm in the dreamer's psyche. This is symbolized by the thought within the dream that the baby may be given up for adoption. The dreamer's uncertainty about self undercuts her inner intention and results in a lack of confidence about her ability to follow through and develop the new areas which are being introduced in the dream. The issue is still in doubt.

Did the worksheet help with this? The dream is fairly obvious and straightforward in its images. Some details have not been looked at, such as the sister or the projected visit to the doctor. Perhaps you have some ideas about these. The dream does show very clearly Helen's deep insecurity about presenting her own self in the face of disapproval and feared rejection by others. It also shows that she has come far enough in her personal development to begin to bring this forward in spite of the obstacles. It would be natural for her to feel doubtful about the outcome and to wonder if she could support the validation of herself which will have to come from within.

Helen's comment was that the strongest feeling in the dream was the fear of death and loss of safety, coupled with a fear that she would not be able to support herself and the new baby. She felt that the baby was a threat to her survival and her old belief structure. This is consistent with the interpretation given above.

Here is another short dream about pregnancy we can look at.

Marion's Dream.

I am standing behind a shadowy figure who is me and looking at another, pregnant woman who is also me, stretched out on a table. I am observing her. The pregnant woman seems complacent and unconcerned, but in the dream I am concerned because the labor has not taken place.

This is one of those dreams which can be very confusing because it tells the dreamer that something is going on but doesn't tell her exactly what it is. It does show her a particular inner relationship with the event of the "pregnancy." Without knowing what it is that is to be born, there is still a lot of information given in just a few images.

First of all, it is clear to Marion in the dream that all the characters are her. This is often not so evident, as you probably know. In this dream there is no doubt about this, even to her dreaming mind. So whatever the dream is about, Marion in her waking life knows that she is looking at herself playing out different aspects within. There is Marion The Observer, Marion The Shadowy Figure, and Marion The Pregnant Woman.

The meaning of the dream can be found by looking at the relationship of these three figures. We see two opposites here; Marion The Observer is concerned that the labor which will bring on the birth has not yet occurred. Marion The Pregnant Woman is not concerned at all. What can we see from this? In addition, between the two is a third: Marion The Shadowy Figure.

The shadowy Marion represents something not seen clearly by Marion The Observer. This figure symbolizes something within Marion which stands between her and the process of birth which has not been initiated in the dream. One side of Marion wants this process to hurry up. One side does not care at all about this – it is involved in its own rhythm and timing for the birth which has nothing to do with what the concerned Marion thinks ought to be going on. This is a split within Marion's psyche and a way of relating to events which should be apparent in her external life if we are interpreting the image correctly.

Marion in real life does have a pattern of impatience and a tendency to try to push things to completion before they are ready. This results in frustration and confrontation for her and a deep inner resentment. She feels powerless to affect events in the way she would like and her frustration takes covert forms of expression with her co–workers and friends.

What Marion does not see is why she is not willing to let things take their natural course of events and progress in their own timing. That this unconscious material is present is the essential symbolic meaning of the shadowy figure. In other words, Marion carries unconscious patterns which split her off from herself, literally "stand between."

What is the split really about? What is the difference between the two figures? One is an observer and acts out of judgement about the situation; one is simply involved with the process without concern about timing. One is mental and concerned, one is feeling and unconcerned. One is detached, one is fully participating. One has ideas about the birth, one is in the process which will actually lead to birth. The split is between feeling and mental levels of Marion.

The pregnant figure also represents something which is developing within and in fact is near term. Marion is impatient for this to emerge so that she may get on with it. She senses change within and thinks it should have become clear to her by now. That is a reflection of the mental override of an internal, developing and experiential or feeling process. The lesson here is one of patience and timing and allowing things to emerge in their own way. It is also necessary to let go of the desires to control and define life through the mental areas. That is a difficult task for Marion, as it is for many of us.

Marion was disturbed by this dream so she asked herself for another dream to give her more information. This can be a very effective way to get to a deeper understanding. She got a powerful dream which further developed the theme of a split between mental and feeling areas.

KEY POINT

You can ask for another dream about a dream you have already had in order to obtain more information. This is frequently a very effective way to see more about the issue within your psyche.

Marion's Follow Up Dream.

I'm standing in a large, paved area, like a shopping center or mall. There is a stucco wall along one side of it, and in front of the wall I see myself running across there. I know that it's me and it looks like me but it's a horse. It's a wild, dark, shiny horse, but it looks like me. I'm very surprised, but I know that it's me, I know that it's a horse even though it looks like me.

There are some other people in the dream. I don't know who they are, but they also know that even though this woman looks like me it's a horse. They want to capture her and they do that some how. They are chasing her and they want to do some kind of surgical procedure to find out how I can look like a woman and yet be a horse.

Then I am me, in the body of the woman. I'm stretched out on this table and all these people are standing around above and looking down at me and that's when I wake up.

This again points out the difference in Marion's consciousness between the feeling and the mental, analytical levels. Part of her is free and natural, like a horse. This is a surprise for her because in her waking life Marion has shut down feeling levels and has ordered her life towards safety, security and staid ways of expression. It's been a long time since Marion felt wild and free, if ever. However, this energy is emerging and wants expression. The dream is portraying this aspect of her as a horse.

The people who want to capture the horse/woman are unknown to her; they want to perform some surgical procedure to find out how a horse can be a woman and vice versa. These are the analytical areas within which are not concerned with feeling levels except as a subject for dissection and study. Once something is dissected it is killed, at least when we are talking about horses and women. As in the previous dream, Marion is aware that she is more than one energy at the same time. She is observing, she is a horse, she is a woman who is a horse. She finds herself on the table where the others want to dissect her. This is similar to the image of the pregnant woman on the table in the earlier dream.

From this dream and the first it would be safe to conclude that what is coming forward is an aspect of Marion which wants a less restricted, freer expression in life. Because of the powerful negative ideas she has about the appropriateness of free expression, Marion is presently caught in the conflict between feeling and control of feeling. This conflict has been present for her entire life and is now coming to the surface as she makes the effort to discover more of who she is. The pregnancy may result in the birth of a new idea of herself, or it may be aborted through her desire to "dissect" this feeling and free level of expression. Only time will tell. These dreams were on consecutive nights and are an example of how our consciousness will give us plenty of information if we are open to it. Marion was able to arrive at a fairly complete interpretation of her dreams without my input by using the worksheet approach. It is always much more meaningful if we can arrive at our own feeling of a correct interpretation. When we work with another, we must always allow them to try their hand at interpretation first before we give our own conclusions.

By watching the action of your dream about birth or pregnancy, you can accurately determine how you stand in relationship to that which is being birthed within you. Use this information to help you with this new and vulnerable part of yourself. New life is tenuous without nourishment and we need to make sure we care for whatever the new energy is which is coming forward.

16
NIGHTMARES

I doubt that anyone has not had a "nightmare" at some time or other. One of the interesting things about nightmares is that we usually remember them, even months or years after they occurred. Sometimes we don't remember, we only know that something has taken place because we wake up startled, heart pounding and perhaps sweating or shaking. All of these symptoms are natural physiological responses to terrifying stimuli.

Recently I saw an interesting television program on dream and sleep research which came from the University of Florida. During this program the observation was made that the body seems unable to distinguish the difference between the experience of sleeping or waking reality. In other words, what is experienced in the dreaming state is just as real to the perception as what we experience when awake. If you think about your own dreaming experience you will probably arrive at the same conclusion.

Since our body doesn't seem to know the difference between what we are experiencing in a dream and what we are experiencing when awake, it stands to reason that a terrifying dream will literally wake us up.

Why would our psyche present terrifying images to us? One reason is to get us to pay attention. A nightmare, particularly one which repeats over time, is presenting material which in some way is very important for us to see, acknowledge and work with. I am convinced that dreams are in many ways a self learning process guided from within. We may or may not get the lessons, whatever they are, and we may or may not pay attention. If the lesson is important and we need to pay attention, a nightmare will at least cause us to take notice.

I feel that nightmares must be looked at deeply, even though our natural inclination is to try to forget them as quickly as possible. The material is by its nature so charged for us that it is very difficult to be objective. It is impossible to be objective unless we can learn to cultivate a state of observation which is non-judgmental and impersonal. This is the state we are in when we are successfully working with the Dreamer Within. Nightmares and other dreams which are repeated will be covered in another chapter. In this segment we will look at some examples of one time nightmares and see if we can develop some general understanding of how to work with them.

The kind of material within which appears in nightmares is of a very primal and fundamental nature. It is always part of the deep unconscious. I can not emphasize too strongly that one needs to go slowly with this kind of material. It may not be something which you want to take on at all, and real understanding may take months or years to appear. I mention this because it can be difficult to get to the meaning of such a dream. Go easy on yourself, don't make yourself wrong for how you feel about it, and above all don't worry if you can't figure it out. In time it may become clear, if it is important enough for you to understand.

There is plenty of reflection in our society of the inner dream world of nightmares. I find it interesting that so many films are filled with nightmarish sequences. The classic example is the series of *Nightmare on Elm Street* movies. Whether the movies are good or bad is irrelevant. A very large percentage of our society finds the imagery fascinating and seductive. This is because such films accurately pick up on unconscious images and cues which trigger the terrifying response. We are looking here at a subject of endless psychological study. That is not my purpose in this chapter.

If you are a person who has repeated and terrifying nightmares, you may wish to consider professional advice about the dreams. I say this in a book which is dedicated to the task of teaching how to do it oneself because I know well that there is a limit at any given time to what we are able to discover without assistance. There are many dedicated and competent professionals available to help if it is needed. Dreams of this nature may reflect an inner turmoil which must be handled in some way if we are to achieve inner calm and harmony.

There is a very powerful reward available if you succeed in unraveling the meaning of a nightmarish dream. You won't have to have it again! If I am correct when I say that nightmares are about fundamental and important issues within our psyche, then the same issues will be presented more than once over a period of time in an attempt by the psyche to get the message across. This means a series of nightmares which will in some way show the same material. For the sake of rest and quiet sleep, if nothing else, it's worth the effort to look at the unpleasant dream.

Nightmares are a signal that the inner pressures which demand attention are reaching a peak of intensity. This "peak" may continue for years unless resolution is somehow brought forward. There are many examples recorded of people with recurrent nightmares. Veterans returning from combat or people who have in some way been traumatically affected by crime or accident often have such dreams. It would seem that within the psyche something has been in some way severely injured. The nightmare is the psyche's call for help and healing.

There are many things besides obvious involvement with external events (such as war) which can wound the inner being. Psychological abuse or a lack of love and nourishment, uncaring parents or simply a perception by the dreamer that his or her life is somehow not valuable can lead to deep psychological woundings which may not show externally as real events. They are real nonetheless and to the inner self terribly traumatic. It is the inner self which is expressing and communicating in dreams.

When the inner self is calling for healing and attention, and if the issue is basic enough, a nightmare may be the result. As with all dreams, the nightmare presents information which the dreamer has a need to consciously know. There is always an implication with dreams that information brought to us by a dream may in some way be used on a conscious level. If we accurately interpret the information and put it to use it may simply fill out what we already know or it may institute change.

With nightmares, integration and recognition of the difficult material may lead to the healing which the inner self is requesting. This may lead to transformation of the way we are in life, the way we view life and the way we interact with others. If we change the way in which we perceive or interact with self, through the work with dreams, then it follows that our external relationship with life must change also. We are no longer exactly the same person we were before the recognition encouraged by the dream was integrated. We see things in a different way, feel them in a different way and therefore have a new experience of a life which is now perceived differently. Our perception determines the quality of our experience and our participation with it.

The following dream presents some very basic inner issues for the dreamer. The dreamer was deeply disturbed by the dream. You always know something is really fundamental by the sensation you feel in your body. Your body cannot deceive you, although your mind often will. This dream was powerfully felt by the dreamer and there was no way for him to ignore the images.

This dream has to do with very early, childhood material. I am telling you this in advance so that you may have an idea as you go through the dream about its meaning. It also has to do with the dreamer's relationship with his mother. Since "Mother" is the basic patterning experience of the feminine and the perception of woman by the child, the relationship with the mother will affect all relationships with women on an unconscious level. Understanding the dream could lead eventually to a shift in the dreamer's outer relationships with women, based on a shift within. Mother does not appear in the dream, and the association with mother is a third level interpretation. See if you can feel into the deeper levels as you go through the dream.

The first section is not especially terrifying but it contains the clear symbols which will be amplified in the later section. The entire dream takes place in a "house" which the dreamer is "renovating." Does that tell you something?

Erik's Dream: Section One.

I am renovating a house, my house, with some others. There is a workshop going on in the family room.

We can stop right here and determine the main theme of the dream. Erik's house is where he lives, that is, his life structure. He is renovating the house, meaning he is making major changes and is updating the structure (renovation is usually done to modernize a home and bring it to current desired standards, to upgrade it). The family room setting says that the renovation will have to do with something in Erik's consciousness that is founded in family dynamics, and this is emphasized by the workshop taking place there. Work is being done within on fundamental levels which are configured in Erik's experience of family. In real life, this was not a satisfactory experience for Erik. OK so far? Let's go on.

Erik's Dream: Section Two.

Two naked women are posed as if for a dance. I am upset by this, I want nudity to be voluntary. The workshop is about some kind of bodywork or massage. I am going to begin to conduct the workshop but then an ugly, fat woman begins to lead. She knows what she's doing. She tells the people in the workshop to take their clothes off. They start to undress — there are six couples.

As she is pulling off her dress I see that she is menstruating. That is when I tell people that nudity is optional. Then I realize that someone not in the workshop is in the basement. A young blond in a red dress. I bring her up and tell her not to look. I am annoyed that she is there.

We are approaching the "nightmare" stage, which comes next. Already, though, things are getting out of hand. Erik is trying to control events in the workshop but is not succeeding. The nudity upsets him. Nudity represents exposure here, something which Erik would like to cover up but cannot. What is being exposed remains to be seen but we can get some ideas.

Since the nudity involves women, there is something here which Erik does not want to see about the feminine/woman. This is really very powerfully presented by the symbol of the ugly woman, distorted in Erik's eyes, who is menstruating. Menstruation symbolizes many things, and is an essential statement of woman. It means life and the potential of life. The blood is the visible sign of the woman's power and role as bearer of life. It is a mystery and for Erik, something he does not want exposed.

There are six couples. Remember what six can be about? Six and sex are similar to the unconscious and sex is about relationship on basic levels. This dream is about Erik's basic relationship with the feminine — how he feels about it within, how he relates to it on very deep levels.

In the "basement" is another important figure. The basement can represent a deeper level of the unconscious, from which come energies within which affect other areas. Why do you think so many terrible and horrifying movie scenes take place in the basement? Ever notice that? The second most favorite place for horrifying events in horror films is the attic. A good example is *Psycho* or *Burnt Offerings*. To our minds basements and attics are places where things are often dark and hidden away, unpleasant places of dirt and crawling creatures. It makes no difference that modern homes may not be like this. The images are burned into the collective psyche. This is why the films use them so frequently. As we shall see, the core of Erik's nightmare will take place in the attic.

The blond woman in the red dress is an image which appears from time to time, in various forms, in Erik's dreams. She is a symbol for him of the many aspects of his internal feminine. In this dream, he is unpleasantly surprised to find her there at the workshop. He does not want her to see what's going on. This is more emphasis by the dream to show how much Erik does not wish to see what's happening within.

One of the things Erik does not want to "see" or recognize is the split between less mature, "young" aspects of the feminine within himself (the young blond) and empowered, mature aspects of the feminine within (symbolized by the ugly, menstruating woman). The image of ugly tells how Erik sometimes looks at the feminine in its empowered aspect. He does not like it. This will reflect into his outer life and his relationships with women. We are seeing that there is a very strong conflict within Erik's psyche about these feminine energies, inner and outer, and that this conflict is getting out of control for him. The red dress picks up on the blood color of the menstruation and its mysterious connection with life.

Erik's Dream: Section Three.

Now I am working on this house, a large house, on the top floor. Others work below. I tell one of them to get me a different ladder, one that is light and strong, instead of the old, heavy wooden one — a stepladder. The scene is one of repair and dust. The dust is being blown about by two windows which have been left open.

I am painting the room. Suddenly what looks like blood begins to pour from a spot in the ceiling, slowly at first. I see it is really orange paint. I am afraid, uneasy. Then blood begins to pour from other spots — it is from the attic.

The dream is deepening. The stepladder suggests that a new way of access is being called for. A stepladder has steps. New steps are necessary for Erik. Do you follow? The two windows and also the orange paint are about sexual areas. This is an oblique reference by the psyche to the second chakra or energy area, which has to do with the integration of sexual energies as one focus. Orange is a color often associated with this energy center. It is also a color of vital forces, vitality. Two windows open = letting something "blow through" this area.

Painting the room is the same as covering something over in the attempt to renovate. This isn't going to work, though. Can you imagine blood pouring through the ceiling from the "attic"? No wonder Erik is becoming uneasy and afraid! But there is more, as if that weren't enough.

Erik's Dream: Section Four.

The blood horrifies me and I am afraid to look in the attic, but I know I have to. I am drawn by fear and morbid curiosity. I open the attic door, or am somehow in the attic. It is dark and hellish, confused, a maelstrom of blood and screams. I see an infant's arm, or perhaps a young child's. Just the arm. I am afraid that I will see a slaughtered child, and that I will have to face it and eat it. Then I surrender and turn to face the murdered child, knowing I have to go through this.

There is a confused and horrible impression of scattered pieces of the child. There is lots of blood. I start screaming, a thin, childish cry. No one can hear! Then I wake up shouting.

Erik's comment about this dream was that it was difficult to convey the sense of horror.

When Erik enters the attic, he enters hell. This whole sequence contains the very heart of the dream. Within Erik is a murdered and dismembered "child." In his psyche a crucial aspect has been "slaughtered." He doesn't want to look at this and we can easily understand why. He thinks he may have to "eat" it. This means taking it in, nourishing himself somehow with it, digesting it. Something within him is ready to take this on, though. He knows in the dream that he must face this, whatever it is, and he does actually surrender to the confrontation.

Throughout the dream he is repeatedly reminded or shown that he does not want to face whatever is going on, and in gradually stronger images he is finally led to what must be faced. Because of the earlier sequences he can assume that part of the problem has to do with the feminine. Erik's experience of the feminine is not a positive one when he considers his mother. He felt manipulated, unloved and controlled as a child. The support which was actually given him in his childhood was not the kind of support he needed and wanted on an emotional level and he felt disempowered by his mother. This feeling of disempowerment and helplessness is seen in the image of dismemberment of the child in the dream. When he screams in the dream it is the cry of an abandoned child, not the scream of a man. And just as in his childhood, no one can "hear" him. To hear Erik would be to recognize and validate him.

Whatever the real source of the psychological and traumatic wounding of Erik's "child" may be, the dream is saying that it is time to work with it and look at it. It is time to do something to initiate the integration of the powerful emotional forces which are represented. Most importantly, the dream says that he is ready to do this now — this is the meaning of surrendering to the sight of the terrifying images.

What Erik can or will do with this information is up to him. There are many options for him and he will have to choose one or another to work with. If he does not, he is sure to have more dreams in the future about this painful area. If he does succeed then a fundamental area of nourishment and security within himself may be established. This can only have positive and far reaching ramifications for his life.

I mentioned above that the image of the woman in the red dress has appeared more than once in Erik's dreams. This figure has appeared as nurturing or destructive, young and old, indifferent and involved. Erik is much interested in dreams and has kept records of his dreams for some time. He has said that even if he did not keep records he would remember the dreams in which this figure appears. For Erik this figure always symbolizes something very fundamental about the feminine. By the way in which he interacts with her in the dream, Erik understands something about his inner relationship with the feminine energies.

You may also have a figure, male or female, like this. You will recognize it because it will always appear in the same general way, although it may take on many faces and activities not consistent from dream to dream. For Erik the figure is always blond, always somewhat beautiful (even in a distorted or destructive aspect) and always in a red dress. She is a fundamental feminine energy within for Erik. If you have such a figure it will also represent a fundamental energy within you and it will show you your relationship with that energy at any given moment.

If this is true, then we should be able to see the progress or otherwise that we are making within in regards to these energies. This will be true of our dreams whenever a theme or image repeats itself, with variations, over a period of time. That is why a journal is so valuable as a tool for dreamers. When you look back over time you can see the images and themes appear and watch the story unfold. Dreams like this may be of any kind, nightmare or not. I classify these as progressive dreams, and they are the subject of another chapter.

Here is a nightmare which is so loaded with personal, first level material for the dreamer that it has taken her many years to even look at the content. This dream was so powerful for her that she used it as an excuse to begin drinking destructively. Her excuse for being an alcoholic for many years was the event of this dream. She thought that she went over the edge in drinking because the alcohol helped her sleep without dreams.

The dream is one of three she had within a period of about a week. Maria began drinking excessively before going to sleep so that she would not have to deal with the images. This is what her outer mind told her. In reality, the dream is reflecting back to her very painful inner material which she was not then capable of resolving. Her response, as with many people in a similar situation, was to blot it out. A key figure in the dream is Jennifer, Maria's actual daughter.

Maria's Dream.

Jennifer and I stand up to leave the Sacred Heart Catholic church in our home town. We are on the right side of the church as we face the altar. As we are leaving the pew my father approaches us to escort us up the aisle to the main entrance. As we approach the entrance I can see all the people who have left the church before us, waiting for us to come out.

As we enter the foyer to the church I notice a metal pole in the center of the doorway. Jennifer and my father are talking to each other, sort of laughing softly. Jennifer turns towards me and as she does she bumps into the pole. She bounces back but her head has been severed somehow by the pole. My father turns and looks at me. He looks puzzled. I turn and see Jennifer's head bouncing down the steps of the church. I scream and wake up.

Because of Maria's real life associations with father, church and daughter, this dream has always been difficult for her to understand. Her unconscious immediately is activated by any one of these subjects and she is aware that she is very unresolved regarding each of them. Reaching a place of objectivity has been impossible for Maria in all three areas. This dream is a good example of how we must watch out for unconscious projections onto a dream.

Let's look at the first section and see if we can get a feeling for the theme of the dream. Remember, if we can get a feeling for the theme we will have a good general sense of what the dream is about. The dream takes place in the Catholic church of Maria's childhood. She comes from a traditional and strict Catholic background with the old world context that goes with her Hispanic heritage. Maria does not have a "liberal" Catholic background. She was brought up in a small town in the Southwest, and in circumstances bordering on poverty. Her father was strict and remote. Her mother was not understanding and Maria was conceived out of wedlock, although her parents married before she was born. Interestingly, Maria's daughter was conceived in somewhat similar circumstances, and Maria has never quite gotten through the feelings of guilt and sin which she has about the conception and birth of Jennifer.

You would not need to know the information given above in order to see that something about the Catholic experience is crucial to understanding the dream. The entire dream takes place in the Catholic setting. If you are Catholic you understand something about Maria's childhood which a non-Catholic can only guess at. You will also have difficulty separating your thoughts about Catholicism and your unconscious material from the symbol in the dream. If you are not Catholic, your observations about Catholicism are second hand and liable to be skewed. There is nothing like a religious setting in a dream to activate unconscious material, since all of us have lots of ideas about what is right and wrong about any given religious practice.

In Maria's psyche, Catholicism is seen as repressive and controlling. She has a love/hate relationship with the Church. On the one hand she loves the ritual and sense of communion with Spirit and God which she has felt in the past when she attended the Mass. On the other hand, she bitterly resents the rules and dogma. She is angry at the suppression of women which she sees in the Church's teachings. She feels guilty about some of the things she has done, especially sexually, which are in conflict with those teachings and angry at herself for feeling guilty.

The same might be said for her relationship with her father, another symbol in the dream. Her father carries all of the old world attitudes about women, sexuality and the role of women and daughters in society. The love/hate relationship is present here also.

Maria's daughter, Jennifer, activates all of these feelings in Maria. It is only in the last few years that Maria has begun to resolve some of the ambivalent feelings she has about her daughter. She projects the best and the worst of herself onto Jennifer. She has repeated some of the mistakes her parents made with her, and she feels guilty about that.

When we are in the presence of someone who activates feelings of guilt within us, we usually react by attack, withdrawal or rationalization. Usually the feelings of guilt lead to hurt and anger and the other person is seen as the reason why we feel the way we do. This is one of the patterns which Maria displays with Jennifer. This is intolerable to the piece of Maria which loves Jennifer deeply. The result is conflict on the deepest levels within.

In the dream, the three symbols of father, church and daughter are all brought together. The theme of this dream is centered around the common elements which all three carry in the dreamer's mind; guilt and the suppression and conflict of feeling. The dream is going to get Maria's attention and ask her to do something about this inner conflict. If she had been able at that time to resolve the issues, Maria might never have taken the step into alcoholism which was one of the ways she pushed the material away. It was not the dream which triggered the drinking. The drinking served to provide another avenue of expression which Maria could not activate on her own because she could not consciously understand her own inner conflict.

The father comes to escort Maria and Jennifer to the entrance of the church. This symbolizes the controlling influence of the masculine value systems which Maria sees as negative. The Catholic church is referred to as "Mother Church" by Catholics. However the experience is usually not one of being mothered but rather sternly directed. The feminine image is overlaid with strong masculine systems of rule and order, in service to a masculine, Father God. Between Church and father, Maria doesn't stand much of a chance for free self expression.

Outside the church all those who have left before are waiting for Maria and her family to come out. These are areas of Maria's consciousness which have already "left" the structure of belief represented by the childhood church. Now it is Maria's turn to leave, that is, move into a different area of consciousness which is not so firmly identified with the controlling energies church and father represent. She starts towards the entrance.

The entry is split down the center by a metal pole. This is a wonderful symbol of the split and conflict within Maria. There are two sides within her regarding the whole issue of church and father, and daughter as well. It is the love/hate relationship with them mentioned above; it is more fundamentally a love/hate relationship with herself. This is the third level of interpretation for this symbol.

Distracted by the friendly conversation with the father, Jennifer bumps into the pole and is decapitated. This is a scene of incredible horror for Maria, when recounting the dream. The father is puzzled — what happened, he seems to be saying. This energy does not understand what the decapitation is about. It does not understand in the dream and it does not understand what Maria needs within. It cannot relate to her needs and feelings or to the symbol in the dream in a meaningful way.

We need to look at Jennifer as a symbol, because it is she who is decapitated. It is her head which rolls down the steps of the church. What does she represent in Maria's psyche? What do you feel she represents?

Jennifer is an aspect within Maria, a younger aspect, a feminine aspect, an aspect which is destroyed through the interaction with the symbol of the father and the symbol of the pole at the church entrance. It is not a mature aspect for Maria. To Maria, in outer life Jennifer represents the potential Maria feels she misplaced somewhere along the way. Jennifer is "the best" of Maria, her projected hopes and fears, strengths and weaknesses. Maria has tried to shape and control her, just as her parents did with her. Jennifer represents the potential and bloom of the feminine in Maria's own life. On this level of feeling it is easy to see how devastating the image of decapitation is. It is the death of everything Maria wants for herself as a woman, which is not yet developed or mature.

It is not an accident that the dream consciousness chooses to cut off the head. This emphasizes the need to leave the mental areas and shows the separation of these areas from the real body levels of feeling. This image is consistent with Maria's outer life at the time of the dreams.

The dream is saying to Maria that she is still caught in masculine and un-nourishing perceptions of herself and her world. It is saying that because she is directed by these unconscious areas, she is literally cutting herself off from feeling and from her own potential. It is saying that these perceptions are founded in her beliefs about herself which she learned from church and father. The implication is that she needs to discover why she has accepted these beliefs. She then needs to take responsibility for them. This is third level interpretation, because it is not stated in the dream. The dream simply shows the dynamics. In real life Maria blames church and father (and mother) for her unsatisfactory relationship with self and the feminine. The dream shows what happens if the responsibility, and therefore the power to institute change, is not realized. Blame of others will never resolve Maria's bad feelings about herself.

Maria had three dreams in which Jennifer was killed within a week's time. This is what the psyche will do when it is trying to get an important message through to the outer mind. It will use the nightmare as a signal of alarm and distress. I feel that nightmares always call for some kind of action by the outer mind. Not all dreams demand action. Some are simply making progress reports, others are helping us solve problems, others are inspirational and nurturing. The nightmare, though, is a signal to pay attention which ought not to be ignored.

17

REPETITIVE DREAMS

Progressive and repetitive dreams deal with the same material over a period of time. These kinds of dreams reveal a pattern within the dreamer's consciousness. Some of the most valuable information we can get from our dreams has to do with the discovery of unconscious patterns.

A true repetitive dream is one which is exactly the same each time. Whatever the message is, it is repeated in exactly the same way with the same emphasis. This kind of dream is immensely important for the dreamer. It is quite possible to have such a dream over a period of time and then not experience the dream again. Often the dreamer hasn't any idea what the content of the dream is really about, but the dream is usually remembered because of the frequent repetition.

Repetitive dreams seem to signal very basic conflicts within the dreamer's psyche. They are often nightmarish or bordering on terrifying, which of course assists the dreamer in noticing and remembering them. Children sometimes experience repetitive dreams and there is really little they can do to integrate or understand the experience. If understanding is to come it will have to wait for a later time in the dreamer's life. Children do not have the capacity or life experience to work deeply with dreams. I feel this is appropriate since the analysis of self which dream work requires must wait for adult levels of awareness. It is a good idea to remember this if you are trying to help a child who has had a difficult dream.

The following dream is an example. The dreamer had this dream several times between the ages of five and eight. The dream, nightmarish in quality, always presaged a severe asthma attack, which would begin immediately upon awaking.

John's Dream.

When the dream begins I am standing on an endless plain. The plain is marked by blue lines, regularly spaced in a square grid pattern. The lines stretch as far as I can see. The sky is dark, gray and featureless. The atmosphere feels oppressive and heavy. I sense that there is some terrifying force behind me and I begin to run across the plain. I run faster and faster but the force is getting closer.

Suddenly I reach the edge of the plain, which is like a black, bottomless abyss. From somewhere above a shower of heavy gold coins begins to rain down on my head, and the force of the coins hitting me knocks me over the edge of the plain. I fall into the abyss with the coins raining down upon me. At the same time I hear a deep and frightening laughter. The laughter is coming from the force which was chasing me. The force, whatever it is, is laughing at me as I go over the edge. I wake up screaming.

Immediately upon awaking from this dream John would be hysterical and would first vomit and then go into a severe breathing episode as the asthma took hold.

How would a five year old child be able to interpret this dream? In actual fact it took John forty years before he was able to feel that he had some understanding of the dream which was meaningful for him on a feeling level. How would you interpret the dream?

Take out your worksheets and see what you can determine. Here is John's worksheet, so you will be able to see what he came up with. Do yours first and then compare them to find out if you were able to tune in to some levels of the dream. Don't be discouraged if it's confusing to you. If it took John forty years it might take you a while! On the other hand, John is too personally involved; you may get to it very quickly because you can be objective.

1. Write down and review the dream (as above).
2. The images or events in the dream which I feel are the most powerful are:
     endless grid-like plain
     unknown terrifying force chases dreamer
     heavy gold coins
     falling and laughter
3. I feel that the most important image is:
     all important but most powerful is gold coins knock the dreamer off the edge
4. The way I feel about this image is:
     strange image
     coins are child's image of wealth
     wealth = nourishment
     something about nourishment threatens child
     key image which precipitates fall into black abyss
     feels like total loss of control
     child cannot control events
     angry and scared
5. This image reminds me of: (put down anything, no matter how unrelated it appears, which comes to mind)
     attack
     overwhelming force
     comic book images
6. The next image or event I feel is most important is:
     grid-like plain
7. The way I feel about this image is:
     surreal
     seems very structured, regular
     odd image for a child
     seems like a foundation for the child
     terrifying because endless and inhuman — doesn't feel like a human place
8. This image reminds me of:
     art images for strange regularity — like Escher, Dali
     chessboard
     trapped
The next image I feel is important is:
     terrifying force

The way I feel about this is:
    was very scary for child
    relentless force
    not controllable
    wants to destroy child
    feels masculine
This image reminds me of:
    Nazis
    uncaring authority
    irresistible
    my father
The next image I feel is important is:
    terrifying laughter as child falls off plain
The way I feel about this image is:
    must symbolize whatever attacking force is
    feel like this is a key to dream
    laughing at child must be humiliating
    I felt humiliated as a child if people laughed at me
    I felt humiliated by my parents, especially my father
This image reminds me of:
    horror movies
    devouring force
    death

9. Any other details I now remember are:
    there was no bottom to the blackness after I went over the edge

10. I feel that the dream is about:
    I feel that the dream is about not being loved by my parents. There's something else, too.

11. Another thing about the dream is:
    Something about money — why else the gold coins? The money is about nourishment.

12. The way I feel about this dream is:
    I hate this dream. I hated it then and I hate it now. It makes me angry and afraid and I feel helpless about it.

13. Some other thoughts that occur when I review the images of the dream are:

This dream has always been so powerful that I have always not known what to do with it. If I understood the dream I might be able to understand something about myself as a child and now. My parents never paid any attention to me when I said that the dream came before one of my bad attacks. When I told my mother about the dream and its relationship to the asthma she dismissed the whole idea as ridiculous.

14. Review what you have written.

15. When I ask for help from within about this dream, I sense that the dream is about:

My relationship with love and my parents.

16. My interpretation of the dream is:

I think the dream is about how I felt as a child and how that affected me. I felt unloved by my parents and remote from the rest of my family. My father and mother were divorced not too long after the dream started, when I was six. My parents were always at odds about money, and my father was very controlling about everything. My mother had been born into money as a child but that was all taken away in 1929. She never quite seemed to forget that. She always seemed to want something more.

I think that the dream shows how I felt about all this. I felt completely helpless to make anything happy in our home. It seemed that I was in the way and not very good at anything because I was sick, and I don't think my father liked me very much, although in hindsight I know he had a difficult time. So what! I think the sound of laughter was my father's laugh. He often laughed at me and made fun of me. I think that the pressures of all that were too much from time to time and my way of dealing with it was to get sick and get attention. I think the dream says something about all of this.

John's honesty with his worksheet tells us a lot. His interpretation is good as far as it goes, which is mostly first level and some hints of the second. What is revealing in his interpretation is that it is apparent he has not yet resolved the feelings which the dream brought up, then and now. He is still angry at the parents and there is also some anger and judgement directed at himself.

John sees that the dream was a response to the emotional pressures and conflicts he was experiencing in his family situation. He also has seen that a way for him to get the attention he needed was to get sick. Asthma is an illness which seems to be very closely tied to emotional stress, although many would say this is not proven.

John identifies the pursuing force as his father. This is a first level interpretation. The second level would see a more generalized source, still external, which humiliates him and "drives him over the edge." The third level of interpretation would be......what do you think?

Remember that we tend to project our unconscious material onto the external world, and that the potential resolution requires seeing that we do this. At the same time we need to appreciate that the forces which we experience as coming from outside are also within us. One cannot hold onto the thought of being a helpless victim if this kind of work is really done.

We all have feelings that we are someone's or something's victim. When we see our victimization in this way we are in essence disempowering ourselves and saying that we are victimized because we are a victim! In order to fully empower ourselves as conscious individuals we are going to have to resolve this issue somehow. Because our outer levels of consciousness are not aware of the inner dynamics which are concerned with victimization, we experience great resistance to accepting responsibility for self. The logical result is the assignment of blame and guilt onto others. This same relationship of conscious/unconscious dynamics leads to assignment of guilt and blame onto self as well. It is a vicious circle which never leads to healing or redemption.

The third level interpretation of this dream leads us deeply into John's psyche, to a place within him which disempowers himself through blaming others, particularly his father. The third level says that this is what John does.

KEY POINT

The healing of feelings of victimization begins with the willingness to take responsibility for how one feels. This does not mean we have to take responsibility for the event. It means that since we are the ones who hold the feelings, we are the only ones who can do anything about those feelings. Because the outer levels of consciousness are usually mostly concerned about assigning blame and guilt, there is great resistance to accepting responsibility for self and how one feels. This is one of the most difficult challenges for personal growth.

The best definition of responsibility I have ever heard is Werner Erhard's; responsibility means the ability to respond. Personal responsibility in this sense means that one is able to respond to one's self. This is the key to personal empowerment, but it means that we have to give up our cherished ideas about blame of others. There are many ways to begin this work. It is not easy work but it must be done.

John still sees himself as a victim of his parents' uncaring and unloving actions. In this case a third level of interpretation goes beyond blaming the father and makes the leap to self responsibility for the feelings of victimization which are experienced. This is the crucial juncture for an internal healing process to take hold. John does see that his illness was a way for him to get attention, so he sees that in some way his illness served him on a very basic level. He does not yet see that in serving himself in this way he took on an active participation in the process of his "victimization." Even if the father was uncaring and unloving, John bought into this on a deep, internal level.

It would not be possible for John as a child to see and understand this. What about John now, as an adult? He is still angry and upset about his childhood experience as "victim" and he carries this mostly unconscious energy with him all the time. It is predictable, since this is a pattern of perception in his psyche, that he will see other situations as victimizing him in present time. The psyche on an unconscious level does not distinguish time and place in the linear sense.

KEY POINT

The deep, unconscious psyche does not view time in the same way as our outer consciousness. To the deeper aspects, all time and experience is simultaneous. What the outer mind sees as present time is simply another simultaneous event for the deeper levels. This is often seen in dream images where events and places of different life periods are presented simultaneously.

This is why a pattern of perception in our consciousness which is established at an earlier time in our lives may affect us in present time. The deep psyche doesn't know the difference. Experiences in childhood, for example, may lead to a particular perception of the world. That perception results in a particular form of behavior based on the experience. Decisions are made about life and"how it is." A pattern of perception/response is established which becomes automatic. This perception is then unconsciously overlaid onto future situations which somehow appear similar. The result may be confusion and inappropriate behavior because the situation in present time is not seen clearly for what it is.

We can see this easily in our relationships if we have learned to look for it. A good example is unconsciously responding to your mate or partner as if they were your mother or father.

The pattern of perception which is triggered on the unconscious level will determine our relationship to what we are experiencing consciously. That perception may or may not be accurate.

What can John do with this dream, so many years later? First he must arrive at an accurate interpretation. He will know this because it will click on a feeling level within. There will be a sense of certainty about the dream which he does not yet have.

Here is my interpretation, as brought forth by the Dreamer Within.

The dreamer is caught in an internal conflict between his perception of external forces and his own inner needs. He attempts to establish a regular and orderly basis for his life but this is sterile and inadequate. This is the meaning of the grid like plain upon which the dreamer finds himself.

The dreamer feels threatened and pursued because he has reached a point where the gap between his attempts to control the situation and his inability to do so has once again become apparent. Since he is not able to face this unresolvable conflict he flees to escape it. Since he does not understand the nature of the conflict the pursuing force becomes depersonalized, faceless and masculine. It is masculine in feeling because the dreamer is masculine and is in essence attacking himself.

The gold coins represent another aspect of the inner conflict. The dreamer's consciousness perceives riches and wealth as a source of danger, since he has come to believe that this is a reason for the lack of nourishment and love which he wants and needs. In the dreamer's psyche wealth and riches are a source of punishment because he feels responsible for the lack of such riches in his family situation. If wealth and riches were to appear it would be contrary to his existence. He feels this way because of a mistaken and childish perception of his responsibility for his family's well being. The child thinks it is a financial and emotional burden to the family. If he were not here, things would be better for them. Resolution of financial problems may only be achieved at the expense of his existence. This is not acceptable and leads to the crisis of emotion and feeling which produces the asthma attacks. The annihilation of the child's being is symbolized by the fall into the abyss.

What John can do with this in present time is take a look around himself. Does his present life in some way reflect these dynamics? One area to look at would be money and finances. If the interpretation is correct, and if what I have said about unconscious projection onto external reality is true, it would be predictable that John would have trouble with money.

In fact, this has always been so. John is quite capable of making large amounts of money and has done so in the past, but somehow he is always in debt and is always worried about money on some level. It is also predictable that John would be very suspicious and wary of men, not quite knowing how to safely relate to them. This is also true, although work John has done to resolve feelings about his father has resulted in many changes in this area.

John does try to establish orderly and somewhat limited boundaries for himself in order to control his life and maintain his safety. This too is changing as he works to open up to more fluid and feminine influences. He has often created upheaval of the order in his life in an attempt to bring about a change. Intuitively he has tried to escape the symbolic plain of his dream.

If John is to change the effects of this unconscious patterning within him, he will have to finally accept his participation in his childhood victimization and appreciate the dynamics which were involved. He will have to see that he carries these same forces within himself. More importantly, he will have to come to a place of humor, love and appreciation of himself as the source of his experience. This will lead to acceptance and forgiveness, both of himself and his parents. This can lead to de-energizing the pattern, which in turn will have practical effects in his life.

In this dream we see an example of true repetition. The dream was exactly the same each time over a period of several years. The dreams stopped a few years after his parents' divorce, after some stability had been achieved in his home situation. Even though it has been so many years, John still feels the impact of the dream and it has periodically surfaced in his memory. Something in John is still trying to resolve the meaning of the dream, even though he no longer has asthma and is now an adult. The material was important to him then and it is important now.

If you have a pattern of repetitive dreaming, there is a very important message for you which is contained within the dream. Even if you have not had the dream for years, the material is still important because such a dream always represents an unresolved area of conflict within. Outer situations may change and alleviate the stressful stimuli which triggered the dream. Then the dream may no longer be presented. The inner situation is likely to remain the same. If the psyche perceives a different, new external stimulus as similar in some way, the old pattern will be activated, and the dream may even return. Even if the dream is no longer seen, the pattern will be the same and the results are liable to be just as unsatisfactory. By understanding the dream it may be possible to de-energize the pattern and achieve a different result.

18

UNCONSCIOUS PATTERNS

The power of dreams as inner teachings for our personal development is most deeply evident when they reveal unconscious patterns. An unconscious pattern is just that – something within our consciousness which is always operating in the same way with a predictable result, without our conscious knowledge. This is really the prophetic level of dreams, because once the pattern is seen the result can be accurately "prophesied" or predicted. A pattern, if followed, always produces the same result.

Earlier in the book I used the analogy of a shirt pattern. A pattern for a shirt always produces a shirt. The shirt may have variations in color, size and material, but it will always be a shirt. Another pattern produces a suit or a pair of pants, and so on. Any pattern, once energized, always produces the same result with variations. If our unconscious is actually involved with patterns, as I am suggesting, then we are often operating on automatic. Although our outer ego levels may not like this very much, what I am saying is that we are effectively acting out myriad unconscious patternings in our daily life. Because they are unconscious we don't know the patterns are there. This means that we don't know what we're doing! Of course, we think we know what we are doing most of the time. That is the problem with the unconscious.

If you or I have a pattern which is operating we will always get a similar result when the pattern is activated and run through to completion. We are not consciously in charge of starting the pattern;

it is activated by the stimuli, whatever they may be, which we experience as we go about the business of living. If we remain unaware of the presence of the pattern we can not make any changes which might be desirable. This can effectively hamper our health, quality of life and general well-being if the pattern is not supportive in these areas.

There are some clues which can be noticed in your life that indicate a pattern is involved. If you find yourself saying "Why does this always happen to me . . .," or "It always turns out this way..." or "No matter what I do . . .," chances are a pattern is running in your unconscious.

Patterns don't care about anything. A pattern is simply a pattern and finds its pattern fulfillment through whatever action constitutes the progression of the pattern to completion. Just like a shirt factory which produces shirts until the machinery is shut down, our consciousness will keep running the same patterns over and over again unless action is taken.

Over time dreams will reveal the fundamental patterns which are active in our unconscious. The dynamics of the patterning are displayed by the dream images. One dream can do it, but usually we need to see several examples before we catch on, if then.

I feel that dreams are one of the best and most powerful tools for the revelation of the powerful patternings of forces which run us on the unconscious levels. Initiating change and shifting these forces is not an easy task, by any means. Just seeing the pattern will not change anything, but seeing the pattern is the first and most necessary step towards change, if change is desired. What might we wish to change in our lives? If you ask yourself that question you will most likely come up with something that could be different.

John's dream of the pursuing force and the shower of coins reflected a sense of deep uncertainty about self. This demanded a response which became a pattern of behavior. The result was a skewed emotional response leading to illness, emotional withdrawal and problems with money. This pattern is shown by the dream and reflected in outer life.

Some of the destructive patterns with which we may be involved include drug and alcohol addiction, sexual inadequacies, awful relationships, destructive work habits and any other observable and repetitive but unsatisfying circumstance in our lives.

I am assuming here that unconscious patterns which support us in pleasant circumstances and constructive results will not be considered subject to change by our outer mind. Unfortunately for simplicity's sake, some of the patterns which result in our perceived comfort are two edged and carry a destructive aspect as well. This is one of the reasons addictions of any kind are so difficult to release. An addiction serves one aspect of the psyche while destroying another.

Dreams can reveal the heart of the dynamics involved with the pattern which we desire to change. In the dreams will be shown the essence of the pattern. Once the pattern is revealed, we can bring our conscious mind to bear on the elements which are involved and through whatever approach we favor work to change it. If the change is accomplished then the pattern is in effect de-energized and dis-empowered. The shirt making factory is shut down. This is true whether we are dealing with psychological problems of relationship or psychological patterns which lead to physiological involvement and even disease and death.

I realize that many will not agree with this statement or its implications. I simply present this to you for your consideration. If you take this as a working hypothesis and set aside belief or disbelief, perhaps you will be able to verify through your experience that there is truth in what I have said. I say it because it has proven to be true in my own experience and I have observed it to be true for others.

I feel that this approach could prove to be extremely valuable in cases of addictive behavior. There is a catch, though. To be successful this approach to shifting patterns of behavior requires several prerequisites which will not always be present or available in any given situation. The revelation of patterns shown in dreams as an effective tool of personal change requires:

1. Commitment by the dreamer to accepting the forces of change; this has to come from within and often requires skilled assistance from without. This assistance can take many forms, such as group work or the presence of a skilled therapist or facilitator who is experienced in working with their own dreams and the dreams of others. Jungian work may be particularly valuable in this area, but there are others who can do it. Some are listed in the Resources section at the end of this book.

2. Commitment by the dreamer to self examination and to implacable honesty about what is discovered.

3. Experience in getting past the outer and reactive levels which are activated when we look at dreams. We must reach to the objective and appreciative level which sees the symbolic images of dreams for what they are. This is necessary for accurate interpretation, and requires practice.

4. Lots of patience.

5. Acceptance of oneself fully as one is. This cannot be stressed enough. One will never change a destructive pattern by refusing to accept its reality. At best an uneasy truce may be established, a standoff within which can always collapse. Acceptance does not merely mean acknowledgement of the problem. Acceptance means a recognition of how the problem serves the individual coupled with a deep and heart felt appreciation for the service which is provided. If that sounds as though it might be difficult, it is! I didn't say this would be easy. I learned this from Brugh Joy. Adding the component of heart-felt appreciation, which is the soul of Dr. Joy's teachings, took my work with self acceptance from an intellectual to a feeling level where change could really take place.

True release and healing do not take place without this component of self love and appreciation, although some of the destructive effects of the pattern may be averted. This is the case with addicts of any kind who manage to discipline themselves into avoidance of the addictive component. A sort of demilitarized zone is established within the psyche between the forces of addiction and the forces which do not wish to be addicted. The problem is that the cease-fire can break down. As long as an adversarial relationship is maintained the danger of renewed fighting is always present. In addition, a great deal of energy and attention is spent on maintaining the fragile peace.

6. A sense of humor.

If the above conditions are met, there is an excellent chance for the transformative and healing energies to come forward. As with any kind of psychological work which addresses basic issues like addiction, progress may be slow and difficult. Using the dream material may dramatically speed up the process because it can reveal the real dynamics within, and time may not have to be wasted chasing fruitless leads and clues. Dream work is detective work. Success in solving the case depends on intuitive as well as logical approaches. As the clues are pieced together, the pattern of the mystery is unveiled.

Dream work is a wonderful way to learn how to balance the intuitive and linear approaches. It is a path to a deeper integration of self.

Patterns are usually only seen in dreams over a period of time. The clue that indicates we may be looking at a pattern is in repetition of the material. This is true, for example, in the case of a repetitive dream which always repeats in exactly the same way. It is more likely to be found in a series of dreams over time. The dreams may or may not show progress about a given situation. That will depend on what the dreamer is doing with the information, consciously and unconsciously.

Dreams which are involved with patterns show the same issue in a different light or circumstance. It is like the "concept" movies seen on television or in the theater. The concept will have to do with a general theme such as family comedy, or new roommates, or medical personnel or cops/robbers, goodguys/badguys. The individual example will express many variations on the theme which has proven successful in the past.

Over days, months or years a certain theme may come forward in our dreams. At first we have nothing to compare it with. Usually it will go unnoticed unless we have trained ourselves to pay attention to the correlation between our inner and outer lives. After a few dreams in which similar events occur we may notice the similarity. This is the signal of a pattern in operation.

To analyze a pattern you have to watch carefully to see how the results always come out the same way or nearly the same way. What are the similarities in the dream? What is the dream result of the dream action? How did you feel in the dream? What does this remind you of in your outer, waking life?

Once you suspect that your dreams are revealing a pattern to you, see if you can ask the questions of yourself which will give you the shape of it. If you can see the shape, the structure and the components of the pattern, you may be able to go to the next level and unravel your desire for the result which the pattern always brings to you. It is worth the trouble. Think of yourself as a detective with an interesting case. Solving the case brings reward and recognition and leaves you free for other pursuits.

I am not going to give examples of dreams in this chapter. You can see patterns revealed in several dreams discussed in other chapters. Usually there will be a comment about the pattern seen in the dream. Besides, you now have enough information to begin to recognize the presence of unconscious patterns in dreams without too much help from me. Just pretend you are Sherlock Holmes and see what you can deduce. Like the intrepid Mr. Holmes, you may ultimately arrive at the observation that the deduction is "elementary."

19

DRUGS, ALCOHOL AND ADDICTION IN DREAMS

Addiction of any kind is not going to be resolved through a dream. What dreams can do is provide clues to the dynamics within the individual which result in addiction. I do not limit the definition of addiction to physiological response to physical substances such as drugs or alcohol. We are addicted, every one of us, to patterns of perception and behavior which in some way serve us, even when they sometimes have destructive results. This seemed like a good place to talk about this kind of dream because addiction is a pattern of behavior, and we have just looked at the idea that there are unconscious patterns which are revealed in our dreams.

The first key to releasing addiction is to see how the addiction serves. There is always an option available to us, sometimes difficult to see or energize, which will give us the same benefits without the trauma of destructive addictive behavior.

If physiological addiction is involved, appropriate medical treatment may relieve the process on that level and must be addressed. In dream work what concerns us is the level which is far more subtle and difficult. This is the area of the consciousness which led to the physical addiction in the first place.

If I had a simple solution to the problem of addiction, I would most likely become wealthy overnight and be hailed as the savior of many unhappy lives. Unfortunately, I do not have a simple answer available! I offer my observations of the process as involved in dreams in the hope that this may prove a useful tool for some who are working with addiction.

In a general sense it is well to remember that the symbols of addiction which appear in dreams, such as bottles of alcohol or drugs, are first and foremost symbols. Therefore these things are not just mere representations of the addictive substance. They represent the essence of the substance. They represent what the substance does for the dreamer, or might do. This is also true for those who do not take drugs, etc. but who dream of these things. The dream can shed new light on how the substance/addictive pattern is used by the deep psyche. Insight or even revelation can be gained on the root causes, psychologically, of the addiction. This is the most valuable knowledge one can have.

Without doing dream work there is often a level of insight about the addictive process which is related to external events and personal history. This may appear as almost anything. Some examples would be alcoholic parents, peer group pressure, desperate living conditions, abusive circumstances, physical illness, work conditions, stress, and so on. Do you notice what all of these have in common?

The common thread is that all the reasons for the process of addiction are external. The addicted person can point to something and say, "It's because of them, or this, or my situation or my friends..." The addict in this statement disempowers self. The cause of the addiction is projected outward. Cause and source become confused, even though the addict may recognize that he or she is the only one who ultimately can change the destructive patterning.

The statement made earlier about feelings of victimization applies most strongly here. As long as a person believes (and thus experiences) that someone or something did it to them, they will never release the addiction. They may handle the symptoms by avoiding the substance. Inside though, the forces which led to the addiction will not be realized or integrated, although the fires may be quelled for a while. Like a fire left smoldering, flames may burst out in the future in unexpected places.

To get to the useful information about addiction which may come forward in our dreams requires some practice. First level interpretations will not usually do the trick. The tendency on this level is to see the dream simply as a dream about the real, physical problem. An alcoholic dreams of drinking and thinks the dream is about the drinking problem. That's true, but what good does it do? We have to get deeper into the dream to derive really useful stuff which we can work with.

You may wish to review the conditions for successful work with deep level patterns which were presented in the preceding chapter. Everything presented there applies here.

The following dream comes from a woman who is an alcoholic. She has been "sober" for many years and has been successful in establishing herself as a therapist. She works with battered and abused women and with alcoholic women. She has a lot of insight about her addictive behavior; at the same time she is aware that she has never really discovered why she began drinking and what that was really about for her. She is now beginning to discover more about the roots of her alcoholism as she discovers new areas of herself.

Allyson's Dream.

I am at a very nice restaurant having lunch and I'm getting ready to leave. As I pay the bill, I ask for a bottle of wine. A waiter brings me a large glass of wine and a small bottle of wine. I drink the glass of wine, open the bottle, and pour another glass. As I begin to drink it I think to myself that I can't go back to work because my secretary would know/smell. I can't see clients if I've been drinking. I put the glass down and leave the restaurant. I start to walk through a parking lot and I can't find my car. I walk behind a Cadillac that's backing out and it nearly runs me down. I move away from it and cross the street into a park.

I am still looking around for my car when I stop dead in my tracks and listen. I say, "I hear you back there." Then two men and a woman come around and stand in front of me. They ask me what I'm doing and I tell them I'm on my way to my car — that I'm out looking for an apartment. We start to cross the street, heading back to the restaurant.

This is a tricky dream and its meaning hides on a deep level. Allyson could not really make much out of the dream. She had another dream about a month later which is related. In the second dream alcohol does not appear, but she receives more information. The second dream is an example of how information about a similar theme may be presented over time. I'll give you this dream now and then we can look at both to see what may be revealed.

Allyson's Dream: One Month Later.

I remember being with a very handsome man who I sensed as someone dangerous. We go to a country cottage/restaurant where I witness a man being taken away by thugs. There is an older, rich looking man there who tells me the man being taken away is going to be killed. He seems to assume that I know why the man is to be killed.

The scene changes and I am in the dining room. The handsome man comes to get me and tells me "the Boss" wants us to see the car that is taking the dead man away. We stand in the driveway as a big white limo drives slowly past us. "The Boss" is looking out the window at me — it seems like a warning. After they're out of the driveway and down the road the handsome man takes me back inside the restaurant.

At first glance you may not think these two dreams are related. Allyson knows somehow that the dreams are related, although she had not gotten too far with the interpretation when she told me the dreams.

The first thing we look for are similarities when we are comparing reams which may be about the same issue within the dreamer. We can assume, with reservations, that similar symbols may stand for similar things within that particular dreamer's consciousness. Here are the things which are similar;

Cadillac — big, powerful, dangerous car (first dream)

White limo — big, powerful, dangerous car (second dream)

restaurant setting — both dreams

return to restaurant — at end of both dreams

companion or companions appear in both dreams

These are the clues which tell us that in some way the two dreams are related. If we could determine something about these similarities we might be able to piece together the rest of it. It's like a jigsaw puzzle — we take the pieces we can see and fit them together, then we move on to the more difficult areas.

A car is one of those symbols which means many things to many people. In this case the car is large, powerful, and in some way dangerous. In the first dream a Cadillac nearly runs Allyson over. It's "backing out" at her. What does this feel like as an image? If something is backing out in a dream it often stands for material which is hidden in the unconscious. It is literally "in back of" the dreamer. Presumably the unseen driver of the car either doesn't see her or ignores her. This is a statement of the unconscious. Allyson is the one who doesn't see what's happening here — remember, it's her dream. The car represents some dangerous force. The danger of something is determined by one's relationship to it.

If we are in harmony with something it is not threatening to us. If we are not, it is. Protection means to be in harmony with. Whatever the car symbolizes, Allyson is not comfortable about it on the inner levels. This should reflect into her outer life.

In the second dream the car is a big white limo. The danger comes from the sinister figure of "The Boss" who rides within. He is a killer. Who gets to ride in big limousines? We think of people who are powerful and wealthy. People who ride in limos are successful, but they may or may not be nice people. The collective image regarding limousines is power. Like the limousine, a Cadillac has been for many the symbol of wealth and power, success and prestige.

The key word here is power. That is the common element of both images. What kind of power? In Allyson's case the power is perceived as dangerous. We now know that one of the elements in the two dreams is a fear of power. This is also indicated by the handsome but dangerous man who accompanies her in the second dream. This suggests that we are looking at something which has to do with power as manifested in its masculine attributes.

This slant towards the masculine, negative aspects is also seen in the rich, older man (wealth and power again) who assumes Allyson knows why a man is to be killed; and it is very clearly seen in the figure of "The Boss." "The Boss" represents the ultimate in dangerous, uncontrollable masculine authority.

In the first dream Allyson stops dead in her tracks because she senses the presence of someone "behind her." This is like "backing out." The two men and a woman who appear are more of the unseen and unconscious actors in Allyson's play.

In the first dream Allyson can not find her own car. Do you think there might be something going on here with these two dream actions involving a car? Are the images related? If cars can represent "power" which is perceived as dangerous by the psyche and Allyson can't find her own car, the message is that Allyson can not allow herself to be powerful. Therefore she by definition must feel disempowered. Now we are getting closer to the roots of her alcohol addiction.

What about the wine and the restaurant? We go to a restaurant to be nurtured and to eat, to take in something. In a restaurant one is served. The food is brought to the diner, there is no work, it is all about service and nourishment. In both dreams she goes to a restaurant; in the first she drinks wine and worries about it being noticed; in the second she sees someone being taken away to be killed. The first restaurant is very nice — Allyson likes it there, it is comforting to her.

In the first sequence she orders the wine just before leaving, when the bill is presented. There is some association here between paying and drinking. In some way being at the nice restaurant where she is nourished must be paid for and at the same time she orders a drink. One of the ways Allyson felt good in the past was by drinking. The third level of interpretation of this short section makes the association between nourishment, payment and drinking. In Allyson's mind the three are all mixed up together. This offers a clue to be pursued by ongoing work.

Allyson was raised as a Catholic. When we go for the third level interpretation in a dream, we make use intuitively of all information about the dream and dreamer which is available to us. Knowing Allyson was a Catholic is important information. The heart of the Catholic and Christian mystery is Sacred Communion — the offering of the Mass and the partaking of the wine and bread which symbolize the redemptive promise of Christ and the taking in of Spirit. One is nurtured and redeemed through this ritual, in a mysterious way made one with God.

In Allyson's mind there is a very powerful piece which associates wine and Spirit, wine and redemption, wine and nourishment. To the deep psyche there is little distinction between the word Spirit, meaning a numinous mystery and Sacred manifestation, and spirits, the word which applies to alcoholic beverages.

I do not mean to suggest that Allyson's alcoholism is a result of her Catholic upbringing! That is exactly the kind of mistake which is often made on the second level of interpretation. If Allyson decided that the Church was to blame she would simply be finding another scapegoat and avoiding the recognition that she has created the problem. What I am saying is that there is a fundamental confusion in Allyson's mind between the connection with nurturing Spiritual energies and alcoholic spirits. This confusion is held on an unconscious level.

Let's go a little further with this. The ritual of the Mass makes good on the promise of redemption offered in Christian theology. The redemption is seen as necessary because of a fundamental supposition of human guilt as stated in the doctrine of Original Sin. This original sin which resulted in the separation of the human race from God the Father took place in the Garden of Eden. The condition of being human is by definition a condition of sin. Therefore by definition Allyson is guilty. Her guilt is part of the payment she makes to God for being human. To redeem herself she must take in the wine of Spirit, literally and figuratively.

To the outer, logical (!), conscious mind it makes no sense that someone would confuse alcohol and the connection to God, except in approved rituals like the Mass. The very reason the ritual of the Mass can be moving and effective is because the unconscious does not make the distinction. This is the experience of the Mystery. All effective rituals are activated through the surrender to unconscious forces which transform ordinary awareness into exalted states. In these states very real and awesome energies are experienced. The unconscious, once activated and allowed to come forward, will sweep away ordinary perceptions and judgments as it reaches for experience in the outer world. Does this sound like what happens when someone has been drinking too much?

I am not the first to make an association between alcohol and Spirit, nor to suggest that there is some connection between drinking and the quest for connection to God. As far as I know the first to suggest this was Carl Jung. I feel that Jung was right. In Allyson's dream the third level of interpretation takes all of this into consideration.

In the second sequence a killing is initiated in the restaurant. She is with a very attractive but dangerous man. An attractive, dangerous man says something about her inner relationship with power and the masculine. Can you see that this is similar to the symbols of the cars, the "Boss" and the older man? The man who is to be "killed" is a piece of Allyson which expresses itself in masculine ways but which is overshadowed by the fear of the power aspects. If Allyson were to express this piece, she might meet with resistance and figurative killing in the outer, competitive world where she works. Any woman who has run up against the negative aspects of the masculine power structure knows exactly what I mean.

Here is a trap opening before us in our interpretation. The second level of the dream sees the external masculine as the enemy and blames its feelings of disempowerment and fear on this convenient target. The third level goes to the responsibility within for being disempowered, regardless of the externals. This is difficult!

One of the reasons Allyson drank was for the feeling of power which she experienced. If any of you have been serious drinkers, you know what I mean. As the inhibitions drop away, new and sometimes very assertive or aggressive levels appear. It is an unlayering process which goes out of conscious control. One of the reasons people drink excessively is to be out of control. Different pieces inside them are demanding expression and alcohol or drugs can allow this to happen. When Allyson was drunk she could do and say things which she would never allow when she was sober.

At this point in our interpretation of the two dreams we can say that the theme is about disempowerment, something about the masculine (whatever that means to Allyson), the fear of power and the desire to conceal all of this from others, and something about the desire for connection to Spiritual nourishment and source. This is quite a lot. It's easier to see why Allyson may have reasons to drink, although it remains to be seen what she will do with the information.

The concealment is shown in the first dream by her thought about the secretary and the clients. They must not know Allyson has been drinking. First level interpretation looks at Allyson's self judgement about having been a drunk and fear of exposure. The second level recognizes that she now takes appropriate behavior in her life by not getting drunk. The third level looks at this differently and sees that there is still something within which takes a drink, and that the other interpretations are secondary to this fundamental energy within.

In both dreams Allyson heads back for the restaurant at the end of the dream. This is a crucial common component. It means that Allyson has not handled the basic issue; she will return and does return to the previous pattern. This is where she is stuck symbolically. She needs to see what the "restaurant" is really about and to understand the symbolic meaning of what takes place there. Understanding would eliminate the necessity to return.

Allyson is actually looking for an "apartment" in the first dream, which means that something within her is trying to energize a new way of being in the world. Reaching further, the third level of interpretation looks at the word "apartment" and sees it as a statement of wanting to be "apart" from the pattern. She is still unable to fully achieve this. This is shown by the image of heading back to the restaurant with the people who came up behind her. She is still under the dominance of her unconscious forces.

In summation the two dreams show the basic issues which manifest as alcoholism for the dreamer. It could take years of therapy and self work to resolve these issues, and even then they might never reach a stage of resolution. That will depend on Allyson. In the meantime she has had the strength, which is considerable, to stop drinking and short circuit the destructive behavior brought on through the symptoms of the addiction.

In general, the symbols of drugs, alcohol and other addictive substances or behaviors in dreams represent something which is not understood. One might dream of smoking a cigarette and acknowledge that one was addicted, but not understand why the cigarette was being smoked. The first step in dealing with addiction is acknowledgement of the addiction itself. The second step is the activation of a strong desire for change of the addictive behavior. The third step is recognition of the purpose of the addiction, whatever it might be. This is the service which the addiction performs. The fourth step is the growth into a new possibility of behavior which provides the same service in non destructive ways. Once the last step has been achieved the addiction ceases to be a problem.

Jack's Dream.

> *I inject myself with a syringe, twice, two ampoules. It is a clear drug, like morphine. There is litter all over the floor from doing this, from taking the drug. I hurry to clean it up so my brother won't see it. There is some difficulty doing that.*

Jack was actually at one time addicted to drugs, but it has been many years since he has taken anything. This dream shows that something is still active in his psyche which is keyed to the experience of drugs. Please remember that the psyche when it is dreaming is experiencing the dream as if it were reality. Taking a drug in a dream is the same on this level as actually taking it in waking life, and it will be taken for the same reason, whatever it is. The underlying and unconscious motivation is the same.

There are two big advantages to acting out the addiction in a dream which are not available in waking life. For one thing, there are no physiological side effects of the addiction. More importantly, the dream may give information from the unconscious about why the addictive substance is required. This is what we were looking at with Allyson's dream above. The same is true for Jack, although much less information is given.

First of all, see if you can picture the actual image of injecting a drug into oneself in your mind's eye. See Jack inject not one but two ampoules. The image of a needle penetrating the body is just that — an image of penetration. This is a good example of how we need to look very closely at the actions and images in dreams. Most of us would see the image of the addict injecting himself and not reach for the level which the image contains as a symbol. As a symbol this is an act of penetration and it is in this sense a sexual act.

Now we also have to remember that sex in dreams is mostly about relationship. Injecting oneself with a drug is on this level of interpretation an act of relationship with the self. What kind of relationship? We don't really know yet but there are several clues. Those clues are:

> two ampoules
> clear liquid like morphine
> litter on the floor
> afraid the brother will find out
> difficulty cleaning up the mess

Two ampoules could just be taking more of the drug, but this is a first level interpretation and inaccurate. Two is the key here. Two is "more than one." Two is a number which does not stand alone. Two is a number of balance. Two ones balance each other and make two. Are you with me so far? Two ampoules means that the act of taking the drug is an act of balance. This is difficult to see because it requires a third level look at the image. The drug is balancing something inside Jack's psyche. Therefore the dream is revealing that the symbolic and addictive pattern is a gesture of internal balance. This fits with the idea that taking the drug says something about Jack's relationship with himself.

The balancing element of the drug is clear in color. Clarity is like purity in this case. It is like a representation of clear energy, not unlike the idea of alcohol as a symbol for Spirit. Of course, morphine also dulls and alters the awareness. It is, after all, a poor substitute for Spirit or clear consciousness. This is why it is difficult to pick up the litter on the floor.

The litter is the result of taking the drug. Succumbing to the addictive way of trying to achieve balance results in trash and clutter, debris and litter within the psyche. This is a warning to Jack that the pattern leaves its own consequences behind within him. The thought in the dream that this must be cleaned up or his brother will find out has to do with Jack's relationship to his real brother. In waking life Jack tends to see his brother as authoritative and sometimes judgmental.

Jack's brother is older and in many ways took on the energy of father for him. The dream is saying that the addictive behavior is in some way related to Jack's feelings about authority in his life, especially masculine authority. A good second level interpretation at this point would focus on those feelings and relate them to the real addictive behavior Jack once showed when he took drugs. What is the third level of interpretation?

The third level is not dissimilar to Allyson's dream given earlier. In her dream the issue was power and feeling disempowered. This is also true for Jack when it comes to masculine power figures. The third level demands that Jack pull back the blame he assigns outside of himself and look for the reasons why he negates his own masculine power. You do not have to know Jack to be able to derive this from the dream.

In an insidious and destructive way injecting oneself with drugs is an expression of power. It is also an intimate expression of relationship with self. It is an expression against authority of others over self. It serves as a substitute for true empowerment and for another kind of relationship with self which is not destructive. Jack's dream, even though he has long been "clean," tells him that he has not resolved this fundamental issue of self expression and relationship to self in a nurturing and constructive way.

Since the dream has presented the images to him, it is safe to assume that the pattern of self destructive behavior, disempowerment of self and a skewed relationship with self has somehow been activated. This does not necessarily mean Jack will return to drugs. There are many other ways he could act out the pattern and achieve the same result. That is the importance of the dream. It is a message to him to pay attention and notice how he is reacting in his waking life. Sometimes self defeat is the most addictive pattern of all.

You may dream of taking drugs even if you have never had the actual experience. You may dream that you are addicted, caught in the disempowering loop of repetitive behavior which is no longer under your control. If such a dream appears, pay attention. Whatever the symbol is specifically about for you, in general it will represent a way in which you substitute unconscious action and behavior for a more aware state of being. The service given to you by the addiction will inevitably be in the form of doing something for you which you have been unable to consciously do for yourself. Jack's use of drugs to overcome his feelings of disempowerment through an act which looks powerful to something within his psyche is a good example. It may also be noted that ultimately the addictive pattern is a result of not handling the real issue, whatever it may be. That is one of the reasons we are working with dreams; to see the real issue and take appropriate action if it is necessary.

20
PROGRESSIVE DREAMS

Progressive dreams differ from repetitive and serial dreams because they are neither directly sequential or exactly the same. They are similar to the other types in that they present images which are concerned with the same area within the dreamer's consciousness. Something is being worked with and the dreamer is shown by several dreams over a period of time just how things stand. New information may be presented which tells the dreamer what progress, if any, has been made.

Like repetitive and serial dreams, progressive dreams are especially valuable for showing the dreamer what the pattern level is which is being utilized. They also show how the dreamer feels about the effects of the pattern. The pattern may not be so dramatic as a physical addiction. Like a physical addiction, however, a pattern effectively takes over control once it is activated. Whether the pattern has to do with drugs or one's relationship to authority makes little difference. Free will and choice in the conscious sense is unavailable while the pattern is running.

When we look through our dream journals and records we may see that we have had several dreams over a given period of time which have similar although not identical images and events. This is often not remembered or noticed until we review. The outer mind

215

quickly forgets past dreams unless there is some particularly good reason to remember it.

When you see such a series of common images and/or themes, you know you are looking at a pattern. You also know that you are looking at something within your consciousness which is calling for attention and perhaps change. If you can decipher the clues you will achieve a much deeper insight or understanding about who you are and why you act in the way that you do in certain situations. At that point choice again becomes available to you.

For example, I had a series of dreams over about a year which consistently involved cars (vehicles) which were either overheating or sliding backwards, out of control. Sometimes the brakes didn't work, sometimes I was in the car or not, sometimes someone else was driving. Often it was Winter in the dreams. Always there was a female companion with me. All of this told me that something consistent was going on within. Something was being worked with and in the dreams I could see a certain repetition, but also a progression. You can be sure I was relieved when the brakes began working in the dreams, even imperfectly! Then the cars could be repaired or re-started. It was good to notice that the dreams began to have a Summer setting, and that my female companions were less upset, happier and friendlier.

This was a time in my life when I was experiencing some deep second thoughts about the work I was doing and how I expressed it in the world. I was struggling financially and attempting to better understand what exactly it is that I do. I made several false starts. Part of my work involves opening to what I call feminine energies — energies of inspiration and intuition, energies more concerned with the flow of the moment rather than the logical goal of the future.

The Winter scenes were telling me that something was literally frozen within me, also that I was in a time when things are quite literally slowed down and in a slow state of animation. That is not a time for forcing growth. One must be patient when Winter has set in. My task was to see if I could feel into the deeper emotional levels, and to see how I was literally "spinning my wheels" and making ineffective use of the "power" which was available to me.

Anger was one of the emotional components and this was one of the meanings of the overheating engines, although not the only one.

Over the period in which these dreams were occurring I kept noticing that there were many correlations in my outer life. The dreams were showing me "how things were." They also stimulated me to look more deeply and to reach for a different perception of my situation, which I kept trying to do. The information they gave me helped me understand what was happening externally. Gradually that began to shift as I made changes. As I made the changes the dreams changed also until things were running smoothly again.

Interestingly to me, I know of other people who have had somewhat similar dreams. It would seem that the "car" in our society has become a kind of universal symbol for many things. This is easy to observe — just watch the TV ads. If you are even moderately observant you can easily see that the cars are sold by association with other values which have nothing to do with the car itself as a functional piece of machinery. These associations include Power, Control, Sex, Freedom (whatever that is!), Clean Air (pretty good, huh?), Mobility, Wealth, Exotic Experience and Adventure, The Ocean, Masculinity, Femininity, Personal Security and Safety, and very frequently, Youth. I could go on, but you get the idea.

The TV ad people are well aware of the unconscious associations which we project onto outer reality. This is the foundation of successful advertising. Sometimes it's extremely subtle — in the background a quick shot shows a man, sexual and dark skinned, playing a piano (erotic, fun) while a fan is blowing (hot — sexy) and the curtains dance over the open windows (free — no boundaries). Meanwhile the voice over drones on, extolling the product. The message is in the images and only secondarily in the words. Just like a dream.

The TV people know that images are far more powerful than verbal information. Images shape our lives and our thoughts and opinions. Images are often substituted for truth, unlike our dreams which always present truthful material. Our deep psyche is happy to pick up and use these collective images which constantly bombard us for our own education. Therefore, there may be a Ford in your future, but that future may lie within your dreaming consciousness!

One of the fun benefits from working with dreams is that you will begin to develop a powerful ability to see through the images which are being presented to you by TV ads, programs and movies. Newscasts will begin to take on a different level of meaning and the bias which is there will become more apparent. It will be harder for the deceivers to trick you! You can hopefully appreciate the attempt and make up your own mind about what is being offered. You will also begin to see things you never saw before, which adds a whole new dimension to the enjoyment of film and visual entertainment.

KEY POINT

Working with dreams teaches you to feel into the real meaning of images. This meaning is found on an unconscious and symbolic level. Learning to attune to this symbolic level of meaning enriches your experience of all of your life, not just the dreaming states of awareness.

What I have written above may seem like a digression from the subject of progressive dreams, and it is! Thinking of the series of dreams I had with the car images led me to the other material. That is one of the ways dream work influences our outer perceptions. We begin to make associations which are not directly apparent, such as dreams and TV ads. Dream work encourages intuitive leaps to other areas of life and to a different understanding of those areas.

Getting back to progressive dreams, these may sometimes show that nothing has really changed, even though a significant period of real time has passed. A dream may appear in childhood one or more times, and then show up again, with variation in the adult consciousness. What this indicates is that there is once again an opportunity to see just what is going on and perhaps do something with it. The psyche is patient and it will present important themes again and again for your consideration. When the adult has the dream he or she has options which were not available to the child. If the adult has a dream that was present for the child, this means that the same dynamics are still operating. It is easy to see that this might not be the best thing for the adult. Here is an example.

Diana's Dream: Childhood.

I am in my mother's bedroom at night. She is asleep in her bed on the left side. I go to her with great fear trying to wake her up. I am trying desperately to tell her that I am dying but I have no voice. I am shaking her and holding my throat. She awakens and looks at me. She keeps saying, "What? I can't hear you." I keep trying to communicate that I am dying. She tells me she can't hear me and to go back to bed. I wake up.

Diana had this dream, more than once, when she was about six years old. Years later she had another dream which repeats the same theme with variation. Here it is.

Diana's Dream: Puberty.

I am out in my parents' front yard where I live, a well manicured lawn with landscaping. It is the afternoon. I am bitten by a baby rattler. I know this snake is more poisonous than a grown rattler. I go to my mother and show her my thumb (left) with the bite and try to tell her I've been bitten. I can't be heard. She ignores me. I go to my father and he doesn't pay attention either. I am very frightened because I think I will die. I wake up.

The first thing we need to do is look at the things which are similar in the dreams. The things which are different in the second dream are giving us information which applies to Diana's life at the time of the dream, her adolescent life. It makes sense that the dream would do this, since she is no longer a young child. On the other hand, the same dynamics of consciousness which were present when she was six seem to be present now. This is the similarity and the basis of both dreams. What is similar? As with other dreams, we can take a worksheet approach and see what comes up. We'll vary it somewhat to take into account the similarities and differences.

    1. Review and write down the dreams. (as above)

    2. The things that are similar in the dreams are:

        dreamer goes to mother/parent

        can't be heard

        afraid she will die

        can't get any response that she wants

        terrified and very frightened

        something about left side, left thumb, left

3. The things that are dissimilar are:
    snake is shown as cause
    time of day — night in first, afternoon in second
    father appears in second
    outside/inside
    manicured lawn

Continue on through the worksheet as you have done with the other dreams and see what you can intuit and discover. You already have an idea about some of what the dreams are about, don't you? Let yourself feel into the similarities, which reveal the basis of the pattern, and the differences, which reflect the later development. Let your mind make any associations it feels, and don't forget to ask the Dreamer Within to come forward and help you with the dreams. I will take a break and come back in a few minutes to share my interpretation.

These two dreams contain some very powerful information for the dreamer. In a little while I will give you two more dreams which she had years later as an adult. These will continue the inner story. Right now, what can we see?

The most apparent thing which leaps out is the relationship which Diana had with her parents. Without knowing anything about her personal history, the dream shows deep emotional turmoil and upset about communication with the parents, especially the mother. This is a first level interpretation, but very important nonetheless. Diana cannot be heard, that is she is not validated or acknowledged by her mother and father. This is so important to her that she literally feels she will die from this lack of nurturing and support. Remember, she first had this dream when she was only six. She is trying to communicate that she is "dying." Somehow if the parent could hear her this might be averted. OK so far?

This dynamic of wanting and needing external support for who she is, and the feeling that she cannot be validated or taken seriously is still operating in her life at the time of the dream. This could obviously be a problem in future adult relationships and an obstacle to a satisfying life.

The deeper levels are a little more difficult. What exactly is it that needs to be communicated or acknowledged? Where is the difficulty centered? The first clue is in the emphasis on "left." What is our collective association with "left"? On a personal level it could be a play on words — Diana has been "left," left out, left behind, etc.

Another possibility looks at collective associations. In the collective "left" is not a good thing. Left has associations with the sinister, the dark and is often associated with the feminine, with woman. The reasons for this perception go back many centuries and emerged through different cultures and stories. In Western metaphysical studies the left hand path is the path of Satan, the path away from the light. This association, however, has its roots in the Judaic/Christian ethic which emphasizes masculine and ordered forces over feminine and chaotic, natural forces. The left hand path is the path of the chaotic, the feminine, nature, sexuality and the pre-Judaic Earth Mother and all her representations. It is anathema to the right hand path of the masculine, God the Father, restraint of sexuality, and control of human nature.

How could a little girl of six or a pubescent girl of eleven have any association with or knowledge of these connotations of "left"?

The answer to that question is one of the mysteries which begins to be revealed through the experience of expanded states of consciousness. If we humans are actually in some way connected to a greater consciousness and wisdom, for all purposes infinite and aware, then that is always true regardless of age, sex or conscious appreciation. If that is true, then it must follow that on some level we must have access to that wisdom and consciousness. In turn that means that all information and all ideas must be in some way, not necessarily consciously, available to us. Therefore a child of six or eleven can attune, unconsciously, to any image and idea which is held within the greater awareness.

The implications of this statement are mind boggling. I do not ask you to accept it, only to consider that it may indeed be so.

From this perspective, "left" in Diana's dream takes on a new meaning. There is something here about the feminine, and of course Diana is a girl/young woman. The mother, the principal image of the feminine for the child, is indifferent and invalidating.

The feminine is thus reduced and pushed away. This has deep ramifications for Diana's sense of self as a woman.

Is there something in the second dream which may amplify this? I feel that the snake image is the other clue to the deeper meaning of the dream. The snake is another symbol which generally gets a bad judgement in our society, for the same reasons as left, and because it is a symbol of the energies which lead to claiming the human condition. This is the heritage of the Garden Of Eden allegory which is so firmly rooted in the basis of our Western traditions.

In the myth the snake is the agent which leads to the human acquisition of the knowledge of Good and Evil, the forbidden fruit. It is conscious knowledge of self which separates human from animal. It is also the knowledge of self which is seen as separating human from God. The human children defy God the parent and as a result become responsible for their own well being. This includes the awareness of sexuality, viewed as a great sin, one which produces shame. This shame has to do with the physical body and the human condition. The body now becomes something shameful and unclean. The snake has become associated with evil and sexuality, which are one and the same in most Western religious thought.

Although the snake has many other meanings as a symbol, in Diana's case I feel we are looking at an echo of this myth and that the area concerned is one of her sexuality. I am talking about sexual as an expression of femininity and being in a feminine body, not just the physical act. The snake is immature in the dream, a poisonous snake. This suggests that Diana has an undeveloped sexuality at this stage of her life (when she had the dream) and that the whole idea of sexuality is threatening to her. She has set up an ordered and neat inner existence in relationship to natural forces; she attempts to control them. This is the meaning of the neatly manicured and landscaped lawn. The chaotic forces of the inner feminine threaten this security. This certainly fits with the onset of adolescence and the physical maturation of sexuality.

Diana receives no support or understanding from the parental forces in her dream, who presumably might guide her or help her with this. In fact, this was her experience in real life. On the second level of interpretation she might now, as an adult, see that she blames her parents for her feelings of inadequacy and non-support and work to change this.

The third level of the dream is difficult and subtle, and requires a certain intuitive leap. This is usually the case with the deepest levels of any dream. There comes a point where something else has to come forward. Since the something else is not linear, it is difficult to express exactly how we arrive at the interpretation. That is the function of the Dreamer Within — to bring forward an understanding of the dream which is not necessarily based on a direct linking of evidence.

On the third level Diana's dream is about her perception and relationship with self at the most basic levels of self. She is in adult life a woman who has experienced deep fears about her sexuality and femininity and who has struggled to find the support within which will enable her to validate and express herself from an authentic center. The energies which prevent this development are childish in nature. The child is not comfortable with adult expressions of sexuality or self support and never will be. Those are not appropriate expressions for a child. The problem is that Diana is still somehow stuck with the child's perceptions and relationship with life and this in turn is not appropriate behavior for an adult. The childish patterns are still operating.

It is most important for Diana to stop projecting her needs for support and emotional nurturing onto others. This includes her parents but is not limited to them, since she will carry this patterning into all her relationships. This doesn't mean that she shouldn't ask for or look for the external support. It only means that her challenge is to find the resources within which will give her a sense of self validation as a woman without being dependent on others. The issue of sexuality is more fundamentally an issue of her self expression. Whatever she does to increase her sense of security within herself will be reflected in all the other areas, including sexual expression.

Sixteen years later Diana had two more dreams, two months apart. These dreams continue the developing theme and comment on the progress which has been made. By now in her late twenties, Diana had been working over some years with self awareness and self discovery approaches, and was beginning to actively focus on women's groups and women's issues as she reached out to explore the meaning of femininity. These dreams touch indirectly the issue of sexuality but are mostly related to Diana's developing sense of self. The dreams presage a new development and change in Diana's psyche. Here are the dreams.

Diana: Dream #1.

I am approaching the door of a big, white house. It is two stories high. I am on the path that leads to the front door. I am about at the street, not close to the door. As I approach I know that when I reach the door and enter I will die. I also know that it is not yet time to enter. I wake up.

Diana: Dream #2 (two months later).

I have died. I am not in my body. I am concerned that George, who is in charge of my body, will not wait the required three days before cremating it.

The central issue for Diana at this time in her life is self authorization. This may be the central issue for most of us! Out of a real self authorization comes authentic expression of self, including sexual expression. Authentic expression means being who one is in a way that is true to one's inner needs, feelings and uniqueness without compromising those needs and feelings to standards set by others. We do not live in a society which readily supports this kind of authenticity. This is becoming more evident as our society becomes increasingly parental and authoritative about "what's good for you." If you don't think this is true take a moment to notice how many ideas and rules about what's good for you are floating around these days.

In the first dream Diana is approaching a transformational period. She knows that to enter the house is to die. She will not be the same after entering. She also knows that it is not yet time to enter.

What does the house represent? Two stories is an oblique reference to the sexual areas. Remember that two is the number of the second chakra or energy center, which affects these sexual energies. Two is a number of relationship; it is also a number of balance. Entering the house will have something to do with balance and sexuality, although nothing more is said about this in either dream.

What do you think of when you think of a "white house"? Who lives in a "white house"? In America it is the President, father figure of the nation, symbol of high masculine authority. He is the one who is supposed to know what to do in times of crisis and he is the one entrusted with the guidance of the national family. In Diana's dream, the big white house represents something about authority. To enter the house and die means to shift something within Diana's consciousness regarding authority and secondarily something about sexuality.

If Diana shifts something internally in regards to authority it means that she will view authority in a different way. Her perception will change, her relationships with authority will change and she will be a different person in the way she expresses her relationship with external authority of any kind. This would be an integral and necessary part of a process of self validation. Please notice that this is an internal process which leads to the different relationship externally.

In the second dream the transformation has been initiated; Diana has died. She is in limbo — not in her body. This is the dangerous part of the initiation. She is concerned about George rushing the process. George is her husband. The cremation which is to come after three days is the completion of the transformation, a successful conclusion. Cremation = transformation through fire = new state of being. This cannot be rushed. The figure of George represents the areas within Diana which are committed to masculine perceptions of what is right and wrong. These areas base their judgments on masculine value systems.

When I talked with Diana about this figure of George she said that he represents a masculine side of herself which is responsible for carrying through on actions which she does not completely trust herself to do. Since Diana does not trust the masculine either, she has a serious problem! In the dream she was worried because she was dependent on this masculine figure and had no control over the outcome. She's caught in a double bind of mistrust in herself and mistrust in the masculine. Part of the transformation which has been initiated will have to do with establishing deeper levels of trust and self authorization.

Diana is rightly concerned that these older, powerful and well established areas within her will interfere and abort the process of transformation which has begun. Feminine authenticity cannot be found through masculine values, but she will have to learn to trust the masculine within her to support her in expression of the feminine.

The three day time period is most interesting. Where else do you see a three day period as a crucial element of the transformation which leads to rebirth and a new state of being? In the West it is the period between the Crucifixion and the Resurrection. Before the Christian era it appears in many religious and ceremonial observances. As we go back in time it appears again and again as the symbolic transition period between death and rebirth to a new and greater awareness. For a powerful example look up the myth of Inanna, Queen of Heaven and Earth. This epic story of the transformation of consciousness dates to early Sumeria. For a modern Jungian interpretation of the myth you can read the excellent book *Descent To The Goddess* by Sylvia Benton Perera.

This sequence of dreams over many years presents some of the developments in a long and ongoing process within Diana's psyche. It makes sense that it would take many years, perhaps an entire lifetime. Future dreams should carry on the theme, keeping Diana abreast of events and development within. In turn, she should be able to notice that her life is changing in ways which reflect the inner progress. In real life this has proven to be the case. Over the last two years Diana has developed a different sense of self. She backs herself up more, even when this makes waves in her relationships. She has a different sense of her own ability and authority. When uncertainty arises, she deals with it differently. She is consciously choosing to explore and work with the feminine in a way which moves beyond simplistic assertion of her rights as a woman to a meaningful relationship with herself as woman. Her dreams reflect this changing reality.

21

CHRIST AND THE DEVIL IN DREAMS

Sometimes our dreams will bring to us a presentation of the inner struggle to attune to Spirit and to understand our relationships with the Sacred. Although the images may well have to do with our personal levels of expression and consciousness, this is one of the border zones in the psyche between the personal and impersonal realms. The images which our consciousness presents to us will differ by virtue of our culture, heritage and upbringing. All cultures have collective images of the Sacred and spiritual forces. All of the images stand for a quality which is transpersonal, non-human and mysterious. All of the images in some way suggest or convey the power of the Divine, by whatever name or form it is called or known. In the West we have Christ, God the Father, angels and saints. We also have the devil, demons, and images of evil on earth. These negative aspects are easily seen on your TV or at your local theater on any day of the week.

In Eastern religious traditions God is seen as a universal force which contains all possibility and form, manifest and unmanifest. In the West the three great monotheistic religions of Islam, Judaism and Christianity have split the evil or negative aspects off from God, and personified this as Satan. These aspects are seen as separate from and at war with God. In the East the negative aspects are just different faces of God, part of an eternal cycle of change and transformation, as much a part of God as any other aspect.

The challenge in the East is to recognize and appreciate these different aspects made manifest in human form. Evolution takes place through experience and integration of the myriad faces of God within one's own being. Success in this task leads to realization of the nature of God, the experience of self as not separate from God and enlightenment.

In the West the task is seen quite differently. We are taught to deny the negative aspects and to diligently focus on the "good" aspects. The existence of evil is seen as error and a result of man's original sin in achieving the consciousness of good and evil as taught in the Garden of Eden allegory. Mankind is by nature evil because of this sin and may only redeem itself through particular acts of contrition and submission as defined within each of the three great religions. Failure to do so will lead inevitably to damnation and eternal torment.

In the East the torment takes place through continued return to the suffering of life on earth until the lessons have been learned and one is then set free from the cycle. In the West there is only one chance, and if you blow it you face an awful punishment. Eternity is a very long time to suffer.

Leaving aside questions of theology and opinions or beliefs about who is right, it makes sense that our dreaming unconscious will choose the symbols of its cultural heritage to represent these mythic and awesome forces of Divine and supernatural Good and Evil. If we are entering a crisis in our spiritual growth and inner development these symbols may appear in our dreams. They will represent our viewpoints and feelings about the crisis and give us details about it. These symbols may also appear during times of fear or inspiration in our inner and outer lives.

This chapter works with dreams in which Christ and the devil appear. That is because the dreamers are all Christian in background. Someone from a Judaic background might dream of Moses, or the coming Messiah. Evil might be represented by a figure from the Judaic background of demonic form, such as Azazel. Christian and Jew alike might pull in representations from the Old Testament. Hitler might substitute for the devil, but not necessarily as Hitler represents many things to many different people.

I feel that in the West, because of our religious traditions, these images are particularly well suited to reflect the inner struggles which are the nature of human consciousness on the most fundamental levels of being. Conscious integration of the material which is labeled by the psyche as good and evil is perhaps the most difficult of all psychological work.

Our dreams may present this material to us for our consideration. How we handle it may lead to a different understanding and integration of how we carry these energies. A deeper understanding and integration might give us a new option of conscious choice about expression of good and evil in our life. If we are experiencing fear on some level, the dream may shed some light on the problem. If we receive inspiration we may be uplifted and strengthened for whatever task is at hand. The following dreams give examples.

David's Dream: #1

Another man and I have taken Christ down from the cross and are attending to Him. We lay him down on the floor. There is a scar, fairly large, reddish and healed, on the area of his left shoulder. It is like a burn and puncture combined. The scar covers the front of the joint where collarbone and arm meet. He seems alert and somewhat tired.

The other figure disappears. I want Christ to instruct me, to heal me. I ask Him to shift to the energy which will heal or help me. He does so, and it is quite bizarre. His whole face changes, becoming purple and green. There is a sense of aura and energy about Him. His eyes are very strange, three eyes, very wierd. He begins to send energy to me. I feel the energy. At first it is uncomfortable, then painful and makes me nauseous.

I say to Him that I feel I am possessed. I ask Him if that is so, and can He drive out the possession. He has given me what He can, and instructs me to look above, where I can see a black shadow, like a nimbus, around my head. In the outline of the shadow I can see demonic horns, like the devil. By this I know that I am possessed and that Christ can not do anything about it — He has already done what He can. With deep emotion and a painful feeling I say, "I've tried so very hard, can't You help me then?." There is a deep feeling of frustration and sadness in the dream. I realize that Christ can do no more.

This is an important dream which clearly shows the inner battle which has been engaged within David's consciousness. David has spent quite a lot of time working with different teachers in the pursuit of spiritual knowledge and inner harmony. He has also done a lot of psychological work, attempting to understand himself and what it is that makes him the way he is. He knows enough to recognize that he contains many possibilities of self within, some of which are destructive and self serving. He classifies his unconscious material under the general term of "shadow," a Jungian term for the unconscious areas which are not understood or seen clearly for what they are. He also tends to see this shadow material as negative in content, failing to recognize that he also carries unconscious areas of service and compassion which balance things within. He is hard on himself, feeling that he should know more than he does or be farther along the path he has chosen.

Without knowing anything of the background I have just given you about David, you can tell a lot from this dream. What do you think, so far? Is David "possessed" by the devil? If you think so in any literal sense, perhaps you need to look a little more closely at your own unconscious material! Why is it uncomfortable for David when the Christ figure sends energy to him in the dream? What is the meaning of the demonic outline in the shadowy cloud above his head? Why can't Christ help him any more than He already has? Why does the dream begin with taking Christ down from the cross? What is the meaning of the scar and the healed wound? Why does Christ take on such a bizarre aspect when He shifts to the healing energy? Why does David feel so terribly sad and frustrated at the end of the dream?

This is another approach you can use to get to the meaning of a dream. Make a list of questions about all the images which you do not understand, or which you feel are important. Sometimes asking the question will trigger the answer. There is always a meaning and a purpose behind every dream image or event or feeling. If nothing else the questions will help you focus your attention upon the dream.

KEY POINT

You can discover the meaning of some dream images/events by phrasing questions about them.

Sometimes asking the question will provide the answer.

It might be helpful to know what David thinks the image of Christ symbolizes. There are collective meanings galore and David or you or I would very likely associate them with the Christ image. There may also be associations which are personal for any of us. What does Christ represent as a symbol? More importantly, what does Christ as a symbol represent to David? Here is his list:

compassion
salvation
forgiveness
love
unconditional love
power to heal
wisdom
connection to God
teacher
caring
help

These attributes are all positive. I asked David if he felt there were any negative aspects and this is what he came up with:

commitment
surrender
sacrifice
pain
suffering
will change me
I will fail
something else but I don't know what

These lists are very revealing. They tell David how he feels about establishing a real relationship with the energies within himself which are symbolized by the Christ figure. The first list shows all the wonderful things that David thinks the Christ energy could do for him; the second, the reasons why he has trouble allowing that to happen.

The theme of the dream is the development of David's inner balance as he struggles to integrate oppositional and powerful aspects within. The dream shows the current status of the struggle. David's psyche is at war with itself.

In the first section David and a helper take Christ down from the cross, a Christ who is tired from His ordeal, but alert. This signals the unconscious completion of some inner process. The process of the crucifixion is necessary for the transforming energies to take place. If there is no crucifixion there is no redemption. The sacrifice is essential for the completion of the pattern. A sacrifice has taken place within David's consciousness, and now the next phase is beginning. Notice that one of David's negative connotations for the Christ symbol is sacrifice.

More than the sacrifice is needed however. This is true in the collective sense of the Christian epic and in the personal sense for David. The key element in both is that the sacrifice must be acknowledged and accepted. Otherwise it has no personal meaning for the individual. That is the cornerstone of Christianity. It is the acceptance of the sacrifice which leads to redemption, not the sacrifice itself, which does not affect those who do not accept it except through their potential acknowledgement or rejection.

The sacrifice demonstrates the Divine transformation through human form and suffering. It is the message of the Christian God made manifest in human form. It is the example which provides the most visibly important teaching. If the sacrifice is not accepted within the individual, the transformation and recognition of the Divine in man cannot take place. One of the most fundamental teachings of the example of Christ is this taking on of human form and all of its trials. This allows the potential transformation into a new state of being and consciousness.

In David's dream, frustration and sadness arise because Christ can do no more. He has done all he can, through sending the healing energy which makes David uncomfortable and sick. This reaction shows that David is not yet willing to accept the teaching of the Christ figure, although he is drawn strongly to it. This does not mean the teaching of the Christian religion! It means the teaching of the example which Christ the Teacher brought to the world as a figure of Unconditional Love, compassion, healing and the willingness to surrender to the Divine forces within. These are qualities which appear on David's positive list.

This part of the dream says that David has work to do! He has reached a point in his development where responsibility for the further transformation is clearly his. The transformation may be accomplished by integrating the teachings symbolized by the Christ. The sacrifice must be accepted, but this is not yet possible, or David would not be made ill by the energy.

The bizarre appearance of Christ as He shifts to the radiation of healing energy is a symbol of the transformation of consciousness which is necessary for these energies to come forward.

The source of frustration is the unconscious forces which block development. These are symbolized by the black cloud or nimbus around his head. The wise Christ energy calls his attention to the cloud. The demonic aspect or suggestion of the devil emphasizes the contrasting elements David carries which resist the message of love and healing. For David it is like possession since he constantly runs into inner barriers which prevent recognition, experience and conscious union with the Divine. Those barriers exist in every human consciousness. The reason great teachers such as Christ appear is to help us in crossing the barriers into broader areas of awareness and consciousness. The devil is a symbol which represents that which is opposed to the message of the Christ.

The scar on Christ's shoulder shows a healing which has taken place. The left side may suggest the feminine; Christ is a feminine energy of spirit and healing in masculine form. This is one of the Christian mysteries. The location of the wound suggests the cutting off or disabling of the left arm. This is a symbol of disempowerment. It seems to have been a bad wound. The hopeful sign in the dream is that the wound is now healed. This indicates that work has been accomplished in the past which is part of David's process of spiritual development and inner healing.

David is being told very clearly that the work now rests with him. It is time to take the teachings to a deeper level and reach for the resources which will activate the Christ energy of healing, love and compassion within him.

David had a dream a few months later which is related. He dreamed that he had to enter an underground tomb, where he would die. This was inevitable in the dream. He knew that he had to enter the underground passageways of the tomb, and in the dream he calmly accepted his fate. This is a classic image of inner transformation, and is similar to countless mythic examples, including the three days Christ spent in the tomb. It represents the time of transition from one state to another and a surrender to the forces of transformation which have been initiated within.

A few months after that David had another dream where Christ appeared. Taken overall, these dreams represent both a progressive aspect and a transformational aspect, as discussed in earlier chapters. Here is the second dream of Christ.

David's Dream: #2

I am a high school or college coach, coaching a softball or baseball team. They seem to be dropping the ball and I think it is hopeless. Suddenly there is a beam of light from above, and I look up. There is an older wooden building with stairs and a room at the top, on the second story. I climb the stairs and enter the room. Inside the room Christ is standing. I realize that he can solve the problems with the team dropping the ball and other problems as well. He radiates kindness and compassion. I fall to my knees and begin sobbing. I wake up crying.

What do you feel the dream is about? If you had these dreams over nine months, as David did, what could you discover about your inner journey?

The Christ in this dream has entered the fully transformed state. The time of transition is over. Now we see the Christ in His full power, radiating love and compassion, which David reacts to in a way that is much different from the earlier dream. By falling to his knees David is acknowledging that power. At the same time he recognizes that the Christ message holds the answers for him. Something has changed in David's psyche.

Being a high school or college coach implies an immature development. High school and college students are not adults and they are not mature. The team is David's collective representation. They're dropping the ball! In spite of the coaching, the team is not performing as they could. A baseball team which drops the ball isn't going to win many games, and dropping the ball is a collective idea of failure.

The new possibilities which have begun to manifest in David are not yet focused or mature. The answer to the problem is found by ascending to a different level of consciousness where the Christ teachings can be experienced and seen, and thus applied. David is being told that his problems will be solved, whatever they are, by integrating and applying the teachings which Christ brings. This is an overwhelming recognition. It has been my experience that people who truly open to the heart energies of love and compassion are often overwhelmed by emotion and relief. They cry more often than not.

The figures of Christ and the devil are mythic in our collective consciousness. They represent the polarities of good and evil, darkness and light, life and death, and every mixture of relationship within which is concerned with issues of power and expression of self and the Divine. How one views any of these things will be expressed through the dream symbols. The issue of power is particularly present. Few of us are able to escape the conflicts which arise when we are in some way required to express personal power.

The expression of self in our society is a loaded issue, to say the least. We are constantly presented with the split between what we are told is good and right and the evidence before us which shows power expressed in ways which are just the opposite. Somewhere along the way we make decisions about power and what it means to us. Some decide to be powerless, in order not to confront the potential which power holds for distortion and harm to self and others. In this sense power is seen as evil. It is often presented as the devil or other demonic forces in dreams.

It doesn't really matter what kind of power expression we are talking about. Most of us are not dealing with the external power issues of great responsibility such as being President or commanding an army or directing a large corporation. For most of us the issues are very personal ones involving sexuality, family, work relationships, finances and the like. These are the ordinary things of everyday life. It is here that we fight the battles with ourselves over what is right and wrong. The heart and soul of the transformational journey is this struggle to connect with an internal authenticity of expression in the ordinary. To do that we must face the demons within and integrate the teachings of human and Divine compassion which will place them in their proper perspective. To dream of Christ and the devil is to dream of our human potential and struggle to be conscious.

Here is an interesting dream of the devil.

Moira's Dream.

The devil is after me. He wears a long, black robe. A necklace with round silver pieces is around his neck. He is VERY tall and his head is small in proportion to his body. I can't see his feet. He just floats along. His face is always dark. I can see slender horns, perhaps 6" long, on his head. I think, "You can't have me." I remember his fingers come around my ribs from behind me. His fingers penetrate my body on the right side and go into my ribs. PAIN! NO, RESIST, SURVIVE, SURVIVE. I feel a shock to my body. I wake up instantly, very alert.

The first thing that stands out in this dream is the fact that Moira cannot see the devil's feet or face. What do you think this means about the inner symbol of the devil? The feet are what usually connect to ground, to earth. In the dream the devil floats along. This is a symbol of detachment. It says to Moira that whatever the devil represents for her in the dream is something she has detached herself from. There is some force within her which she has removed herself from. This is seconded by the fact that she cannot see the devil's face. She literally cannot see whatever this is about.

The distorted aspect of the small head and tall body is also a clue. Something is distorted out of proportion within. This tells us that perhaps the issue symbolized by the devil, whatever it is, is not really as serious as Moira thinks. It literally says that she has blown the whole thing out of proportion.

We still don't know what the problem is, but we do know three things about it so far. Moira is detached from the issue in some way; she does not see it clearly and cannot recognize what it is; and it is something which has become distorted or blown out of proportion within her psyche. The small horns, which are symbols of the devil's power and basis in the sensual side of the psyche, also emphasize that the problem is smaller than it looks.

The image of the devil as familiar to us in the West is derived from the image of Pan, the Greek god who ruled the spirit forces of nature. Pan was a horned god with the lower body and hooves of a goat, noted for his association with fertility and sexuality and with wild displays of drinking. Pan is the master of the flute or pan pipe, and his music leads one into the sensual realms, away from the cares and responsibilities of life. One of the principle associations with the devil in the West is unrestrained sexuality.

In the dream the devil penetrates Moira with his fingers. This again is sexual in content. This dream symbol has to do with the forces of sexuality with which Moira is struggling. She is not comfortable with these areas, which challenge a younger area within her. Part of the problem is that Moira was sexually abused as a child. This gives you background information which helps to confirm the interpretation, but it is not necessary to know this in order to see the sexual content and the fear of it which is symbolized in the dream.

The penetration causes pain; Moira resists and wakes instantly, alert and ready to act. This shows how she has well developed defensive modalities which protected her in the past. Alertness was her best protection as a child. Resisting is equivalent to surviving. On a very fundamental level Moira's survival was deeply threatened by her childhood experience.

The problem is that she is now an adult, married and no longer subject externally to the abuse she suffered as a child. However the issue is unresolved. That is understandable if we know her background. If we did not know something of her history, we could still see from the dream that she resists surrender to dark and threatening forces which she associates with sexuality. We could also see that she does not understand exactly what the problem is and that it has become distorted and over emphasized within her.

Something has been triggered for Moira by circumstances and it is now time to take another look at the problem. This is why she has the dream. The necklace of round silver pieces suggests something also. Round is a symbol of something feminine here. This is a third level association.

The same night she had the dream above, Moira had another dream of a beautiful and powerful woman holding a budding wand, accompanied by a magnificent lion. There was also a second lion nearby with a man cowering next to it. This dream was showing her another possibility, a possibility of strong feminine energies within her which carry the energies of life and sexuality. Moira is in a process where these energies must be emphasized and can be emphasized if she wishes. This may require the submission of certain other energies within which she sees as masculine. There is often a period of adjustment as we move into a deeper sense of self where it becomes necessary to emphasize one aspect at the expense of another. If all goes well, eventually a balance will be struck. This is especially noticeable if we are trying to energize a strong sense of self as man or woman.

Christ and the devil in dreams represent two sides of the same coin. Balancing these energies within is a principle task for our spiritual growth and awareness.

22

MYTHIC DREAMS AND FIGURES OF POWER

I am very stimulated by the work of Carl Jung. I did not read Jung's works until after I had already discovered some of the awesome deceptions my conscious mind had created to mask the unconscious material I held within. Jung's work felt like a validation of my own experiences and provided powerful information which my outer mind soaked up like a sponge. Jung worked extensively with dreams. One of his great recognitions, a seminal discovery in psychological work, was the existence of what he called the collective unconscious. This is today still a very controversial idea not fully accepted.

The idea of a collective unconscious has staggering implications. In essence the concept is simple, although difficult to realize on a feeling level. We as individuals have an individual expression of consciousness which will in large part be an expression of our unconscious. Our unconscious is based in personal experience and history but it is also based on a much larger collective experience. In effect we are connected through our unconscious to the entire history and experience of the human race since humans emerged as distinct life forms. It is even possible that any form of consciousness may be part of the great collective mix.

If our conscious expression is a manifestation, in large part, of unconscious dynamics; and if in turn our unconscious is in some way connected to a larger, collective pool of experience and unconsciousness; then our personal expression as a conscious individual depends on reaching an awareness of both the personal and impersonal or collective elements with which we are attuned.

Put more simply, we are beings of a collective nature attempting to express ourselves individually. Jung called the struggle to become aware of these inner relationships the path of individuation. It is possible that Jungians may see this somewhat differently, but this is my interpretation.

What does this have to do with dreams? Our dreams will present to us images which are based not only on our personal history but also images from the collective experience. These are the great themes of myth and story, themes so universal in human experience that they are presented again and again in every culture. These images weave their magic through all of us in some way or another. They are intimately connected with the experience of God and Spirit, and with the common experience of being human. This great collective pool of experience represents a universal and invaluable teaching for those who care to pay attention.

In earlier times the societies of the world recognized the importance of the myths and stories of their culture for what they were and used them as an anchoring point which gave stability and continuity in a dangerous and changing world. Today things are different. We have not succeeded in creating a new and unifying myth to live by which might provide stability, although there have been many attempts to do so. Now the teachings must be found on different levels since there is no outward and accepted agreement. Aside from the teachings of cultures and times which seem remote from us there is a powerful and available tool waiting for our attention. This is the doorway to the collective wisdom which may be found in our dreams.

The great themes are themes of transformation, reclamation, the quest for communion with God and the evolution of the human spirit. These are what are seen in such stories as the myth of Innana, the Arthurian legends, the Hopi stories and the Sufi teaching stories, to mention only a very few. These stories are roadmaps of consciousness, laid out by those who managed to attune to the essentials of human experience on levels which went beyond their time and place.

Our dreams will take up the mantle of story teller and teacher, casting us in some role within the greater epic. In our ability to understand the role we are playing can be found a valuable piece of who we are. We are also given the choice to continue playing the role in the same way, changing the way we play the part or taking on a new part altogether.

Consciousness, in the sense of awareness and potential choice, demands that we know what role we have chosen within the greater tapestry of human expression. Dreams are a vehicle towards that greater awareness.

Jung also presented the idea of Archetypes. This is a subject which creates confusion when first introduced. For me an Archetype represents a great, collective patterning of human energy. It is presented as an image which exhibits the qualities of that collective human patterning. All Archetypes have a transpersonal quality in common. They go beyond the individual human to mythic proportions. They appear as gods and goddesses, divine and semi-divine heroes and heroines. They may be distinguished by their numinous and trans-human aspect. Some examples are The Nurturing Mother, The Fool, The Wise Old Man, The Crone, The Devouring Mother, The Sun God, and most of the Major Arcana found in the Tarot. Numinous means that something carries the quality of the Divine, the Central Consciousness.

These Archetypes do not always represent what we would tend to call positive aspects. The Devouring Mother is an excellent example, as is The Devil.

Our dreams will sometimes present these figures. When they appear we know that we are in some way attuning to the powerful collective forces which they represent. Because we are dreaming about them, we must have some personal relationship with the larger, impersonal energy. A dream of The Devouring Mother would be showing something about the dreamer's relationship with all women in the sense that She represents something about the feminine. It would also be telling the dreamer about his or her relationship with the feminine within self. These Archetypal figures are not gender conscious, which is in keeping with their collective and universal human aspect.

A dream which presents an Archetypal figure of great power may take a long time to understand. One trap will be the dreamer's inner issues which have to do with personal power. I know of no one personally who has resolved all their issues of personal power and its expression. The dreamer's dreams will faithfully reflect the truth about those issues, but it is often difficult for the dreamer not to be seduced one way or another by the unseen inner forces of self expression. The dreams we will look at in this chapter contain this component of personal power. One of them presents Christ as a central figure. In this case, Christ may be seen as the Archetypal pattern of The Messiah. This is similar to The Sun God.

I feel that dreams of this Archetypal nature are especially important for understanding our inner conflicts and strengths. For example, a person who resonates unconsciously with the pattern of the Messiah will demonstrate this pattern externally, whether seen consciously or not. The most powerful example of this in modern times is Adolph Hitler. Another example of this expression is Jim Jones. Both of these men manifested the pattern destructively. Destruction is a component of the pattern since transformation requires the death and collapse of an earlier perception. When combined with personal charisma and lack of awareness the results can be devastating.

Archetypes as energy patterns are not concerned with human ideas of good and evil or right and wrong. These are personal judgments and are not the concern of the impersonal realms. By paying attention to these energies when they appear in our dreams we gain two great benefits.

First we may see that the power of these forces which are vibrating within our consciousness is pushing us towards some distortion. The nature of the impersonal is its disregard for the personal forces of life. This can lead to expressions which are in essence anti-life, as was seen in Germany or Guyana. By seeing this in its early stages of development within, we may choose a different expression. This is where we apply our conscious and individual free will.

The second benefit is that doing such work may allow us to see these patterns operating in others. If enough people were aware in the collective of these energies, perhaps the individuals who carry the destructive aspects would not rise to positions of such great power as they have in the past.

I notice as I write this that I am aware of my own unresolved material about figures of power and authority. I have to watch out and not be seduced by the charms of my personal judgments about various political and other contemporary world leaders, which tend to be very negative. This is exactly the problem which we encounter when looking at impersonal energies.

What I want to suggest is that it seems to me human evolution may be pointing in the direction of an evolving, collective consciousness. This process may well take many millennia. Part of that evolution will be the recognition and integration within each individual of these awesome rhythms of human experience which appear in archetypal images in our dreams. Since we have no way of knowing the end result of this evolution and no way of accurately gauging what is really important in such a long process we are left with our own personal evolutionary piece of the collective. This will provide more than enough work to do!

Here is a dream of The Messiah which demonstrates some of this.

Kurt's Dream.

I dreamed I was with a crowd of people. There was a hill and a paved street. It was daylight. We were waiting for something. Then Christ comes over the hill. I am surprised to see Him, and glad. I think He has been in prison. He has black hair, blue eyes, black beard, a white robe. He looks a little fanatical. I know this is the Fuhrer.

I say to Him, "Has anyone ever been so loved as you, mein Fuhrer?" I open my arms to Him. There is excitement among the crowd. He embraces me, my heart is beating fast. Then He steps back, waiting. I realize I am supposed to lead the people or speak to them, but I am not sure what to say or do. I am His representative to the people, to lead for Him.

Kurt is not German and is not a Nazi. The association in the dream which links Christ and the Fuhrer is a perfect example of the dark and light side of the Messiah pattern. There can only be one messiah, only one true messenger of God. The messiah brings this true word to his followers, who then act as his emissaries in the world. This part of the pattern states that the messiah brings absolute truth in his message. The followers bring their own interpretation to the "truth" and distortion sets in. This leads to fanaticism on the part of his followers as is seen in both the dark and light aspects. If you don't believe me, think of the Inquisition in Christian history. The Nazi example is well known.

As the dream opens Kurt is waiting expectantly with a crowd of people. The "people" are aspects of Kurt; this is Kurt's inner collective. Over the hill comes Christ, a figure of power, carrying what Kurt sees as a slightly fanatical look. The dream image is now beginning to present the hidden material. That suggestion of fanaticism is what Kurt is going to have to look out for in his development. It is the look of the true believer who knows he has the truth and the right.

Kurt is surprised to see Christ because He has been in prison. This is straightforward and a wonderfully clear piece of information. The energy of the messiah figure, whatever that is for Kurt, has been imprisoned, locked away in Kurt's psyche. Now it is free. This portends changes for Kurt. What those changes are remains to be seen but this energy is now active within. Kurt is making progress within, as he is now ready to interact with this energy on a more conscious level. He is beginning to integrate the forces which the figure represents. The dream gives further information about this inner relationship.

The quote which says. "Has anyone ever been so loved as you, mein Fuhrer," was actually spoken by Hermann Goering. It is sometimes seen on the newsreels of Hitler which can be found most evenings on your TV. It is the statement of the believer and flatterer, who takes on an association of power through his proximity to the messiah. It is interesting that during the time when these words were spoken Hitler was indeed loved by millions, who saw him as their literal savior. This piece of the dream is like the Christ/devil split we looked at in the last chapter. The association with Hitler is like the association with the devil.

Kurt opens his arms to receive the embrace, and the crowd stirs. Kurt's heart is beating fast as he moves towards union with the Divine figure. They embrace and Christ steps back, waiting. Now what? The blessing has been bestowed and Kurt is supposed to take up the banner and lead but he doesn't know what to do.

This section shows how much Kurt wants this union with the Divine and powerful force. It also says that he does not know yet how to communicate the message to the crowd; that is, how does he get the message of the Christ across to himself? He is uncertain. That uncertainty has to do with Kurt's relationship to this powerful patterning of energy.

When you ask for a deeper level of knowledge about this dream, what do you get? Can you see the inner relationships which Kurt is working with?

In real life, Kurt is actively involved in teaching. He influences others, who sometimes assume he has some sort of inside line to the Divine. The temptation to take on the authority of teaching the true word has occurred to him because it is easy to believe in what you say if it has some element of truth and power to it. Kurt would like to be loved by millions, and this aspect is not far from the surface.

The dream is cautioning him to pay attention to this tendency towards fanaticism, certainty of absolute truth, and the Divine right to lead others. This is true on the inner level where he has a tendency to deny anything which conflicts with what he believes to be true. It will also be true on an outer level unless Kurt watches for the emergence of the "messiah" which he carries within himself. He is being shown one of the ways he interacts with this Archetypal patterning.

The dream also shows considerable potential. If Kurt can successfully integrate such a powerful energy within this can not help but reflect outwardly in levels of success and power in his work as a teacher. It is not yet time, though, for these levels to appear. Kurt has more work to do, to learn, before he will "know what to do."

The next dream is so full of classic images of the collective that I would suspect it was fabricated if I did not personally know the dreamer. I have seldom seen a dream which was so mythic in nature. In this dream is seen the initiatory transformation of the feminine as it takes on a deeper level of activity within the dreamer. The integration of what this dream indicates will certainly take years. The dream is long, so I will present it to you in sections.

Please get comfortable and take your time with each section. See if you can resonate with the images. Let your mind freely associate from your own experience. If you are well versed in myth and psychology you will easily recognize the images. If you are not, you will still be able to feel into the images and sense their significance. Knowledge of symbols and myth gained from outer levels of information is not necessary for understanding. You contain within you the capacity to accurately attune to the meaning of the dream.

Sandra's Dream: Section One.

I find myself crawling down a long, dark tunnel. The tunnel is round and the earth walls touch my body. I come out into a circular opening in the earth.

This opening sequence is the classic image of entering a place of transformation and change. The image is feminine, womb-like. The earth is usually seen as feminine — "Mother Earth." The tunnel is like a birth canal, but at this point the journey is in reverse. Sandra emerges in a circular place, another image of the feminine. Whatever comes forward in this dream will have to do with fundamental perceptions and experience of the feminine for the dreamer. This will be very clearly seen in the next sequence.

Sandra's Dream: Section Two.

At the far side of this circular chamber a woman is seated on a golden throne. She is black and is dressed in a black robe. A circular golden pin of a snake devouring its tail is in the center of her breast. On her head is a golden crown, with a motif of skulls and crescent moons. Her hair is long and hangs in tangled ropes. Her eyes are closed but I don't believe she is asleep — merely waiting.

If I were trying to find an image of the Archetypal feminine in one of her many aspects, I could not do better than this. The Black Queen is an ancient figure, and her decorations are found throughout history in images of death, transformation and wisdom. The snake which devours its tail is very old and symbolizes the circular existence of all life. It stands for wisdom, rebirth, transformation and the renewal of the spirit. It is a symbol of knowledge.

The crown of skulls and crescent moons are found also. These symbols first appeared in the East and the Middle east. The crescent moon has been for millennia a symbol of the rebirth of the feminine and the beginning of all things. The skulls bring in the aspect of transformation. Transformation requires the death of something so that the new may come forward. Skulls and crescent moons together present a clear message that the figure on the throne represents these energies of feminine transformation. What will be transformed for Sandra, potentially, is her view and experience of self as a woman.

The Black Queen is a representation of the hidden, primal side of the feminine. She is dangerous for those who will not acknowledge her. This awesome figure sits, waiting, on her throne of gold. The gold represents purity, power and the connection of spirit with the world. Gold represents rule and authority. Gold is the pure refinement of the raw material of the earth. Gold represents the transformation through Spirit.

Sandra's Dream: Section Three.

I begin to dance before her. This is a passionate dance and yet it is a dance of submission. I am clothed in veils of seven colors. The outermost is amethyst, then indigo, blue, green, yellow, orange and the one closest to my body is red. As I dance I remove the veils one by one. Each one is harder to remove than the last but at last I stand naked before her. I am very hot and out of breath.

You have probably heard of the dance of the seven veils. It is unlikely you have seen it! The association which we have with this image is a powerful one of eroticism, sexuality, femininity, beauty and surrender. It is a dance of passion and submission, just as in Sandra's dream. What is not often discussed is the hidden meaning of those veils. Why seven? Why is seven a number associated with magic and luck and superstition?

In metaphysical literature and in the great religious teachings of the East there is frequent reference to energy centers within the body called chakras. The word chakra is Sanskrit and means wheel or disk. The chakra may be seen by expanded vision as a spinning wheel of color.

Chakras are in some way a connecting link with the transpersonal and spiritual forces. They are usually presented as a system of seven centers within the body, located at different points and rising in a vertical line from the base of the spine to the top of the head. These major chakras (there are others) are shown in the colors of the rainbow, beginning with red at the bottom and ending with violet or amethyst at the top. Work with the chakras, as presented in ancient yogic teachings and in other traditions, may lead to transformation of the human experience and the union with the central, spiritual Force.

I am telling you all of this because it is helpful in understanding the seven veils of the dream. To remove the seven veils in an act of submission is to prepare oneself for the transformation which is to come. This image is repeated as seven gates in the myth of Inanna. Inanna descends to the underworld, ruled by her black and terrible sister, Ereshkigal, through the seven gates, shedding articles of clothing as she goes until she stands naked before her sister. This dream is picking up the same collective thread.

How are you doing so far? If this story were presented to you as a movie instead of a dream, what would you think the movie was about? Can you feel the part of you which responds to such images on a deep level?

Sandra's Dream: Section Four.

I look up and the woman has now opened her eyes and is looking directly at me. She has terrible eyes — they hold the knowledge of all things. I am afraid of her and at the same time feel she is sacred. She rises and comes forward and stands in front of me. At this time she is also naked. She reaches out with her right hand and begins to touch my body. At the same time she touches her own body in the same way.

She starts by pressing her palm flat on my forehead. I feel the hot blood begin to well up under her hand and begin to drip down my face. She has done the same to herself and as she removes her hand I see the bloody handprint on her face. She touches me in this way all over my body, at the same time touching herself. She looks horrible, the blood is welling up and dripping down her body into the earth. I know that I must look the same. We stand face to face and our hands are raised with her hands touching mine. I look into her eyes and feel that we are sisters.

The Dark Queen begins the initiation, the transfer of energy. The terrible eyes are a feature of this dark side aspect, and convey the essence of her nature. This is not the nurturing mother we are looking at here! She is a Shadow figure, an area of the feminine which is not usually consciously appreciated or even recognized. She is the aspect of the feminine which all men unconsciously fear for her destructive powers. Her usual manifestation in the outer personality levels is unconscious and destructive.

If you would like to see an example well portrayed as one part of a very complex character, watch the movie *Fatal Attraction*. Glenn Close gives an amazing performance which includes this dark side aspect as one of the components. The more the feminine and its needs are unrecognized and avoided, the more this aspect comes forth in the picture. This side of the feminine does not need to appear in the trappings of mythic symbolism to show us her face.

The blood is another symbol of the life forces and primal energies which re part of the ceremony and the passage to a new state of being. The recognition of self in other ends this section. Sandra feels her kinship with this force. This is herself that she is looking at on a very deep level.

Sandra's Dream: Section Five.

And then I begin to swallow her. I do this in the way of a snake; opening my jaws wide and swallowing her whole, head first. This takes a long time and when I have fully ingested her I feel that my body is very large and swollen. Then I look down and see that I am pregnant. I begin to crawl, sweaty and bloody and pregnant, back up the earth tunnel. At this point I wake up.

There is a strong sexual component here. One of the things this dream is about for Sandra is her sexuality, which has been somewhat repressed. The expression of sexuality has a dark side to it in the sense that it is primal and ancient, impersonal and amoral. Full expression of sexuality is not a feature of our culture. No one escapes the conflict between what the society says is right and good and what the primal psyche demands.

The union with the Black Queen takes place. The aspect of the queen which is devouring is mirrored in Sandra's act of swallowing her whole. Then she returns towards the surface, pregnant and bloody. The birthing of what this dream is symbolizing has not yet taken place.

This dream is about something Sandra wants very badly, which is a sense of power as a woman and as a sexual being. It is a deep dream of the deep psyche. The terrible, bloody handed figure of the Black Queen represents something feared and long repressed within her, but something is changing. She is becoming more willing to let these energies surface consciously. She now has a potential available to her which was not really apparent before. The dream indicates that this potential is now gestating within her. Before it was merely unconscious and unrecognized.

In the past Sandra was very attracted to the New Age philosophy of "Light and Love." She carries forces within her which are not consistent with that philosophy. There is a lack of balance and understanding of these forces. A true and deep manifestation of love and the positive aspects of life may depend on the recognition of such forces as the Black Queen within. As Sandra moves to deeper understanding of self she becomes more capable of tolerance and understanding for others. She also has the opportunity to find ways to express herself more completely and more consciously. Her challenge is to find a way to integrate and birth the Black Queen within. The dream holds this promise out to her.

It also reflects her desire to be special and to have special knowledge. Sandra knows this on an outer level. The desire to be special is something we all bring to work on the self, although sometimes we don't know it! One of the functions of dreams is to bring in a sense of compensation for lack or excess in outer life. A very wealthy man may dream of being poor. A woman who feels powerless or suppressed at a deep level may dream of having great power and expression. This dream may be seen in the light of compensation, but the deeper level honors the symbols for what they are and what they portend.

This next dream is one I had a few years ago.

The Crystal Woman

I am in a room somewhere. A powerful, tall woman, blond, wearing a long dress or gown of lavender/white is standing before me. She says, "Tell me how to energize a crystal." She has a large, amethyst crystal, roughly diamond shape. I also have an amethyst crystal, more columnar in shape than hers. I tell her lots of things about working with crystals and she goes away to work with it.

When she comes back, she has mastered it. She says to me, "The most valuable thing you told me was to focus the mind on the crystal and then bring the energy through from the bottom." In the dream I am startled by the simplicity of this as compared to all the information which I had given her. Then there is a section of the dream I don't remember.

She comes again and asks me the same question. This time I reply, "You focus your mind on the crystal and bring the energy through from the bottom." She nods, pleased, and goes away. She comes back as before having mastered it, very pleased. In the dream I remember what she said the first time, which is why I tell her what I did. She has a very commanding presence.

This is certainly a dream of power. There is a sense in the dream of energizing the crystal in order to use it for some powerful purpose. The woman is mythic, commanding, archetypal. She is not an ordinary woman.

There is a very strong clue here in the color of her dress, which is similar to the crystals which she and I are both holding. This indicates that she and the crystal symbolize something in common. There is an association between the images which is brought through by the colors. This is a third level reading, which says that energizing the crystal and energizing the woman are the same thing. Whatever she represents will be empowered by the process of "bringing the energy through from the bottom."

It is also the woman who tells me this in the dream. Originally I tell her many things — I have figured it out, so to speak. This is a masculine process, a linear, informational process. From all this, she comes back with the information, simple in its essence, which goes straight to the heart of the matter. This is the advice about bringing the energy through, twice repeated in the dream.

When something is repeated twice, particularly a clear and well remembered statement such as appears in this dream, you are looking at the key message which the dream contains. This will not be easy to read unless the association is made between the message and the other symbols contained in the dream. In this case, the message has to do not with crystals (although that's how you do it!) but with the feminine.

In the dream the feminine is pleased with the teaching and is pleased even more when I repeat her teaching back to her. It is a loop; it appears that I gave her the information, but it is she who communicates it clearly to me.

This is a dream which is very positive, as it shows that there is an open channel of communication with feminine energies within and that something in me is willing to listen to the message.

It is easy to see from what I have written throughout this book that I attach a lot of importance to our inner relationship of masculine and feminine energies and that I feel the feminine energies on this Archetypal and impersonal level are most important. The dream is telling me that the way to empower the feminine is to balance the energies of mind (focus your mind) and feeling (bring it up from the bottom). The Crystal Woman is telling me that I can do this. The implication, based on the correlation of woman/crystal, is that this will further empower and focus the energies of the feminine.

Do you see how I arrived at this interpretation?

I have had other dreams where a feminine figure acts in a teaching capacity. The figure is always numinous and mysterious. She always radiates an aura of power and wisdom. I have also had dreams of the terrifying and destructive aspect of the feminine. This figure is so clearly beyond human that Archetypal seems like too mild a word for her. I have also had the Crone and the Nurturing Mother appear in my dreams. Each of these dreams of transpersonal feminine energy has remained in my mind and each has felt important to me in ways which most other dreams do not.

There have been many examples of such figures given throughout the book. They always herald something moving at the deepest levels of the psyche. If and when they come to you, you will recognize them by their powerful presence and mysterious aura. They stand out in our dreams. When we meet these figures in our dreams we are touching upon one of the great mysteries of the collective human experience. They reaffirm our common humanity and touch it with the breath of something which is beyond human at the same time.

23
LUCID DREAMS

Before I end this book, I want to make some brief comments about lucid dreaming. The idea of lucid (conscious) dreaming has become very popular recently, and a book about dreams ought to at least take this into account. If you have read this book with moderate attention, you know that I feel the dreaming state is a powerful tool for self discovery and information. My experience is that the dreaming consciousness is connected to areas of wisdom and knowledge which far surpass the knowledge usually available to our conscious minds.

I have said that the dreaming consciousness is an interface with expanded awareness and wisdom. That expanded awareness knows more than our conscious mind. It contains a wealth of resource and information not known to the conscious mind. If this is true, why should we want to impose our less aware and less developed conscious mind upon this awesome resource? The answer to that question is not too difficult, if we remember that there may be a hidden agenda of the unconscious behind much of our actions in life.

Lucid or conscious dreaming is in essence an attempt to control the unconscious or change or direct the information which is received from the unconscious in dream states. It is an attempt which is initiated by ego levels in order to maintain or develop personal power. We want to control something because we think that we will obtain some advantage, or because we fear it and feel threatened by it.

The problem with lucid dreaming is twofold. On the one hand, the motivations for establishing power and control are unconsciously held and therefore not understood. Remember, if something is unconscious, by definition we do not know it exists. On the other hand, if the dreamer succeeds in inserting conscious control into the dream the information which is presented is manipulated and distorted to suit the dreamer's idea of what is wanted.

Traditionally conscious dreaming is utilized in tribal societies as a tool of shamanistic or "medicine" power. In these situations the shaman has learned to seek information within the context of the particular training of his or her tradition. This may or may not involve the use of hallucinogenic drugs. It will always involve ritual and focused intention. Sometimes the purpose for entering the altered state of dreaming awareness is to connect with a "spirit guide," often a force within nature such as a bird, animal or spirit. This guide in turn provides information. It is a dream or like a dream.

You can see a good presentation of this in the powerful film *The Emerald Forest*. There are many books available which describe these kinds of experiences. The books by Carlos Castaneda are excellent examples.

In other tribal societies, lucid dreaming is used to deal with troubling dreams and inner fears which appear in dreams. This is a way for the individual to handle the troubling material, by gaining mastery over it, symbolically, in the dream and changing it to his or her liking. It is most often this approach which is brought up in our society when people discuss lucid dreaming.

From my point of view I feel that in most cases lucid dreaming is a mistake. I am aware that many people think lucid dreaming is a wonderful tool for dealing with nightmares or other difficult material. Others feel that this is a path of inner discovery. This is perhaps true for them and it is not for me to say whether one should or should not follow this route with dreams. But if it is true that the unconscious is a vast resource of wisdom, it seems to me best to learn what it has to teach us without interfering in what it presents. I know that we have much work to do before we begin to see clearly or understand our unconscious motivations. I also know that there is a real risk of aborting stages of development in our expanding awareness. There is always a risk of distortion, which is never seen for what it is because that is part of the distortion!

In the tribal societies which have a tradition of conscious dreaming there is a lot of training and preparation for the task. Not everyone does it or is encouraged to do it. The shaman or medicine man/woman undergoes difficult and extensive training. That training is designed to stabilize them and bring them into harmony with the very powerful forces which are accessed through the unconscious. We in the West are rarely trained in this way. It requires much more than technique to work successfully on the levels which may be opened through conscious dreaming.

I do feel that lucid dreaming may open windows within which are exciting and provocative of growth. However, it also seems clear to me that there is much work to be done in looking at the self through normal dreaming states before lucid dreaming should be attempted. That work may take many years. Please consider these remarks if you are interested in lucid dreaming or have begun to explore these levels. The time we take to discover what is already evident within us and then to integrate and accept that material is a necessary step before searching for deeper levels. If we do not make this effort, anything else we attempt with the unconscious will suffer as a result. This is especially true of dreams and the information which they bring to us.

Since I do not support lucid dreaming as a technique which most people should explore, I am not including any techniques in this chapter which would help you to practice it. If you are really determined to explore lucid dreaming, there are books already available which contain various techniques, mostly autosuggestive, which can assist you. You will find them as needed. If you do take on the exploration, please ask yourself why you think your dreams need to be altered or in some way controlled, and see if there are, perhaps, hidden motivations not immediately apparent to you.

Trying to control our dreams rather than be open to them may lead to a tragic loss of possibility and inspiration.

SUMMARY

I have tried to show how our dreams may be seen as a powerful and accurate tool of self discovery. Working with dreams is a slow and sometimes confusing process. The techniques which have been introduced will work for you if you give them a fair trial. Some may feel better to you than others. You may also develop your own unique method for remembering and interpreting your dreams.

The inaccuracies of interpretation come from the outer mind. Throughout the book I have mentioned that we project our unconscious material onto our dreams. The unconscious mind imposes a filter upon our conscious perception. It doesn't really matter if we understand this fully or not. What matters is that we remember that our minds will do this without our knowing it. The assumption then becomes simple; nothing is as it appears and we must look more carefully to get to the real meaning of what we are looking at. This becomes very apparent when looking at dreams. A great benefit of dream work is that this new way of looking for meaning spills over into other areas of our life. We begin to get a little closer to whatever "reality" is.

The concept of "levels" in dreams has been very helpful to me and for others. There is always a first level interpretation which is based on what is familiar and known to the outer mind of the dreamer. This is almost never what the dream is really about and it is one of the reasons there is so much difficulty with dreams.

The second level will begin to reveal really useful information and insight on the dreamer's relationship with life. It is reached by feeling into the symbolic language of the dream and letting the associations with the symbols come forward. It requires the beginning of an intuitive grasp of the meaning coupled with a process of logical association and deduction.

The third level will hold the key to resolution and action, if action or resolution is required. The third level is the most difficult because it requires an intuitive and non-linear leap of understanding. On this level associations are made and conclusions are drawn which are not at all evident at an earlier stage of the interpretation. We will know the interpretation is correct when we feel the sense of being right in our body. Our bodies never lie to us.

Once we have begun to tap into third level understanding of dreams we have a new resource available for really significant change in our lives. In itself the third level recognition does not bring resolution of any issues contained in the psyche. What it does do is help us begin to realize that the solutions are within and that we can take steps to energize those solutions. Third level recognition reveals that we are the source of our confusion and that we are the source of our empowerment or our lack of it.

The third level is reached by accessing the energy which I call the Dreamer Within. You may call it what you like. This energy is impersonal and objective. It is not concerned with the issues which trouble or confuse our outer levels of consciousness. It is connected to the deeper pool of wisdom which is part of our life experience and human heritage. On the third level will be found the deeper meanings of the dream and the full and truthful interpretation. With practice you will be able to reach this level and know what your dream is about.

The techniques which are given are frameworks for exploration. The meditation, for example, may be altered in any way you see fit to suit your personal preference and needs. What is important to remember, however, is your intention when preparing to meditate. It is necessary to ask for cooperation from within. You are attempting to evoke that within you which knows how to interpret dreams. This is qualitatively different from invoking assistance from without.

The worksheet is a very effective way of working with your dreams. Repeated use of this tool will teach you how to approach your dream in a way which encourages the intuitive and non-linear state to emerge.

You can see from the dreams which I have chosen to present as examples that there is a lot to learn about the mystery of our human consciousness! It is not necessary to know a lot about psychology or myth or any other ideas about dreams. Your dreams are personal and unique. Their meaning is held within your consciousness, which is why the dream was presented to you. The great themes of human experience will be presented to you because you are part of that experience. All of us are in some way trying to express our selves as individuals within that larger human collective. To do so we must learn how we uniquely resonate within the great human consciousness.

All of the polarities of life come forward in our dreams. Triumph and defeat, good and evil, right and wrong, black and white, feminine and masculine, nurturing and devouring, humility and exaltation will present themselves. We can learn to see our personal relationship to these forces. If change is called for and action needs to be taken our dreams will point the way. By taking the time to work with our dreams we can empower ourselves through the information given. We can attune to a greater consciousness and a sense of Spirit and wholeness.

The information contained in this book is based on experience and practical usage. It is an effective approach which can help you understand your dreams and the dreams of others. It is meant to be a manual for dreamers. Dream interpretation is an art, and like any other art requires practice over a period of time to reach its potential and flowering. It does take practice and a willingness to not take yourself too seriously. Don't be discouraged if it seems overwhelming or difficult at first. It took me many years to begin to feel reasonably comfortable with my own ability to accurately read dreams. I'm stubborn — perhaps it won't take you as long.

It is best to go slowly when interpreting dreams for others. As you do the work on your own dreams and put into practice the information in this book your capacity to see into the dreams of others will improve. I have found that it is necessary to watch out for my own unconscious material when I am working with another. You will need to do the same.

The secret of understanding dreams is to recognize that there is something within us which is connected to a greater store of wisdom and perception than we normally think of ourselves as having. If we are able, through whatever means, to access this "something," we will be able to move deeply into areas of understanding which might otherwise seem impossible.

True understanding of dreams comes through what amounts to a deep and honest attunement to the feeling of the images. This requires inspiration and guidance from within. It cannot be accomplished solely from the outer mind and most certainly cannot be realized by consulting a list of symbols and their possible meanings. Each of us has a unique language of dreams. Each of us has a potential for discovery for the understanding of our own symbolic language and for the language of others. If you have a desire for deeper understanding of yourself and others, and if you are willing to let yourself be guided by the inspirational forces within and without you, you can reap the harvest of wisdom and self discovery which dreams can bring you.

I would be happy to hear from any of you who would like to comment on the material in this book, or who might like to share your dreams. I am interested in how the tools and approaches contained in *What Your Dreams Can Teach You* work for you. I am always interested in new ideas and approaches which have worked for others. If you would like to contact me, please write to me at the address given at the end of the book or through the publishers.

May the door of the Temple of Dreams be open to you.

Alexander Lukeman
Fort Collins, Colorado
February 1990

One of the best ways to really move quickly into dream work is to work with a teacher. I have presented a lot of information and techniques in this book which are often learned more quickly in workshops and conferences. The personal and practical experience which one is exposed to through group dynamics assists greatly in the development of such skills as moving to expanded awareness, the recognition of projected and unconscious material, the ability to see patterns which we are acting out and how to reach the "Dreamer Within."

Although this kind of personal work and reflection in the context of a retreat or workshop is not necessary for successful dream interpretation, you will find it stimulating and valuable. I present conferences in a retreat environment which makes it possible to concentrate solely on inner development without interruption, a rare opportunity in our busy lives. Conferences are given in modern and comfortable facilities. They are held in settings of great natural beauty and peacefulness. People always seem to enjoy these retreats and to grow from them. I know that I do!

If you are interested in hearing more about these conference and workshop opportunities, please write to me at the address given below and request a schedule.

I look forward to hearing from you.

Alex Lukeman
P.O. Box 9047
Fort Collins, CO 80525
(303) 226-2804

To order the audio cassette *Dream Mysteries*, write to the above address or call Tiger's Nest Audio Publishing at:

1-800-628-4877

VISA and MasterCard accepted. Cost is $9.95 plus $1.50 shipping and handling. Colorado residents add $.30 sales tax.